Notes from the WACKO! File

And Tales from the Madhouse on McDowell

by
Tom Ambrose

with forward by
Jerry Colangelo

TOM, THE ORIGINAL "HAYSTACK"

WACKO !

DEDICATION

•

To Alice, Casey, Logan, Alphonse, Adeline, Barbara, Bean, Pooch, Mike, Duck, Jerry, Bill, Rich as well as my many coaches, teachers, mentors and friends.

"I believe that gathering stories is what makes life so interesting. Some stories we experience, others we hear and pass along. But you never know what other people will hear, appreciate or remember. Sometimes people tell me that a story I once told them changed their lives, made them laugh, gave them direction, offered them hope or gave them inspiration. But I've also learned that one person's inspiration can be another's 'yeah... whatever...' So keep your eyes, your ears and your mind open. And write down your stories!"

— Tom Ambrose

"I think my older brother Tom takes his outlook on life from the musings of that well-known 20th Century philosopher, Stymie, of *Little Rascals* fame. In the film episode 'Free Wheeling,' as the Rascals piled into an old jalopy for a wild ride down one of the steepest hills in Hollywood history, Stymie observed, 'I don't know where we're goin'...but we're on our way!'"

— Mike Ambrose

ABOUT THE AUTHOR

TOM AMBROSE

Tom Ambrose is a public relations professional who spent 37 years (1973-2010) in the front office of the Phoenix Suns of the National Basketball Association.

He was born and raised in New Rochelle, New York, where he attended Iona Prep. Later, he matriculated at the University of Notre Dame, majoring in English.

Following his 1970 graduation from Notre Dame, he moved to Arizona to begin his public relations career with Phoenix News-papers, Inc. Two years later, he entered the world of sports management as public relations director for the Suns. During his first 16 years with the Suns franchise, he directed the team's media relations, communications programming and later, its advertising strategy.

On a league level, Ambrose founded the NBA's Public Relations Directors Association (NBAPRDA), authored its code of ethical standards and served as the organization's first president. In 1996, the NBAPRDA honored Tom with its "Splaver-McHugh Tribute to Excellence Award" for his contributions to the profession.

Throughout his career with the Suns, he managed the team's public relations, community relations and played a key leadership role with the team's non-profit, community foundation, Phoenix Suns Charities.

Under his leadership, Phoenix Suns Charities grew from a start-up foundation in 1988, to a respected, community grant-making organization, which raises and distributes over one million dollars annually in grants and scholarships.

Believing strongly in the concept of business leaders giving back to their communities, Ambrose has served as a volunteer board member for dozens of non-profit organizations, including the Children's Museum of Phoenix and the Phoenix Zoo.

Tom remains active in the Phoenix non-profit community and is currently executive director of Big Brothers Big Sisters of Central Arizona. He lives in Phoenix with Alice, his wife of 40 years. Their daughter Casey and grandson Logan also reside in the Valley of the Sun.

In 1992, Tom teamed up with Jim Brewer to co-author the book, *A Silver Anniversary Celebration of the Phoenix Suns.*

ABOUT THE ARTIST

Ronald Lee Thomas has been drawing his entire life. That's a lot of years and a lot of pencils. He has been an avid Suns fan since the team arrived on the Phoenix scene in 1968.

Ron began his professional art career as a sign painter and later did custom pin-striping on cars. A native of Crown Point, Indiana, he attended the University of New Mexico where he played football and majored in art. He nurtured his artistic talent at the Ray Vogue School of Commercial Art in Chicago and the Visual Arts Center of Phoenix. Always experimenting with new artistic mediums and materials, Ron has continued his art education through workshops put on by Raleigh Kinney, Judith Spalchasky and Doris Dubose. Frequently, Ron combines his art with his love for fly-fishing. His Phoenix gallery features paintings of many varieties of trout and bass...caught on canvas.

In 2002 Ron Thomas was named to the very exclusive fraternity of Ernest Hemingway look-alikes following the annual competition in Key West, earning the coveted title of "Papa."

Ron is very proud to have recently been inducted into the Crown Point High School Hall of Fame, as a member of the Class of 1959.

His media drawings and illustrations have been published in numerous books, magazines and newspapers, including *The Arizona Republic*.

Ron Thomas has developed a unique style of caricatures that he calls "sportratures." In addition to those published in this book, Ron has playfully "sportraturized" Joe Garagiola, Michael Jordan, Randy Johnson, Charles Barkley, Steve Nash, and many other sports personalities.

Interested in your own, personalized "sportrature?" Contact the artist at: **occamsedge@cox.net.**

RON THOMAS

FORWARD

TOM AMBROSE (L) and JERRY COLANGELO (A.K.A. "J.C.")

"For all of us who came together during the early years of the Suns franchise, players, coaches and front office...it was a great ride!

"I have often said that Tom was 'on scholarship' for 37 years. Without a doubt, we were glad to have him as part of our executive team and part of the Suns family as we built something very special...both on and off the basketball floor.

"I guess in a way, we found each other at precisely the right moment. Tom was looking for a long-term opportunity and I was getting tired of changing PR guys every year."

— Jerry Colangelo

AUTHOR'S NOTES

Many names and dates have been changed, altered or redacted. My intention was to maintain the spirit of the communication collected in the WACKO! File, while keeping the weirdos, nutcases, screwballs, crackpots and whack-jobs anonymous.

I should point out that all professional sports teams receive a steady stream of requests, suggestions and demands…dozens per month…hundreds per year. The WACKO! File started modestly with snail-mail letters to the Suns organization, but the Internet has really pumped up the volume.

What's presented here is a collection. It includes some samples of what I've gathered in the WACKO! File, interspersed with stories of my background and my PR career, as well as other stories I heard along the way. The book is a memoir, and like any memoir, my recollection of a story may not be precisely the way someone else remembers the same incident, but I was as accurate and as detailed as my memory would allow.

Although this book covers more than a quarter century, the chronology is not pure. There are times when, for the sake of continuity, the focus on a particular topic or person might cover multiple generations of Suns history.

Lastly, as I was preparing this book for publication, I submitted three different parts of the book to the website www.iwritelike.com. The first sample produced the result that I write like Vladimir Nabokov (no doubt my Lithuanian, Czech and Austrian heritage was sneaking through). The second writing sample said that my writing style resembled that of Stephen King (now that was scary!). A third sample said my style resembled Ian Fleming (I was shaken by that, but not stirred).

It was all very flattering. But I was really hoping the writing analysis would say that my style was like that of my favorite literary superstar Mark Twain, who truly had a gift for bringing regional dialects to life. There are certain passages in this book where I take a "Twain-like" approach to dialogue. I meant no offense to anyone. It's just how I heard things and subsequently, how I described what I heard.

ACKNOWLEDGEMENTS

Many thanks to my "go to gang" of Jerry Colangelo, Bob Machen, Harvey Shank, Rich Dozer, Tom Leander, Connie Hawkins, Dr. Craig Phelps, Thom Meaker, Ruth Dryjanski, John Olson, Joe Proski, Rich Wolfe, Dave Walls, Dr. Mike Kates, Dick Van Arsdale, Laura Jordan, Bob Coffman, Carole Bartholomeaux, Julie Fie, D.C. Headley, Vince Kozar, Sherry Reed, Neal Walk, Ronald Lee Thomas, Kenny Glenn, Bob Melka, Shelby Burgus and Dr. Paul Steingard. A very special thanks goes to long-time friend, Pat Poulson, and the production company that bears his name.

H.G. Wells once said, "No passion in the world is equal to the passion to alter someone else's draft." Consequently, I salute the relentless passion of my über-persnickety editor and friend, Philip Barnett.

A special note of gratitude goes to the eagle-eyed Jeramie McPeek.

It has been said that "a mind is a terrible thing to waste"…that's why I am so grateful that there were so many willing to share their minds and memories with mine.

PROCEEDS

By purchasing this publication, you have invested in the community. Royalties from this book project will support Big Brothers and Big Sisters of Central Arizona, the Phoenix Zoo and the Children's Museum of Phoenix.

THE TAKE AWAY

I suppose I was no different from any other kid who grew up loving to watch and play sports. I thought it would be immeasurably cool if someday I could play or work for a pro sports team. This is how my story unfolded... growing up in New Rochelle, New York; heading west to Indiana to study at the University of Notre Dame and ultimately finding a new home, family and career thousands of miles away in Phoenix, Arizona.

Enjoy the journey. I sure have. Maybe it was because I always took my responsibilities seriously, but I never took myself the same way. After all, for an English major with average grades to carve out a 37-year career in pro sports, largely because he could construct a simple sentence in English, all I can say is, "Wow! What a country!"

If it is your desire to get into sports public relations or community relations, by all means, pay attention. There are lessons everywhere in this book, some are subtle, others, not so much. If you have an open mind you will see them and learn from both the good and bad, as I did. Somebody once told me, "If you don't make some mistakes, you're not trying very hard."

Included in the book are some personal background stories, some personal opinions and some tales of times gone by. Most of it is intended to be light-hearted and funny, but some reflections cross over to the serious side.

However, if you are looking for a "tell all" sports book revealing heretofore confidential secrets of the stars...fugetaboutit!

IN RESPECTFUL MEMORY OF

Cotton Fitzsimmons * Scotty Robertson * Ira Lavin * J. Walter Kennedy * Dennis Johnson * Armon Gilliam * Bob Hurt * Johnny High * Wilt Chamberlain * Maurice Lucas * Dave Hicks * H.G. Listiak * Lawrence F. O'Brien * Bob Cowen * Elmer Tanter * Tim McGuire * Dick Stuart * Steve Pascente * Ted Brown * Bill Denney * Chuck Daly * Dick Percudani * Harry Caplan * Stan Kaplan * Sue Stemmer * Vic Blosser * Johnny High * Bob Cohn * Phil Lumpkin * Nate Hawthorne * Wayman Tisdale * Ted Podleski * Scott Podleski * Matt Dobek * Nick Vanos * Mrs. Selinda King * Sid Borgia * John Condon * Mary Anne and Carmine Gallino * Terry Day * Eula and Whitey Dillman * Manute Bol * Johnny Kerr * Pete Newell * Bob Moran * Dave DeBusschere * George Mikan * Arnold "Red" Auerbach * Kheni White * Marc Splaver * Howie McHugh Irv Shuman * John White * Darell Garretson * Hilda Van Arsdale * Tommy Jones * Jeff Temkin * Jerome Blanton * Dennis Price * Harold McAvoy * Bob and Judy Barnes * Dick Dozer * Eddie Lynch * Earl Strom * Richie Powers * Mendy Rudolph * Chick Hearn * Johnny Most * Stephen Ambrose

TABLE OF CONTENTS

CHAPTERS

PROLOGUE

LOST LOVE

It all started in the spring of 1976 with the arrival of LOVE 22. No, LOVE 22 wasn't a Suns draft pick, a uniform number, an old girlfriend, a magic potion, or even an exotic dancer...it was a letter...sort of. The letter, from LOVE 22, showed up in the daily mail delivery at the Phoenix Suns office on North Central Avenue about the time the Suns were about to get back in the playoffs following a five-year absence.

But it was more than just a letter from a random fan. It was a rather substantial discourse, a treatise, the type of streaming diatribe that many years later would be made famous...no, make that infamous... by Ted Kaczynski, the "Unabomber." The communiqué I received meandered through topics of sports, politics, war, religion, pestilence, conspiracy theories and the coming alien invasion of earth. Call it a term paper, a study, a body of work, a manifesto ...call it whatever you want...but pretty much everyone who read it agreed with Suns assistant coach Al Bianchi, who summed it up succinctly, "Tommy, this guy's a wacko!"

Why bring this up? Well, somewhere along the way, I lost LOVE 22. I looked everywhere but, by the autumn of 1976, LOVE 22 had vanished. Perhaps it was programmed to self-destruct after reading. Maybe I left it in my car during that hot Phoenix summer and it spontaneously combusted. I guess you never truly know what you have until you lose it. The moment I realized that LOVE 22 (or at least his letter) was gone, I vowed that I would never again lose or toss anything interesting, unusual or even borderline crazy... and so, the "WACKO! File" was born. So here's to LOVE 22...my thanks go out to you, my man...on whatever planet you now reside.

FROM THE WACKO! FILE: A CLASSIC

Many years later, I was explaining to a friend that I was consistently flattered by the fact that whenever a member of the Suns front office received a piece of correspondence that they couldn't understand, or didn't want to handle, they would just forward it to me. "Tom will know what to do with it," they would assure themselves. I joked that I had actually become the physical manifestation of, "To whom it may concern."

It wasn't long before that same friend, Brian Neddoff, forwarded this correspondence to me. This letter, supposedly from the Smithsonian Institute, was exactly the reason I created the WACKO! File. Brian wrote:

Dear Tom,

Attached is a letter from the Smithsonian Institute to Mr. Scott Williams of Newport, RI. Mr. Williams has an interesting hobby, he digs things out of his backyard. Of more interest is that he actually sends his findings to the Smithsonian Institute, labeling the items with scientific names and insists that the items are actual archaeological finds.

According to the legend, this guy really exists and I feel might be a candidate for your WACKO! File. Anyway, here is the reply from the Smithsonian Institute. Hopefully the next time you are writing a response to a "To Whom It May Concern" letter, you will know that you are not alone and things could be worse.

Brian

Smithsonian Institute
207 Pennsylvania Avenue
Washington, DC 20078

Dear Mr. Williams:

Thank you for your latest submission to the Institute, labeled "93211-D, layer seven, next to the clothesline post...Hominid skull." We have given this specimen a careful and detailed examination, and regret to inform you that we disagree with your theory that it represents conclusive proof of the presence of Early Man in Charleston County two million years ago. Rather, it appears that what you have found is the head of a Barbie doll, of the variety that one of our staff, who has small children, believes to be "Malibu Barbie." It is evident that you have given a great deal of thought to the analysis of this specimen, and you may be quite certain that those of us who are familiar with your prior work in the field were loathe to come to contradiction with your findings.

However, we do feel that there are a number of physical attributes of the specimen which might have tipped you off to its modern origin:

The material is molded plastic. Ancient hominid remains are typically fossilized bone.

The cranial capacity of the specimen is approximately 9 cubic centimeters, well below the threshold of even the earliest identified proto-hominids.

The dentition pattern evident on the skull is more consistent with the common domesticated dog than it is with the ravenous, man-eating, Pliocene clams you speculate roamed the wetlands during that time. This latter finding is certainly one of the most intriguing hypotheses you have submitted in your history with this institution, but the evidence seems to weigh rather heavily against it. Without going into too much detail, let us say that:

The specimen looks like the head of a Barbie doll that a dog has chewed on.

Clams don't have teeth.

It is with feelings tinged with melancholy that we must deny your request to have the specimen carbon-dated. This is partially due to the heavy load our lab must bear in its normal operation, and partially due to carbon-dating's notorious inaccuracy in fossils of recent geologic record. To the best of our knowledge, no Barbie dolls were produced prior to 1956 AD, and carbon-dating is likely to produce wildly inaccurate results. Sadly, we must also deny your request that we approach the National Science Foundation Phylogeny Department with the concept of assigning you specimen the scientific name Australopithecus spiffarino. Speaking personally, I for one, fought tenaciously for the acceptance of your proposed taxonomy, but was ultimately voted down because the species name you selected was hyphenated, and really didn't sound like it might be Latin.

However, we gladly accepted your generous donation of this fascinating specimen to the museum. While it is undoubtedly not a Hominid fossil, it is, nonetheless, yet another riveting example of the great body of work you seem to accumulate here so effortlessly. You should know that our Director has reserved a special shelf in his own office for the display of the specimens you have previously submitted to the Institute, the entire staff speculates daily on what you will happen upon next in your digs at the site you have discovered in your Newport back yard.

We eagerly anticipate your trip to our nation's capital that you proposed in your last letter, and several of us are pressing the director to pay for it. We are particularly interested in hearing you expand on your theories surrounding the trans-positating fillifitation of ferrous ions in a structural matrix that makes the excellent juvenile Tyrannosaurus Rex femur you recently discovered take on the deceptive appearance of a rusty 9-mm Scars Craftsman automotive crescent wrench.

Yours in Science,

Harvey Rowe
Chief Curator-Antiquities
Paleoanthropology Division

Author's Note: Doing a little digging of our own, WACKO! File investigators discovered that this correspondence is often claimed to be a genuine letter from the Smithsonian's archives, but it isn't. The Smithsonian has no Paleoanthropology division, and no curator named Harvey Rowe. Harvey Rowe does exist, however, and he is the very clever author of this letter!

CHAPTER 1

THE PRE-THOMASIOPONIC ERA

45 MINUTES FROM BROADWAY

I grew up in New Rochelle, New York in the 1950's and 60's. "Nershell," as the locals say it, is a suburb of New York City that is, as the old George M. Cohan song goes, "only 45 minutes from Broadway." That's still pretty close to the truth today. You can catch the New Haven Railroad from New Rochelle into Grand Central Station or you can drive into the city, pray for light traffic and then exchange your first-born child for a parking space. Either way, if things go well, Times Square is still only 45 minutes from New Rochelle.

Because of that proximity, New Rochelle has always been home to a host of actors, singers, artists, writers, CEOs and athletes. Norman Rockwell, Willie Mays, Robert Merrill, W.C. Fields, Jay Leno, Richard Roundtree, William Randolph Hearst, Laurence Fishburne and James Fenimore Cooper are just a few names among the hundreds of famous people who called "The Queen City" of Long Island Sound their home, at least for a time.

MR. MAC

Like my three older sisters and my two younger brothers, I attended our church's Catholic parochial school in New Rochelle. The teaching staff and administration at Holy Family School (HFS) were Dominican Sisters. The school covered kindergarten through eighth grade. The good Sisters made certain that the school had a strong academic program, a firm religious foundation and lots of Catholic discipline. This included the occasional use of soap (Ivory™, I think) to wash out a mouth that had used bad language.

The parish school also had solid athletic programs in football, basketball and baseball, in spite of the fact that, for many years, the school had no sports facilities of any kind. The football and baseball teams would practice and play their games at New Rochelle's City Park, a municipal field that was a good two-mile bike ride from the school and not in the best of neighborhoods. The HFS basketball team would bounce from gym to gym around the city.

All of these school teams were coached by the same man, a dedicated local fire chief named Harold McAvoy. "Mr. Mac" was a squarely built man with a jaw that looked like it was chiseled from a block of granite. He coached those Holy Family teams, year 'round, for decades. Hundreds of HFS kids got an opportunity to learn sports and sportsmanship under Mr. Mac. Talk about a role model...because of his example, many of Mr. Mac's young athletes would grow up to become successful coaches themselves, a continuing legacy to his dedication to kids.

We played in a fairly competitive Catholic grammar school league and, regardless of the sport, it was a rare year when Mr. Mac's Holy Family teams weren't challenging for championships. HFS won the football title when I was in 7th grade, along with basketball and baseball titles when I was an 8th grader.

HFS 1960, 7th and 8th GRADE CHAMPIONSHIP FOOTBALL TEAM. COACH HAROLD McAVOY (FAR RIGHT, BACK ROW). THE AUTHOR (BACK ROW, THIRD PLAYER IN FROM MR. MAC)

SID

One of my grade school classmates, teammates and friends was a kid named Johnny Borgia, known to all simply as, "J-Bo." His family lived on Clove Road in a distinctive pink house that I walked past every day on my way to school. John's dad was Sid Borgia who, in the 1950's and 60's, was one of the top referees in the National Basketball Association (NBA). Sid was only about 5'7" and started refereeing before World War II in what he termed "the dance hall days."

Sid once explained, "There'd be a dance before the game, they'd play the first half, continue the dance at halftime, then finish the game and dance afterwards."

For all that, he'd earn a dollar or two for refereeing the game. Following the war, Sid got a tryout with a new basketball league, the Basketball Association of America. He went to training camp to work with a team called the New York Knickerbockers and he ultimately earned a spot in the league as a ref. Three years later the league would become known as the National Basketball Association. Referees didn't get much publicity back then but I remember seeing one feature story that referred to Sid as a "bow-legged, diminutive arbiter" and then went on to describe him as "the whistling pixie." Back in the 1950s Sid would work just about any game he could find, including high school basketball games. Basketball Hall of Famer, Connie Hawkins, remembers Sid doing some of his games at Boys High in Brooklyn.

Once in a while, if Sid had an NBA game at Madison Square Garden, he'd load Johnny and one or two of Johnny's buddies into his Nash American and take us with him for a night of NBA basketball at the "G-a-a-den." Frequently, these would be NBA double-headers. A typical night might feature the Philadelphia Warriors taking on the Syracuse Nationals in the first game and the Knicks battling the Cincinnati Royals in the second game. Incidentally, in 1960, a Madison Square Garden double-header would feature exactly *half* of the NBA's eight teams!

When the first game started, we'd sit in the comp seats that the home team Knicks would provide for the referees, but as the game progressed, we would keep moving down closer and closer to the court. Inevitably we'd be ousted by the ushers and chased back to our original seats. I'm not sure you could do that today, but back then there were *lots* of empty seats in the Garden. When you consider that some of the stars that populated the NBA at that time included: Wilt Chamberlain, Al Attles, Sam Jones, Bob Cousy, Bill Russell, Bob Pettit, Jerry West, Dolph Schayes and a host of other future Hall of Fame athletes, it was clear that basketball fans really didn't know what they had...or hadn't yet grown to fully appreciate it.

Sid Borgia was a wonderful storyteller and one of those characters you meet in life who you never forget. Sid did a full schedule of NBA games in the winter and then would umpire local baseball and softball games during the summer. I'll always remember Sid explaining the infield fly rule to Johnny and me at the Borgia's kitchen table, using salt and pepper shakers as props. He had this staccato manner of speaking, a gravelly mix of New York City and West Virginia that sounded a bit like the old entertainer Jimmy Durante. It was both funny and engaging and I never got tired of it. When he was out of earshot, J-Bo and I would often try to imitate Sid's distinctive speech. To this day, whenever I call John, the first thing he says is, "Hello, T-a-a-a-m-m-y!"

Two of Sid's sons, Johnny and Joe, would grow up to follow in his footsteps as NBA officials, making Sid one proud papa.

WALTA

I was hearing NBA stories from Sid when I was still in grade school. One of my favorites involved big Walter Bellamy of the St. Louis Hawks, who, during NBA games, would often mutter about himself in the third-person. After Sid blew the whistle on Bellamy for some infraction, he might overhear him saying, "A-w-w-w, man! Walter didn't commit no foul! Walter got all ball!" Or perhaps, "Walter wasn't in the lane for no three seconds!"

> **"Hey, Walta! Do me a fay-va!"**
> **- Sid Borgia**

One night, Sid let Bellamy's monologue ramble on for a while, but when he'd finally heard enough of Walter's whining, Sid confronted the seven-footer. Topping-out at about Bellamy's waistband, Sid craned his neck upwards, wagged his finger at the big guy and said, "Hey, Walta! Do me a fay-va! You tell Walta, that if Walta don't shut up, Walta's gettin' a technical foul!!"

HIGH SCHOOL HOOPS

Later, as high school seniors at Iona Prep, J-Bo and I were voted co-captains of the basketball team. Understand that John was the real player in that dynamic duo. I was simply his friend. J-Bo really knew the game. He was a fine all-around guard who made his teammates better. Basically, I was a football player, playing basketball. Every basketball season it would take me a couple of weeks to make the physical and mental adjustment from one sport to the other.

Once, early in the basketball season, Iona Prep came down to Manhattan from Westchester County to play a game against Regis High School at Madison Square Garden. It was a preliminary tilt prior to a Knicks game. That was a regular thing back in those days and a thrill for the high school players. I was just a few days off of the football field when I came into the game and J-Bo quickly found me open for my best shot, a baseline jumper from the corner. I lined it up and let it fly! I guess my muscles were not yet in basketball shape, because the shot sailed high over the rim, missed everything and landed pretty close to the opposite corner! I recall hearing some mocking o-o-o-h-s, a-a-a-h-h-s and maybe even a stunned "whoa!" from the tiny crowd. I was totally embarrassed...and in the Garden, no less!

The Iona Prep "Irish" hoopsters had a bit of a rough go that year...finishing the season 2-17 under our fine leadership. However, since J-Bo and I were also in charge of the sports section of the school yearbook, students looking back today at the 1966 Iona Prep basketball team will find nothing but great pictures, good memories and absolutely no results from that epic senior basketball season. For all anyone knows, we went undefeated and won the state championship!

Incidentally, when those high school preliminary games were done at the Garden, you got to stay and watch the pros for a few minutes before the school bus would be ready to take you back home. There was a rookie on the Knicks at that time, a country kid from Indiana with blond hair and a physical game, who I had first read about in *Sports Illustrated*. Because of his aggressive game, I took a liking to him, and subsequently followed his career. His name was Dick Van Arsdale. Just a couple of years later, the Knicks would let him go to the new Phoenix team in the 1968 NBA Expansion Draft. Five years after that, I would join the Suns as their PR director. Van would prove to be the perfect choice to build a franchise around. A fierce competitor and a class act in every way, Van will always be "The Original Sun," my all-time favorite Suns player and a great friend.

IONA HIGH SCHOOL

Bottom Row — Left to Right: J. Borgia, B. Morrisson, J. Taylor, M. Morris, P. Mudd, W. LaPolla

Top Row — Left to Right: P. Marquette, T. Gleason, P. Detagyos, J. Hennessy, T. Ambrosie, N. Furlong

Coach: Mr. Lawrence Lembo   Moderator: Bro. J. J. O'Connell

Managers: F. Vitolo, J. Manganiello, H. McHugh, B. Quinn

J-Bo went on to Princeton on a full academic scholarship and played on the Princeton basketball team. I went on to Notre Dame, played some club-team rugby, but basically hung up my jock, my sneakers, and my sports dreams.

On one Christmas vacation however, I was back at the Garden to watch Princeton take on one of the great UCLA teams featuring Sidney Wicks, Curtis Rowe and company. It was a blow-out win for UCLA but one that allowed J-Bo to get a few minutes of playing time at the end of the game. I was really proud to see my buddy out there in a big-time NCAA game in Madison Square Garden. It was a hoot!

TOO HOT, TOO SMALL AND TOO FAR AWAY

J. Walter Kennedy was commissioner of the NBA in 1968 when the Suns came to be. When the idea was first floated for possible NBA expansion to Phoenix, Arizona, Kennedy was all for it. He thought Phoenix's rapidly growing market could more than adequately support an NBA team. But this was a simpler time before the feasibility of a new franchise was carefully evaluated through extensive market research studies and focus groups. It was also prior to the time when potential ownership groups had to undergo a financial colonoscopy before being approved by the league.

Many pundits in the East thought that Phoenix was too small, too hot and too far away to be a good site for a new NBA team. So Kennedy did his own survey and evaluation. On several trips to Phoenix, he talked to numerous cab drivers, shoeshine boys, bellmen and barbers. According to Kennedy, all of them thought that an NBA team would be a great idea! He was also impressed at how knowledgeable Phoenicians were about the NBA. Kennedy's endorsement led the way and the Phoenix application was approved. For the princely sum of two million dollars, the team's major investors, Richard Bloch, Donald Pitt and Donald Diamond had their NBA franchise in Phoenix.

> **"He was impressed at how knowledgeable Phoenicians were about the NBA."**

THE COLISEUM

A special commission began planning for an "Arizona State Fairgrounds Exposition Center" as early as the fall of 1962. They envisioned an indoor facility that would serve as the key venue for the State Fair and be used for other shows and events year-round.

In 1964, Phoenix architect Leslie Mahoney presented the commission with the final plans and construction began that summer. Built for the then-pricey sum of seven million dollars, the Coliseum opened on November 3, 1965 with a production of the *Ice Follies*, hosted by Bob Hope. People drove from across the state to marvel at the Coliseum's unique, saddle-shaped, tension-cable roof, which supported more than 1,000 pre-cast concrete panels... but more on the roof later.

ARIZONA VETERANS MEMORIAL COLISEUM AND ITS SADDLE-SHAPED ROOF

MURALS AND MORE

The Arizona Veterans Memorial Coliseum quickly became a source of pride for the entire state. Named in honor of Arizona's war veterans, the building was designed to be a monument to the activities and culture of the State of Arizona. Consequently, the State Fair and Exposition Board and the state legislature commissioned one of the finest artists and muralists of the time, Paul Coze, to create two giant murals that would be displayed at the East and West ends of the Coliseum arena. One was called "Friendship," done in a unique, linear, interlocking style. The other featured Arizona's five C's of commerce: Citrus, Cattle, Cotton, Copper and Climate, with a special salute to the military.

The Coliseum's circular lobby also featured Coze murals of the Grand Canyon and a Mexican bullfight, while other murals displayed colorful Native American and cowboy scenes.

After the building opened, huge display cases were constructed to house the trophies of respected Arizona hunter and guide, Mr. Bob Householder. An extensive collection of his full-sized hunting trophies, the displays included Householder's "grand slam" (a game trophy from each of the four recognized varieties of North America's wild sheep: Dall, Stone, Rocky Mountain Bighorn, and Desert Bighorn). It was an impressive display worthy of a fine natural history museum. But a taxidermist's collection of wild beasts just seemed a bit odd for a public arena designed for hockey, basketball, rodeos, family shows and concerts.

> **❝... the only place in the NBA where you can get hit in the head with a corn on the cob! ❞**
> **- Dave DeBusschere**

The Suns arrived in 1968 but their October schedule annually clashed with the Coliseum's biggest event of the year, the three-week run of the Arizona State Fair. Part of the Coliseum's charter with the State Fair called for a single admission fee. Once the admission fee was paid, all events on the State Fair grounds were open to the public. So fairgoers could enjoy some Indian fry bread on the midway, ride the Ferris wheel and, if the Suns were playing that night, they could wander in, take a seat and enjoy some NBA action. This situation led to arena crowds that not only included basketball fans but also a fair sampling of both the curious and the clueless.

The Arizona State Fair's carnival atmosphere, once prompted NBA All-Star Dave DeBusschere to describe Phoenix and its Coliseum as, "the only place in the NBA where you can get hit in the head with a corn on the cob!"

GUNS OF THE SUNS

The "Guns of the Suns" were a group of local Phoenix business-men, who became known for the fancy Suns crest on their dark blue blazers and for their staunch support of the Suns during the early years of the franchise.

Jerry Colangelo and his chief marketing executive, Ted Podleski, worked tirelessly to develop this group of influential community movers and shakers. It was a classic, grass-roots, word-of-mouth, one-on-one strategy that helped sell the fledgling Suns to the community.

The group cut a swath through the Phoenix business demo-graphic. It included: bankers, real estate agents, insurance reps, grocers, advertising execs, car dealers...even Jerry Colangelo's barber. All of them were recruited to become an extended sales force for the franchise.

The NBA was the first of the major sports leagues to hit Phoenix. People were curious but not quite ready to invest in season tickets. The "Guns" helped give the young franchise some early credibility within the business community.

When Colangelo ventured out to sell tickets, he'd bring a 16 mm projector and an NBA highlight film to show to any group that was willing to sit, watch and listen to his pitch. Ronald Lee Thomas, Colangelo's barber (now called his "stylist"), gathered a group of his customers in his shop to watch the film and listen to the Suns' young general manager.

"We just hung a barber's cloth on the wall in the back room of the shop to show the film," Thomas remembered, "and we wound up selling six season tickets that night!"

That was good enough to qualify Thomas as a full-fledged mem-ber of the "Guns." Car dealers Kemp Biddulph and Lou Grubb along with Dave Amster, Paul Muscente, Bud Davidson, Willis Neilson, Lou Goldstein, Jack Humphries, Dick Todd, Art Schaier and Dr. Howard Sherman were among many well-known and successful Phoenix business people who also became "Guns." Going on a road trip with the team was the annual reward for major sponsors along with members of the "Guns" who sold their quota of season tickets.

BEAT THE BULLS!

One "Guns" trip at the tail end of the 1970-71 season would feature two games on back-to-back nights in Chicago against the Bulls followed by a third game in Madison, Wisconsin against the Milwaukee Bucks. It was Cotton Fitzsimmons' first year with the Suns and, with the team in the playoff hunt, the hyped-up and gung-ho "Guns" wanted to demonstrate their loyalty and support.

In addition to his considerable tonsorial skills, Ron Thomas was also a talented artist and he packed his lettering brushes for the trip. Upon arrival in Chicago he picked up some additional sign-making materials and quickly produced a large sign in Suns' colors that stated simply, "BEAT THE BULLS!"

It was an enthusiastic group of "Guns" that gathered for a pre-game cocktail party at their downtown Chicago hotel and then prepared to bus over to the old Chicago Stadium for the game.

Thomas and his buddy, Allan Starr, taped the newly-painted sign to the side of the bus. Many in the group were wearing 1930's style, straw, "boater" hats that said "GUNS OF THE SUNS" on the hat band. On the trip over, they were cautioned that Chicago Stadium was not in the best of neighborhoods and they should go directly into the arena and not wander around outside.

No sooner did the bus, with its "BEAT THE BULLS!" sign on the side, pull up to the curb at Chicago Stadium, than it literally came under attack by eight or ten irate Bulls fans who rocked the bus violently, trying to tip it over. Thomas' sign was quickly destroyed by the attackers. The "Guns," shaken both literally and figuratively, hustled off the bus and made their way inside. And that's when things really got interesting.

Another member of the group smuggled in a big banner that read: "GUNS OF THE SUNS." Before the game, a bunch of the "Guns" paraded that banner around the entire perimeter of the court. Today, NBA arena security would never allow that to happen, but this was 1971.

Without warning, the Bulls' mascot, Bennie the Bull, charged right through the Suns banner, ripping it in half. The bull, simultaneously wearing and seeing red, proceeded to tear the "Guns'" banner to shreds. A minor melee ensued. One of the "Guns" counter-attacked and yanked off Bennie's tail!

Suddenly, things got even crazier as irate Bulls fans began working their way down the aisles to "put a hurtin' on" these upstart fans from Phoenix. Although they certainly wanted to show their support for their Suns, about the last thing the "Guns" wanted was to become embroiled in a Chicago-style backstreet brawl. Things finally calmed down. Bennie the Bull was put back together and the "Guns" were able to cheer on their Suns. Unfortunately, the Suns were thumped 116-92 and the disappointed "Guns" retreated to Rush Street to regroup and build up their courage for the following night's game.

For their encore performance, Thomas created another sign that said "NO MORE BULL!" But this time he rolled it up and hid it in his sleeve. Just before tip-off, with security once again non-existent, Thomas and fellow "Gun" Allan Starr, ran the banner down onto the court, right in front of the Suns bench. They held it up proudly and showed it to one side of the stadium, then the other. Angry Bulls fans howled in anger and outraged disbelief! Within seconds the sign holders and anybody from Phoenix wearing one of those silly straw hats, were being pelted with anything Bulls fans could get their hands on. Someone zeroed-in on Ted Podleski's alpaca sweater and drilled him squarely in the back with a great big wad of some kind of gooey, gummy adhesive that wasn't going to come loose anytime soon. Amidst the chaos, Suns center, Neal Walk looked over from the bench and said, "What the hell are you guys doing down here?"

> **❝The last thing the 'Guns' wanted was to become embroiled in a Chicago-style backstreet brawl.❞**

"Just having fun," was Thomas' response, as he tried to duck and dodge the unidentified missiles that rained down on him.

By this time, the "Guns" were not only being pelted with all manner of trash and debris, but they were also being booed lustily. To avoid what was rapidly shaping up to be a full-scale riot, somebody turned off the lights and plunged Chicago Stadium into darkness. This was years before NBA teams did their elaborate "lights-off" introductions, but throwing the "off" switch stopped everyone in their tracks and seemed to calm things down. That gave the targeted "Guns" a chance to scramble over the courtside seats and return to the anonymity and relative safety of their seats in the stands.

In spite of the valiant efforts of the "Guns," the Suns lost to the Bulls again, 111-99. On the last game of the trip the Suns defeated the Bucks 119-111 in Madison, Wisconsin. That game was played without incident and the "Guns" returned safely to Phoenix with only their pride shattered ...and their egos slightly battered.

FOOT TO HEAD

A few years later, after I joined the Suns, I went on one of the "Guns of the Suns" road trips. This time the trip was to San Diego to take on the Clippers. Needless to say, in laid-back San Diego, game night wouldn't be as confrontational as it had been in Chicago a few years before. While a lot of the Guns went off to play golf, I stayed with the team for the morning shoot-around. By mid-afternoon, my roomie for the trip, Jack Humphries, still was not back from the golf outing but I had to get spiffed-up and ready to take the team bus over to the arena. As I stepped into the shower, I realized that our cut-rate hotel had not supplied our room with any shampoo. I looked around, but all I could find in the bathroom was a small, plastic bottle of soap that belonged to Jack. I thought, "What the heck, Jack won't mind if sneak a little squirt of his shampoo." The liquid was thin and a little reddish and it smelled OK, so I lathered up.

I rode the team bus over to the arena and got busy with my PR duties. Before too long, the "Guns" arrived and I immediately sought out my roommate.

"Jack," I said, "I hope you don't mind, but I used a tiny bit of your shampoo when I was getting cleaned up for the game."

He had a puzzled look on his face. "Shampoo?" he asked.

"Yeah," I replied, "It was in a plastic bottle in the shower...kinda reddish?"

He looked at me and burst out laughing.

"No, I don't mind," he said between chuckles, "But that wasn't exactly shampoo! I have this foot condition and that's a special treatment I have to use for it!"

For many months afterwards, any time I saw Jack at a Suns game, he would never look me directly in the eye. But he always seemed to be smiling and checking out the top of my head!

I am pleased to report that my hair never turned red, most of it is still firmly rooted... and to this day, I have never...ever...suffered from athlete's foot of the head!

TED

When I first started with the Suns, I reported to the sales, marketing and promotion manager, Ted Podleski, who was Jerry Colangelo's right-hand man.

Even if he didn't have any time, Ted was a guy who would always make time for you. Then he would usually compound matters by giving you too much time, which is why he really didn't have any time to give you in the first place.

> *❝...the new team was all about...integrity, hard work, creativity and having fun. ❞*

Once you were with him though, you had Ted's undivided attention. No amount of pressing business could shake his concentration on finding out how your family was doing, getting an update on your latest challenges, asking about mutual friends and, of course, talking about the Phoenix Suns.

Ted joined the Suns as their sales and promotion manager during the franchise's first season. To many long-time season-ticketholders, sponsors and staff, Ted embodied what the new team was all about...integrity, hard work, creativity and having fun. In those early years with the Suns, Ted was indefatigable, with a mind that simply bubbled over with creative ideas. Ted's innovative promotions helped to make Suns fans out of legions of youngsters, create a wholesome family-oriented approach to game night entertainment and helped establish the strong community reputation that, to this day, still defines the NBA's Phoenix franchise.

Ted and JC were among the first sports-marketing executives to "package" sponsorships. It was no longer just about selling tickets. Sponsorships now included radio and TV time, in-arena signage and announcements, give-away nights, traffic building promotions, half-time shows and special events. We often joked that "we interrupt our commercial messaging in order to present tonight's game. We apologize to our fine sponsors." But we made it fun...and it worked.

When Ted passed away in 1999 at age 62, after a long battle with heart and lung disease, the Phoenix Suns family lost one of the "originals." I lost a great mentor and friend.

NEVER AGAIN

Jerry Walser had been part of the front office of the Syracuse Nationals going back to the days when Johnny Kerr was a "Nat." When Kerr migrated west to coach the expansion Suns in 1968, Walser re-joined his old buddy. He was an experienced business manager who set up the Suns' ticket operation during the early days of the franchise. In the summer of 1968, the Suns' first as a franchise, Walser had to travel down to Fort Huachuca (Waa-chew-ka), Arizona to make arrangements for a Suns pre-season game that would be played there a few months later.

Fort Huachuca has been a U.S. Army post since the Indian Wars of the 1870s. The fort is part of the town of Sierra Vista, 190 miles southeast of Phoenix and a good three-and-a-half hour drive. But rather than make the long drive, Walser decided to travel there by small plane. Although the flying time was much shorter than the drive, he spent the entire flight being violently tossed around in the thermals that define Arizona flying in the summertime.

But the flight was just the start of his misery. Coming from the East and going right to work for the Suns, Walser never had the chance to make the switch to lighter clothing. So he spent the day in Fort Huachuca's 100 degree heat, nattily, though uncomfortably, attired in a shirt, tie and tweed business suit. By the time he got back to Phoenix, he was an over-heated, physical wreck and he understandably declared, "I will never set foot in Fort Huachuca again...ever!"

The Fort Huachuca game pitted the Suns against the Los Angeles Lakers, who featured future hall-of-famers Jerry West, Wilt Chamberlain and Elgin Baylor. But when the game tipped off in the Fort Huachuca gymnasium, there were more players on the two team benches than there were fans in the stands. Virtually the entire fort was on leave for the weekend so hardly anyone showed up for the game, including Jerry Walser.

GLAMOUR

Late one night during the Suns first season, trainer Joe Proski and his wife Jan were driving down Central Avenue in Phoenix, when they saw some lights on in the Suns office. Thinking it was a little unusual for anyone to be working that late, the Proskis pulled into the Suns parking lot and entered the office through the unlocked back door.

They walked in to see Jerry Walser, still wearing his signature shirt and tie, crawling around the floor on his hands and knees, sorting through hundreds, perhaps thousands of tickets that had been fired into the air by a malfunctioning ticket counting machine. The tickets seemed to cover every surface in the room.

Joe and Jan pitched in to help, but much to their amusement, in between obscure references to the Marx brothers, Walser kept up a steady stream of malevolent obscenities directed at the shoddy equipment, the overly-frugal Suns ownership and just about anything or anybody else he could bring to mind.

It was just another typically glamorous night with an NBA expansion team.

COCONINO

In the early days of the Suns franchise, the team frequently hooked up with the Los Angeles Lakers for pre-season games. Such was the case when the two teams met in Flagstaff, Arizona to play an exhibition game at Coconino High School.

The Suns and Lakers were on an austerity program and since both teams were staying at the same local motel, there would be only one bus for both teams going over to the game. Wilt Chamberlain was a Lakers' star and he was taking his sweet time getting on the bus. Suns coach Johnny "Red" Kerr was getting a little impatient.

When Chamberlain finally walked in front of the waiting bus, Red shouted to the driver, "OK...FLOOR IT!" Wilt then walked to the back of the bus and moved out several Suns players who had committed the unpardonable sin of sitting in "his seats." No doubt, it is always nice to have visiting royalty on a pre-season road trip.

Although the game was a "sellout" of 3,000 people at the tiny Coconino gym, that didn't impress Wilt who took one quick look around and said, "'Dipper' ain't playin' in this place...there's no-body here!" A man of his word, Wilt did not play that night.

FLAT NIGHT

For that game in Flagstaff, Dave "Big Daddy" Lattin (La-TEEN) of the Suns was on the injured list with a broken hand. But wanting to stay involved with the team, Lattin drove his Cadillac three hours north from Phoenix to attend the game. During the course of the evening, Wilt heard that Lattin would be driving his own "wheels" back to Phoenix. Chamberlain immediately shunned the idea of a return trip on the team bus and told Lattin, "I'm with YOU, my man!"

> **" Dipper don't change no tires! "**
> -**Wilt Chamberlain**

There was no problem. Chamberlain was 7'1" and 275 pounds. Lattin was 6'7" and 230 pounds. Chamberlain was God...and you always did what God said.

With Lattin driving, this dynamic duo made it about 30 miles south of Flagstaff before they ran out of luck and had a flat tire.

When the one-armed Lattin held up the cast on his broken hand and informed Wilt that *he* would have to change the tire, Chamberlain said emphatically, "Dipper don't change no tires!"

So Lattin, stood on the shoulder of the interstate, and frantically tried to wave down a passing car to help.

Think about it. It is 1968. It is Northern Arizona. It is late at night and, a very large man with a cast on his arm is trying to wave you down on a lonely stretch of highway. Waiting in the car, is another giant man. The few cars that went by not only didn't slow down...they accelerated!

Ultimately, faced with a long night on the shoulder of Interstate 17, "Dipper" did change the tire, but he admonished Lattin, "If you EVER tell anybody I did this...I'll KILL you!"

HANDS OR TALONS?

Shake hands with Connie Hawkins and you will never forget it. His extraordinarily long fingers wrap all the way around your hand... and then they envelop your wrist! Comparing one of "Hawk's" hands wrapped around a basketball, to a normal person's hand gripping a grapefruit, is really not much of an exaggeration.

When "Hawk" arrived on the NBA scene in 1969, nobody had ever seen a player quite like him. Years later, players like Julius Erving, Michael Jordan, Pete Maravich, Magic Johnson and George Gervin would all emulate elements of the artful grace that was Connie Hawkins' game, but in 1969 he dazzled everyone, even the refs.

In one of Hawkins' early games with the Suns, the basketball was bouncing out of bounds. Hawkins swooped in and with one big hand, grabbed the top half of the ball as it was just six inches off the floor, saving the Suns' possession. Referee Mendy Rudolph was in perfect position to make the call...but he called it the other way. He couldn't believe that anyone could do what Hawkins just did. The ball must have hit the floor!

Hawkins just laughed and nonchalantly flipped Mendy the ball, "That's OK, Mendy. I know you've never seen anything like that before!"

A LEGEND IN HIS OWN MIND

A "New Yawka" friend of mine was at a Suns' event and was regaling a small group of people with his high school basketball prowess. He specifically mentioned that, when Connie Hawkins was the leading high school player in the country at Boys' High in Brooklyn, averaging 42 points per game, he held Hawk to 28 points. The group was impressed.

"That was some awesome 'D,'" somebody said.

Connie was standing a few feet away and, ever the gentleman, smiled, but said nothing.

Unfortunately for my friend, someone in the group asked, "How much of the game did Connie play?" His response, in almost a whisper was, "Just the first half."

So much for "good D."

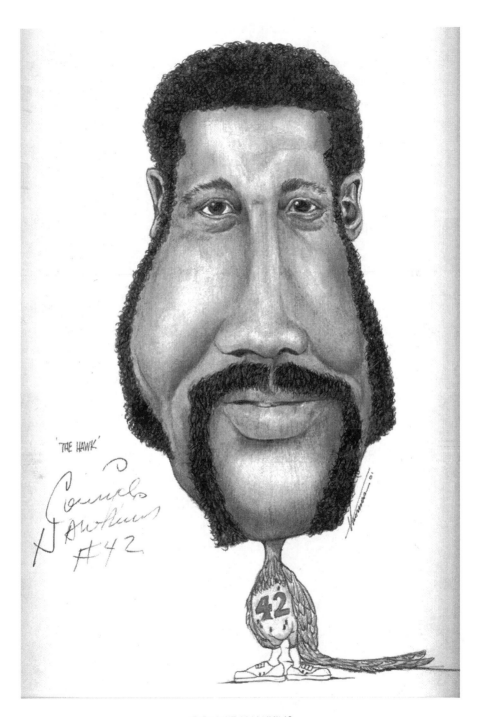

CONNIE HAWKINS

YOU'RE GONE!

As the Suns were warming up for an early 1970's game against the Cavaliers in the old Cleveland Arena, forward Lamar Green walked over to his friend and teammate, Connie Hawkins.

"Bad news, man," Lamar said, "Mendy's doin' the game tonight!"

Hawkins was devastated. He didn't know why, but he felt that referee Mendy Rudolph had some sort of personal vendetta against him. It was an opinion that was shared by many around the league. In Hawk's mind, it was going to be a long, frustrating night, filled with nit-picky calls and Mendy's self-aggrandizing theatrics.

The game hadn't even begun, but because of Rudolph, Hawkins had already worked himself into a froth.

A few minutes later, as the Suns and Cavs jostled for position around the center-court jump circle to start the game, Hawk just couldn't help himself. Just as Mendy got ready to toss the ball in the air for the opening tip, Connie mumbled a reference to Rudolph's parentage as possibly being canine and suggested that Mendy perform an act on himself that is considered to be anatomically impossible.

Rudolph tossed the ball in the air... the two centers jumped and tipped the ball... it bounced around, then hit the floor as a couple of players scrambled for it. Rudolph blew two quick tweets on his whistle, stopping play. But instead of calling a foul, he threw Hawkins out of the game! Hawkins didn't say a word. He just walked off the court and headed for the locker room.

Meanwhile, Suns coach Jerry Colangelo stood speechless in front of the Suns bench, arms outstretched, wondering "wha' happened?!"

Many years later, Colangelo reflected on that night.

"That was the quickest ejection I ever saw!" Jerry said. "The ball went up...the ball came down...and Hawk was gone!"

NOBODY KNOWS THE TROUBLE I'VE SEEN

But Connie Hawkins wasn't the only NBA player who had prickly relationships with certain refs. In a 1970s game versus the Suns in Atlanta, the Hawks' Walt Hazzard went ballistic over a call that went against him and called referee Don Murphy a "racist." Murphy didn't waste any time in ejecting Hazzard from the game.

Hawks captain, Bill Bridges came over and asked Murphy what was going on... why was Hazzard thrown out? Told about the racist comment, Bridges thought about it for a second before responding, "I tend to agree." And Murphy threw him out too!

AN EARLY LESSON

During his first year as Suns coach, Cotton Fitzsimmons also had a run-in with Rudolph, earning a "T" early in a game that the Suns had started badly. The game quickly went from bad start to blow-out and Fitzsimmons kept up a non-stop stream of chatter about the terrible officiating. Rudolph ignored him.

Finally, during a time-out, Rudolph came over to Cotton and said, "Look...you're a new coach and you have a really bad basketball team. If you think I'm going to give you a second 'T' so you can leave and not watch this...you are sadly mistaken. You are going to sit here and suffer with the rest of us!"

CAR WARS

During his first few years in the Valley of the Sun, Jerry Colangelo lived in a northern suburb of Phoenix called Moon Valley. For him, the fastest and most direct commute was to come right down Interstate 17 into downtown Phoenix. He was barreling down the freeway one morning on his way to work in one of the loaner cars from Lou Grubb Chevrolet. Suddenly, something went "pop" and smoke started billowing from the engine compartment. Jerry quickly steered the car toward the nearest exit. He realized that the exit was Camelback Road...exactly where the Lou Grubb dealership was located! Never slowing down, he zoomed off the freeway, made a hard right, careened into the service department at Lou Grubb's, and with the engine still belching clouds of black smoke, Jerry jumped out of the car and said, "Here, you guys take this! I'm done with it!"

BACK UP PLAN

Dave's Imports is an extremely reliable automotive repair service for just about all foreign makes and models. Many Suns players, coaches and front office personnel had their cars serviced there. Jerry Colangelo pulled in one day in a Jaguar XJ6...proudly showing off his new ride.

The owner, Dave Walls, took one look at it and said, "I hope you have two of these!"

"Why would I need two of them?" Colangelo asked.

Dave just grinned and said, "Because one of them is always going to be in the shop!"

HAWK AND LOU AND A DOG NAMED... "FOUL"

One of the great stories in early Phoenix Suns lore, involved Connie Hawkins and his dog named "Foul." JC had set it up for "Hawk," to have a loaner car from Lou Grubb Chevrolet for the season. Connie needed a four-door sedan with a big back seat because he owned a huge Great Dane. The pooch was named after the David Wolf book, *FOUL!* which was Connie's life story. The dog loved riding in the car and he also loved the back seat ...literally. There was something about that back seat that set ol' Foul a droolin' and a salivatin.' He couldn't resist chomping down, biting off and eating huge chunks of the upholstery and seat padding.

By the time the basketball season ended, and Connie was ready to head back to Pittsburgh for the summer, Foul had devoured virtually the entire back seat of the loaner car, in some places leaving only the bare metal springs!

Connie was always running late so, as he was leaving town, he called his friend and teammate, Charlie Scott, and asked him if he could do him a big favor and drop off the loaner car at Lou

Grubb Chevrolet. Charlie bears witness to the fact that the people at the dealership were at first outraged, then simply amazed at what Foul had done. But Hawkins, in his own inimitable way, had skated!

When he was later asked how one dog could do so much damage, Connie just shrugged and said, "He must have been hungry."

KEY MAN

Jerry Colangelo had a really bad habit of pulling into the Suns office parking lot on Central Avenue, tossing his keys onto his car's center console and leaving the car unlocked. As he was leaving the office one night, he realized that his car wasn't in its normal spot. In fact, it wasn't anywhere. It had been stolen.

He reported the theft and picked up a replacement vehicle the next day. At that time, the Suns insurance policy would only pay to replace a stolen car if 30 days had expired without the police recovering the vehicle. On the last day of the waiting period, the police called Jerry at home.

"Could I please speak to Mr. Jerry Colangelo?"

"Who's calling?"

"This is the police department and we just need to inform Mr. Colangelo that his stolen car has been found!"

Without missing a beat, Jerry said, "I'm sorry, he's not here!" and hung up.

HEY! YOU CAN'T PARK THERE

Colangelo was taking his oldest daughter Kathy to the airport. Knowing a little of Jerry's history of bad luck with cars, it should be no surprise that en-route, the entire transmission on his late model Porsche imploded, leaving Jerry and his daughter stranded right in the middle of a busy Phoenix intersection.

With traffic buzzing around them, Jerry got out of the car and told Kathy to take her things. He then grabbed the rest of their luggage and walked away, leaving the car sitting there in the middle of the intersection. Jerry called his assistant Ruthie, told her the location of the car and instructed her to "just get rid of it." The Colangelos took a cab the rest of the way.

The Porsche was never seen again.

FIGURE THE ODDS

It was 1970 and the Suns were in the playoffs for the first time. While on a flight, *Phoenix Gazette* columnist Joe Gilmartin was interviewing Suns Coach and GM Jerry Colangelo, asking about the Suns' chances against the Los Angeles Lakers, their opening-round playoff opponent.

"I think it's a two-to-one shot that we'll win!" Colangelo said optimistically.

But before Gilmartin could ask a follow-up question, a huge hand came from behind and over the top of their airplane seats. Dangling from its fingertips was a 20 dollar bill.

"I'll take a piece of that!" said the owner of the hand.

It was Connie Hawkins.

CHECK PLEASE

A few years later, when Connie became the first inductee into what would become the Suns Ring of Honor, Jerry Colangelo presented him with the keys to a new car and Hawk gave Jerry a big hug in return. All Hawkins had to do was stop by the dealership and pick up his wheels. Jerry and the Suns would take care of the rest. Well, Connie left Phoenix, went back to Pittsburgh, and never bothered to pick up the car.

About a year later, Suns' business manager, Bob Machen got a call from Connie, who was then playing in Bologna, Italy. Hawk asked about the car and Machen told him that after he failed to pick up the car, the Suns dropped their arrangement with the dealership.

"Do you think you could just send me a check instead?" Hawkins asked. "I could sure use the money."

So Machen wired the funds to Italy. A few weeks later he got a postcard from Hawkins. It was one of those classic religious post-cards with a painting of Jesus Christ on the front. On the back of the card, Hawkins scribbled a note.

Bob,

Jesus Christ!

Thanks a lot!

I really needed this!

Tell what's-his-name thanks a lot too!

Hawk

CAN I HELP YOU?

As is the case in most high school gymnasiums, the bleachers in the Catalina High School gym in Tucson rolled out to within a couple of feet of the sideline. Basketball teams would occupy the first row of the hard, wooden bench seats and fans would fill in behind them. But NBA coaches are used to a slightly wider sideline area so they can roam up and down a little bit. How else can you get a player's attention or yell at a referee?

During one of those early Suns pre-season games at the Tucson school, a couple of fans wandered in late. They kept looking at their tickets and it was clear that they did not know where they were supposed to sit. Suns Coach Johnny Kerr, who was prowl-ing the sidelines, saw their puzzled looks, walked over to them and asked to see their tickets. With the game going on at full-tilt behind him, the ever-helpful Kerr pointed to an area in the stands where the fans could sit and then escorted them to an aisle that would get them there. Coach, comedian, master-motivator, usher...Johnny Kerr did it all.

WARDROBE MALFUNCTION

When the Suns franchise played its very first game in 1968, Dick Snyder was a member of the original starting five. Drafted in the second round by the St. Louis Hawks in 1966, the former Davidson star, nicknamed "Duck," he was the third player picked by Jerry Colangelo and the Suns in the 1968 NBA expansion draft. A fine shooter, Snyder would go on to enjoy a solid, 13-year NBA career, sporting a career scoring average of over 12 points per game. Ironically, he lost his starting job for a time, during that first year with the Suns, because...well, I'll let "Duck" tell the story:

"I fell out of the Suns starting line-up because I forgot my uniform on a road trip," Snyder remembered. "We had some 'home' games down in Tucson that year, and then we were going to play a couple of games on the road. At the time, we had to keep both our uniforms. I packed my road uniform, but I forgot to pack my home uniform. So, when we played the game in Tucson, I sat on the bench wearing a Catalina High School uniform under my warm-ups. I had been starting up to that point, but that eliminated me from the line-up. I had to work my way back. We had Bob Warlick and Stan McKenzie behind me, so when I lost my spot in the starting line-up, I think it became Stan's turn. When he played himself out of a spot, it was Warlick's turn and then it came around to me again."

Following a solid NBA career, Snyder made the Phoenix area his permanent home, where he's a respected agent for State Farm Insurance. No one has ever checked to see if he occasionally wears that Catalina High School uniform under his business suit.

OPENING NIGHT

I don't think there is a better person to tell the story of the Suns first training camp, their first pre-season and their first "official" regular season game, than "The Original Sun," Dick Van Arsdale. Here's Van's recollection of those events, in his own words:

"Coming to Phoenix from New York in the 1968 expansion draft, I knew that I would have to adjust to the heat, but nothing could have prepared me for the opening of the Suns pre-season camp at Brophy Prep in September. It had been a very hot summer and the gym did not have any air-conditioning. It must have been 115 or 120 degrees in that little gym. When you think about it, it's amazing that nobody died.

"Johnny Kerr was a classic, 'old school' coach, who'd just roll the ball out and let 'em play. Practices were loose. There was a lot of running and trying to get in shape. I don't think Johnny thought about the heat too much. He just sat in the corner and laughed. We must have put 30 or 40 players through camp before we came up with a final roster, but even the day before the season opened we were still making changes. I remember that a guard named Harry Hollines was waived and Eddie Biedenbach, from North Carolina State, was added at the last minute.

> **❝Lattin broke his hand on Kauffman's jaw, but Kauffman didn't even flinch. ❞**
> **- Dick Van Arsdale**

"We played pre-season games all over Arizona including Mesa, Ft. Huachuca and Globe-Miami. In one of those games, Dave Lattin took a swing at Bob Kauffman of the Sonics. Lattin broke his hand on Kauffman's jaw, but Kauffman didn't even flinch. We wound up 2-7 in pre-season but one of those wins was over Seattle, our opponent in the first regular season game, so we felt pretty good going into the opener.

"For an expansion team, we had a great backcourt combination in Gail Goodrich and Dick Snyder. Neil Johnson and I were the forwards and George Wilson was the center. George was only about 6'8" so he wasn't a true center and wasn't real mobile, but he could rebound. McCoy McLemore was a 6'7," 235-pound forward who started some games for us early in the season, before he was traded. After his playing career was over, for many years McLemore was a color commentator on Houston Rockets TV broadcasts.

"Kerr always tried to keep the locker room talks light and that was the case on opening night. He didn't put a lot of pressure on the players. His main theme was to tell us just to go out, give it our best shot and see what happens. Johnny was a coach that all the players liked. He had been a player himself and was a good communicator. He wanted us to run and keep things very simple. He was a motivator, not a real technical coach. Back then it was just a matter of trying to get the guys to play hard and he was good at that.

"With an expansion team, it's hard to have a cohesive group. Each player is trying to find his own niche in the league and capitalize on the opportunity of being with a new team. But that original Suns team was a close group and many of us have remained friends over the years.

"Our trainer, Joe Proski, was really the 'glue' that held the team together. Everyone liked 'The Prosk.' He had a way of keeping the guys loose in the locker room, but he was also serious about his job. Of all the guys we had, Joe was probably the most popular. A trainer can do a lot to help bolster a team's morale.

"We didn't know what kind of game or season it was going to be but, as players, I think we all had a lot of pride and wanted to show the fans that we were going to be a team that played hard. We jumped out to a big lead in the first quarter (41-21) and never looked back.

"I was matched up against Tom Meschery, a strong 6'6" forward who was an 'enforcer.' I liked playing against him because he was a real competitor. He was a bear on the boards that night with 19 rebounds. There were some other players on that Seattle team I can remember. I played against Tommy Kron in the state high school finals back in Indiana. Bob Rule was their center, a big bruiser who poured in a ton that night (34 points). Rod Thorn, who has been a team and NBA executive for years, was one of the guards, along with Hall of Famer Lenny Wilkens. Coincidentally, the coach of the Sonics that night was Al Bianchi, who, in the mid-1970s, would later join the Suns as an assistant coach.

"I've been told that I scored the first basket that night, which would have been the first in Suns history, but I really don't remember it. We ran some basic patterns offensively, but nothing very complicated. We ran two-on-two on one side, guard around, and splits off the post. It was pretty basic stuff. George Wilson grabbed 19 rebounds and Goodrich scored 27 for the Suns. It went down in the books as a 116-107 win. NBA basketball and the Suns had officially arrived in Phoenix.

"There was a lot of optimism on the team after the win. I think that when you win your first game, especially as a new team, you say, 'Hey, we're really not that bad!' We went on to win four of our first seven games, but then reality set in. Even though we only won a total of 16 games that year, I never thought we were that bad of a team. I thought that every time we took the court, we had a chance to win. We had some good NBA players but depth was a big problem. I think Goodrich and I both averaged over 40 minutes a game that season. But the team had a positive attitude, always competed and I think set the stage for the big Suns turn-around the next season."

ATTENDANCE... GO FIGURE

Suns broadcaster, Rod Hundley, after hearing the official attendance announcement on an evening when the Coliseum seemed awfully empty, commented on the air, "if there are that many people here, then most of them must be disguised as empty seats!"

As the team's business manager, Bob Machen was charged with determining the official attendance count at all Suns home games at the Coliseum. Toward the end of the third quarter, a Coliseum official would hand him the evening's turnstile count on a scrap of paper. Bob would then factor-in the media in atten-

dance, team officials, seeing-eye dogs, neighbors and any other people who might have thought about attending the game that night. Bob was doing "fuzzy math" before that term and computers became mainstream.

Once he had a number in mind, he would then lean over my shoulder at the press table, and with his left hand, scribble the "official" attendance onto the "official" score sheet. Every night, I would look at the inflated number, and look around the mostly empty building. Then, I would look him in the eye and say, "Bob, how do you sleep at night?"

BOB MACHEN

Every night, he would very deliberately click his pen closed, look at me with a wry smile and deadpan... "Like a baby, my friend... just like a baby!"

EXPENSES

In the Suns early years, former college star and NBA veteran Rod Hundley was the color commentator on the Suns broadcast team. On an early road trip to the East coast, Hundley somehow lost his raincoat. He wasn't sure if he left it in a cab, had it stolen in a restaurant or left it at one of the arenas. The reason didn't matter...it was gone. When the team returned to Phoenix, "Hot Rod" turned in his expense report for the trip. Suns business manager, Bob Machen gave the report his usual casual scrutiny, until he saw "Raincoat -- $200." Machen flipped.

"Rod, we can't pay for a raincoat," Machen said, "that's got to be your personal expense!"

"Yeah, but I lost it on the road trip!" Rod responded.

"I don't care. We're not paying for a raincoat and that's it!" Machen declared.

Hundley harrumphed and walked out of the office. Months later the team returned from another extended road trip to the cold and rainy East coast. Once again Hundley came into Machen's office to turn in his expenses. This time he simply tossed the expense report on Machen's desk and said, "The raincoat is in there somewhere... try to find it!"

HOLD ME BACK

Early Suns fans were a passionate lot, and none of them was more passionate or more vocal than Jerry Middleman. One night at the Coliseum, Middleman was outraged at the way veteran referee Mendy Rudolph was calling the game and the fact that the Suns were consistently getting the short end of his calls.

Middleman's ire kept building until yet another Rudolph call went against the Suns. Middleman just couldn't take it anymore. He jumped out of his seat and started heading for the court...

and Rudolph. Fortunately, Suns exec Bob Machen happened to be walking in that direction and he quickly put a bear-hug on Middleman before he could do anything foolish.

As he wrestled with Middleman, blocking him from the court, Machen said, "What the heck do you think you're doing?!"

"I have no idea," Middleman said, "but I sure am glad you grabbed me!"

A VISIT FROM MARY JANE

Back in the 1960's, NBA teams traveled on commercial airlines. Team duffle bags were routinely intermingled with the luggage of regular passengers. It was not unusual if some of the team's luggage was lost or picked up by somebody not in the team's traveling party. So it was not a big surprise one afternoon when Bob Machen got a call at the Suns office from the bell captain at the Mountain Shadows Resort in Paradise Valley. Apparently, an orange Suns duffle bag became mixed up with the bags that were brought out to the resort.

> **"Joe, is that what I think it is?"**
> **- Bob Machen**

The hotel sent a driver to the Suns office on Central Ave and gave the bag to Machen. Bob claims he tipped the guy $10, but I'm guessing it was more like $2, which Bob would argue was pretty good money at the time. Anyway... Machen then called Suns trainer, Joe Proski, to tell him about the errant bag and that he would bring it over to the Coliseum about five o'clock, with a Suns home game scheduled to tip-off at 7:30 that night.

Machen arrived at the Coliseum with the bag, but Proski was baffled. Even though it was a Suns logo bag with a number "31" stenciled on it, this bag was older and smaller than the bags the team was currently using. Proski opened up the bag and on top were a pair of shorts that were way too small to belong to any Suns player. He dug a little deeper and found that the rest of the duffle contained nothing but little plastic bags filled with something that looked like grass clippings or maybe...tobacco!

Machen said, "Joe, is that what I think it is?"

"What do *you* think it is, Bob?"

Machen smiled, then took the entire stash of marijuana and flushed it, one bag at a time, down the locker room toilet. All Proski could do was stand by and shake his head.

Surprisingly, no guest from Mountain Shadows ever tried to reclaim their lost duffle bag.

QUIET PLEASE

One night, referee John Vanak was being dogged by a Suns fan sitting in the front row under the basket. For the entire first half of the game, Vanak could do nothing right and he got an earful. As the first half ended, Vanak spotted the guy in the seats and pointed at him.

"Was that you yelling at me the whole first-half?!" Vanack asked.

The response from the boisterous fan was a loud and proud, "Yeah! That was me!"

"That's funny," Vanack responded, "I thought it was a *woman*!"

Vanack didn't hear a peep from the guy for the rest of the game.

ALL IN A NIGHT'S WORK

Bob Machen had to oversee game night security at the Coliseum. Suns fans in the early 1970s were loud and loyal, but they never felt that their Suns got the respect they deserved from NBA referees. There was one night when referee Richie Powers was working and three straight goal tending calls went against the Suns late in the game, resulting in a two point loss. Suns fans were incensed and Machen knew that he'd better hustle down to the tunnel leading to the officials' dressing room, to make sure the refs weren't accosted on their way off the floor.

He got there just in time. The two referees were walking off the court and were being vindictive older gentleman who was spewing a vitriolic tirade, while trying, with all his might, to claw his way past a security guard and attack Richie Powers with his bare hands. The man's face was red with anger, his features so distorted by emotion that Machen hardly recognized him. Machen was so surprised, all he could say was, "Dad?! Is that YOU?!"

THE FIRST CHRISTMAS

On December 25, 1968, the Suns took on the Los Angeles Lakers in a nationally televised Christmas Day game, broadcast by ABC-TV from the Arizona Veterans Memorial Coliseum. The Lakers were one of the NBA's elite teams and featured future Basketball Hall of Fame players Jerry West, Elgin Baylor and Wilt Chamberlain. The expansion Suns were struggling through their first season with an 8-26 record going into that game. But it was a significant day in Phoenix sports history and the first big opportunity for this new Suns team to make a statement that they belonged in the National Basketball Association.

Any underdog team will try to prove that they can play with the big boys. This game was no exception and the Suns came out firing on all cylinders. Incredibly, Phoenix went up by 24 points early in the second quarter! But then the nationwide television audience was whisked away from the game for coverage of a NASA space program mission in the Apollo series. When ABC –TV returned to the game in the fourth quarter, the lead was still 24 ... unfortunately, it was the Lakers who were now ahead! As incredible as it may seem, the Lakers outscored the Suns by 48 points in less than two quarters! But at least the Suns were spared the indignity of having the entire nation witness their collapse. Like Tang™, computers and zero-gravity pens, it was another positive outcome from a very successful NASA space program.

Mission Commander Frank Borman and Apollo 8 had their splashdown on December 27th. The Suns had crashed to earth two days earlier.

COUNT TO THREE

Joe Proski remembers when he was the trainer for the Bulls and the team's marketing director, a guy named Jerry Colangelo, wanted to hold one roster spot open for a local, Chicago-area player. It would be a good PR move for the new team and definitely would help with their community relations efforts in the Chicago-land area. The Bulls PR guy, Ben Bentley, put out the word and hundreds upon hundreds of players, of every age and stripe, showed up at a Chicago gym to try out for that one spot. Some of them drove all night to get there.

Bulls coach Johnny Kerr, realizing that the numbers were totally unworkable, lined them all up and said, "Okay, count off...one, two, three... one, two, three."

And so they began counting. Proski remembers that there were so many guys that even the counting seemed to take forever. When the count finally reached the last man, Kerr said bluntly, "Okay, THREES GO HOME!"

Proski laughs about it now, but at the time he was a little concerned, because the howl of protest that went up was almost primeval. "Those guys were really mad!" Proski recalls.

S-H-H-H-H

❝...It's all very hush, hush right now. ❞
- Jerry Colangelo

It was early in 1968 and the NBA had confirmed expansion plans for two cities, Phoenix and Milwaukee. The Bulls' young, NBA up-and-comer, Jerry Colangelo, was being considered for the general manager's job by both expansion franchises. But a mid-winter visit to beautiful, warm and sunny Arizona convinced Jerry that Phoenix would be his destination and his destiny.

When a new GM is starting a new organization, he wants to surround himself with people he knows he can depend upon when the going gets rough...people with experience and people with whom he'll enjoy working. Naturally, Jerry Colangelo looked to the people he knew and trusted best... the folks already working with him at the Bulls.

J.C. approached Bulls trainer, Joe Proski about joining the staff in Phoenix. Since Proski also doubled as the trainer for the Chicago Cubs, who did their spring training in Arizona, Joe was really excited at the prospect of a full-time move to the Southwest.

But Jerry cautioned him, "Joe, it's all very hush, hush right now... so keep it to yourself. OK?"

Proski agreed, but he absolutely had to give his friend and coach Johnny Kerr a "heads-up" about what might happen. First asking Kerr to keep everything in confidence, Proski told "Red" about his offer from Colangelo.

"That's great!" Kerr said, "because I'm going to Phoenix too!"

Proski was shocked! He went to see Jerry's assistant Ruthie Dryjanski and quickly learned that *she* was moving to Phoenix as well!

A stunned and frustrated Proski shouted out to no one in particular, "Is there *anybody* here who's *NOT* going to Phoenix!?"

JUST SAY HELLO

Colangelo told me about one game, very early in the Suns first year at the Coliseum. Suns coach Johnny "Red" Kerr was standing in front of the press table watching the Suns warm up. Suddenly a phone rang. Kerr reached down, picked up the receiver and said, "Hello! Coliseum... how can I help you?"

The caller asked, "What time does the game start?"

Kerr responded, "What time can you get here?"

MOM AND POP

Those early days at the Coliseum, in the late 1960s, were in many ways testimony to the "mom and pop" culture of the NBA at that time. Game times were late, often 8 p.m. for a regular weeknight game. That gave fans a chance to get home from work, change clothes and have a bite to eat before heading down to the game.

Every game night, at about 7:45 or so, J.C. would walk up to the Coliseum's upper concourse and then walk outside to a favorite spot on the South entrance ramp. From there he had a commanding view of the parking lot and all the car headlights streaming into the Coliseum's McDowell Road entrance. If traffic was backed up, Jerry would call down to the press table and delay the start of the game so as many people as possible could get inside before the opening tip. If it looked like the traffic was tailing off and folks were already inside, Jerry would call down and say, "OK, let's go!"

Today it would take an act of God (or a written note from NBA commissioner David Stern) to delay the tip-off of an NBA game.

KERR

It was Johnny Kerr's sense of humor that made him the perfect coach for the first-year Suns. His limitless stories and one-liners drew media attention away from the on-court frustrations of an expansion team.

During that 1968-69 campaign, one of Kerr's classic post-game observations came on February 10th in Los Angeles. The Lakers' Wilt "Big Dipper" Chamberlain, upset by a national magazine's suggestion that he'd lost his scoring touch, poured in 66 points against the Suns. It's a Suns opponent record that still stands today.

After the game, Coach Kerr told the assembled media, "This proves, that 'Dipper' can not only score, but he can also read!"

THE REST OF THE STORY

It took two books by Colangelo, another by Al McCoy and some reminiscences from Rod Hundley, for me to piece together "the rest of the story" that followed the death of broadcaster Bob Vache in 1970.

Following a Suns party for sponsors, broadcasters and key Suns executives, KTAR's Bob Vache, the Suns play-by-play voice at the time, was killed in an automobile accident on his way home. J.C. was shocked to hear the news in the wee hours of the morning, but he knew that with the NBA season already well underway, he had to move rapidly to fill the void. Like any manager of a business facing adversity, Colangelo had to move quickly and decisively. He had to get creative and utilize whatever resources were available to him, in order to pull things together that tragic night.

He first called Al McCoy and asked him to take over as the Suns announcer, but McCoy was still under contract with the Roadrunners hockey team and told Jerry that he was not available. Colangelo then called the Suns' color commentator, Rod Hundley to tell him what happened to Vache and to prepare him to take over the Suns play-by-play duties the following night. Hundley hadn't done play-by-play, but was ready to give it his best shot. Colangelo wasn't fully confident that Rod's voice could hold up through an entire season doing play-by-play, versus his role as a commentator. JC needed someone who could not only support Rod, but also help to sell the young Suns to the community... but his options, along with the time frame, were limited and rapidly diminishing.

Jerry was confident that he could coach the team himself and he also knew that his current coach, Johnny Kerr would be a great on-air talent. "Red" Kerr was the consummate showman and a virtual quip-machine who worked well with the community and kept the media in stitches. Jerry had made the perfect pick in Kerr for his first coach with the expansion Suns. But now, in their second year, with Hawkins, Silas, Goodrich and Van Arsdale, J.C. knew that with the right guidance and motivation, the Suns had a great shot at making the playoffs. He did not want to miss that opportunity.

> **❝❝As the Suns set in the west... Red sails in the sunset! ❞❞**
> **- Johnny Kerr**

So, on January 2, 1970, Jerry relieved Johnny Kerr of his coaching duties, prompting Kerr to say, "As the Suns set in the west...Red sails in the sunset!" But Colangelo immediately re-hired Kerr to join the Suns broadcast team and J.C. took over as coach. The Suns, in just their second year of existence, would make the playoffs, and nearly pull off one of the great upsets in NBA playoff history. They went up 3-1 on a Lakers team loaded with future hall of famers. Kerr would go on to a long career as a commentator on Chicago Bulls broadcasts and Rod Hundley proved that he had enough staying power to be the play-by-play voice of the Jazz for 35 seasons before he retired. Colangelo would step in as Suns coach twice during his long career. His final NBA coaching record was 59 wins against 60 losses.

LOCKED IN

In general, athletes are superstitious creatures of habit. Factor in a shooting streak or a long run of consecutive games started and they become downright obsessive about their game night routines.

Neal Walk and Joe Proski had a little pre-game ritual. After a few minutes of team warm-ups, Neal would invariably return to the locker room to answer nature's call. And each night, as Proski was getting ready to leave the locker room, he would always shout towards the bathroom, "Hey big-guy... have a good one!"

Walk's regular response was, "You too!"

But on this night Proski's call went unanswered, so, figuring Neal was already out on the court, he locked the two sets of dead-bolts on the locker room doors and headed for his spot on the Suns bench. A few minutes later, Walk emerged from the bathroom stall to find that he was alone and locked-in, with no way out.

Meanwhile, in the arena, the starting line-ups were being announced.

"Starting at center, from Florida, number 41... Neal Walk!"

But the big guy was nowhere to be found! It suddenly dawned on Proski that Neal was probably still back in the locker room. By the time Proski ran back there to spring Neal from his involuntary incarceration, the game had already started and Walk's long string of consecutive starts was over.

Upon his release, Neal let Proski know in no uncertain terms, "Colangelo's gonna' hear about this!"

ALREADY WACKO

Even before I went to work for the Suns, strange things were happening. Take, for example, the person who, in a 1972 letter to Jerry Colangelo, identified himself as Ad Adarv-Abul of Whittier, California.

The Suns were preparing to face the Lakers at the Forum, and if Colangelo didn't have an effective game plan, Adarv-Abul did. He wrote:

"If you want me to play for the Suns at the Forum on Friday night, December 22, it will cost you $5,000 (five thousand dollars) cash, net.

"As you have probably heard, I have invented an almost completed NBA coaching system, and I would like to discuss the proposition of selling it to you. Send someone with a Phoenix Suns emblem to the Whittier Public Library on Mar Vista Street in Whittier, California. I would like my jersey number to be 41 and for my name on the back, I would like the letter 'A.'"

It was an offer Colangelo could, and did, refuse.

PREVIEW OF COMING ATTRACTIONS

On spring break from Notre Dame, I was visiting Phoenix during April of 1970, my senior year. My trip coincided with the Suns' 1970 first-round playoff series with the Lakers. One night, at my future in-laws' home, as we were clicking through the television channels, I vividly remember hearing Johnny Kerr's commentary toward the end of one of the Suns playoff wins.

Kerr was enthusiastic in his new role as Hundley's sidekick, and the concept of impartial analysis apparently was not part of his self-styled job description. When Phoenix' Gail Goodrich was at the line for a pair of crucial free throws, I remember Kerr pleading hoarsely, "Come on 'Goody,' knock 'em down!"

In a little more than three years, I would go to work for the Suns. But, on that day, I had no premonition of what was to come.

ARIZONA CALLS

After graduating from Notre Dame in June of 1970, I moved from New Rochelle to Arizona in mid-August. You could say I followed my heart to Arizona because I wanted to marry my college sweetheart, Alice Aylsworth, and that's where she was.

I packed my Bachelor of Arts degree and all my worldly possessions into a small, steamer trunk and flew out to Tucson, where my future wife's father had just taken a new job and had moved

> **"What could possibly be the difference between Phoenix and Tucson?"**

the family. When I stepped off the plane in Arizona, I thought it was about 150 degrees. The heat literally took my breath away.

Having visited Phoenix a couple of times in the spring while I was still in college, I was very excited about moving there permanently. Tucson was a last minute change of plans. But in my infinite New York wisdom I rationalized, "What could possibly be the difference between Phoenix and Tucson? They're only 100 miles apart!"

So, I moved to Tucson and started taking business classes at the University of Arizona, beginning the process of working toward an MBA. But after a month or two, I grew tired of academics and wanted to get out and go to work. Following a year in insurance sales, I focused on public relations as a career path and started looking for a PR job in Phoenix, where there was greater opportunity.

I had some familiarity with the NBA because of my friendship with the Borgia family back in New York, so I decided, "What the heck... I'll give the NBA a shot." That led to this letter I wrote to Jerry Colangelo, the general manager of the Phoenix Suns:

Mr. Jerry Colangelo
Generl Manager
Phoenix Suns
2303 N. Central Ave.
Phoenix, Arizona

Dear Mr. Colangelo:

I realize that we have never met, but I hope that this letter will serve as a form of introduction.

I am a 1970 graduate of the University of Notre Dame, and having followed a very curious and involved route since leaving South Bend, I am presently employed in the insurance business in Tucson. I do not feel however, that selling life insurance is the kind of career that I want to spend my life pursuing.

Being born and raised in the New York City area, I was always surrounded with fine professional athletic teams, and it was only natural for me to think that I might someday be part of such organizations.

I am definitely interested in pursuing a career with an organization such as the Phoenix Suns.

I will be in Phoenix early next week and I would welcome the opportunity to discuss with you career possibilities with the Phoenix Suns organization. I realize that you are very busy at this point in the season, so I would be very happy to comply with an appointment at your convenience.

Best of luck to you and to the Suns in your upcoming games. I am looking forward to meeting you in person.

Sincerely yours,

Tom Ambrose

THANKS RUTHIE

I was pleasantly surprised when Jerry responded to my letter in just a few days. Even though he indicated there were no positions available with the Suns, he invited me to stop by the office the next time I was in Phoenix.

I realize now, that with Jerry scouting, selling, travelling with the team and basically calling all the shots for the franchise, it was really his ever-efficient assistant, Ruthie Dryjanski, who gave me my opportunity to meet J.C. For that, I will be forever grateful.

SEASONING

Meanwhile, I was going through normal channels in my job search...what they now call "networking." Back then it was called "who do you know?" Through some Phoenix contacts my dad set up for me, I got an appointment with Dick Stuart, who worked for a local Phoenix PR firm called Jennings and Thompson. I'll never forget Dick because he recognized that I was just starting out and that I was anxious to find my first real PR job. He assured me that there were some good opportunities out there and he'd find one for me.

Anybody that has ever looked for a job has heard that promise. But less than a week after we met, Dick called me and said, "There's a guy named Bill Shover at Phoenix Newspapers and they've got a job opening for an entry level PR guy. You'd be perfect for it. Give him a call."

So I called Mr. Shover and made an appointment to see him a few days later, at two o'clock in the afternoon. Since I had to drive up from Tucson for the meeting, I decided to see if I could get something going on the same day with this other guy I didn't know... Jerry Colangelo. I called the Suns office and Jerry's secretary, Ruthie, set it up for me.

At eleven o'clock, on the appointed day, I arrived at the Suns offices on Central Avenue and went in to see Mr. Colangelo. Following the usual get-to-know-you chit-chat, Jerry said, "I like your story, but I just don't have anything for you right now. Something may open up down the road, but I can't be sure. Who else are you talking to in town?" I told him about my meeting with Shover later that afternoon. He just shook his head and laughed. I said, "What's so funny?"

> **"I wasn't smart enough to know that I wasn't supposed to do that. "**

Jerry said, "This is such a small town. When we're done here, I'm going to drive down to Phoenix Newspapers and pick up Bill Shover for lunch. I'll put in a good word for you."

Clearly surprised, because I had known Jerry for all of 15 minutes, I said, "You will!?"

He said, "Yeah, sure, absolutely!"

Years later, Jerry fills in the story this way: "I talked to Shover and said, 'Look. I just talked to this kid from Notre Dame and he's coming in to see you this afternoon. He seems good but he needs some experience. Why don't you hire him and give him some seasoning? But I want the right to call him up if I need him.'"

I always say to Jerry, "However you want to tell that story is fine with me, because it all worked out beautifully!"

I worked for Bill Shover for almost two years, doing entry level PR work for the newspaper. Colangelo called me up to "the bigs" in October of 1973.

I was relating that story to a friend who made me realize just how incredible that day was, more than 40 years ago. He said, "Are you kidding me? On basically your first day in town, you just walked in and saw two of the most influential people in the city of Phoenix!"

I hadn't thought of it that way. I just thought there was a guardian angel sitting on my shoulder. Besides, I wasn't smart enough to know that I wasn't supposed to do that.

FROM THE WACKO! FILE – A JOB APPLICATION

Dear Mr. Colangelo:

I saw your name in a book called the Rich Register. The reason I'm writing you is to see if you might have some work for me. I'd like to work from home and make $2,000 to $10,000 a month (10 hours a week). I'd also like to make $2 million but am willing to start small.

Please write to me if you can. I'd like to "get my foot in the door," and would greatly appreciate your help. I'm very intelligent and am sure I would do excellent work for you.

Sincerely,

JA

PHOENIX NEWSPAPERS

The morning newspaper, *The Arizona Republic*, was the largest in the state. The afternoon paper, *The Phoenix Gazette*, had a smaller circulation, but an aggressive sports section. Both papers were controlled by publisher Eugene C. Pulliam and both were well-respected in the publishing industry. Under the direction of Bill Shover, our department served the marketing, promotion and public relations needs of both newspapers, which went by the corporate name of Phoenix Newspapers, Inc. (PNI).

Shover steered a creative and enthusiastic staff of about 30 people, including artists, copywriters, researchers, human resources and community relations staff.

At that time, in the early '70s, the papers were the most dominant media outlets in the state. There were only four local Phoenix TV stations (three of them were affiliates for the major national networks) and more than 35 local radio stations, creating a very fragmented electronic media market. Al Gore had not yet invented the Internet.

There is no question that Pulliam was a hard-charging crusader for the things he wanted to see happen and for the people he wanted to have elected in the state. Pity those who took up positions opposing the Pulliam papers. Because of that power and influence, the community beat a path to our door, seeking editorial support, event coverage, endorsements, leadership and financial support.

Bill Shover was a manager who truly led by example and his example was legendary. He served on an uncountable number of community boards and always in leadership positions. He made sure that the newspapers served the community and its non-profit agencies in every way possible. Free advertising space and promotional stories were often provided for community events and non-profit fundraisers. In those days, if you wanted to create a new project or a community-wide fundraising effort, your first stop was to see Mr. Shover at PNI.

❝ ...the local world revolved around the newspapers. ❞

So, it shouldn't come as a surprise to learn that when Jerry Colangelo first arrived in Phoenix in 1968, to manage the NBA's newest franchise, one of the first people he sought out was Bill Shover. It began a friendship that still endures today.

It was *The Arizona Republic* that ran a "Name the Team Contest" which ultimately selected the name "Suns." It was *The Phoenix Gazette* that ran the "Win Suns Win Club" for young fans that netted them some cool Suns apparel and discount tickets to Suns games. On Christmas Day, the Suns would play a home game and donate the proceeds to *The Phoenix Gazette* Youth Fund.

As a young man, new to the Phoenix community and to the PR profession, I quickly realized that I had landed in an absolutely perfect position to learn the trade. The newspapers were an essential part of virtually every major event or initiative in the state.

With apologies to astronomer Nicolaus Copernicus, who first set forth the radical notion that the earth revolves around the sun, I had the sense that the local world revolved around the newspapers. That made PNI a very exciting place to work.

WORDS TO LIVE BY

On Bill Shover's desk was an inspirational saying that summed up both his humble attitude and his work ethic. The quote is often attributed to President Harry Truman and it was a philosophy that I quickly adopted. It said:

"THERE IS NO LIMIT TO THE GOOD A MAN CAN DO, IF HE DOESN'T CARE WHO GETS THE CREDIT"

MIXED COMPANY

During the summer of 1972 the entire Suns team and the head coach were replaced...with actors. A Hollywood production crew came to town to shoot the movie, *Mixed Company*. Since this "sentimental comedy" centered on the coach of the beleaguered Phoenix Suns, one of the prime shooting locations was the Coliseum. For crowd shots, the casting call went out to Suns fans to serve as extras. Thousands showed up and served with distinction.

The Suns player-actors wore genuine Suns warm-ups and uniforms. The movie-Suns even featured a petulant super-star. For game action footage, the filmmakers came back to shoot real NBA-Suns games when the season got underway in the fall. Using mostly wide-angle shots, they spliced that genuine game footage into the final product. Joe Bologna played the coach of the Suns. Tom Bosley of "Happy Days" fame, Rod Hundley and NBA referee Darell Garretson also had parts.

In a nutshell, the plot revolved around the fact that the coach and his wife had three children, but she decided to adopt three more kids, a Vietnamese, an African-American and a Native American. The coach is trying to produce a winning team, deal with the issues of his star player, take care of three more kids at home, not to mention dealing with some bigoted neighbors. Then he gets fired. You get the idea. That's life in a big family and in the NBA... functionally dysfunctional.

In addition to the Coliseum shots there were lots of location shots around Phoenix. Released in 1974, the movie is still available and plays occasionally on late night TV.

TWIN SUBTERFUGE

While I labored at Phoenix Newspapers I collaborated on many projects and promotions with the Suns. One of my favorites, and one that no doubt helped bring my name and abilities to the attention of the Sun executive staff, was *The Phoenix Gazette –* Phoenix Suns Basketball Clinic at the Coliseum.

Our job, at the newspaper, was to promote this Saturday morning event through a series of free "house" ads along with some strategically placed PR mentions in the sports sections of both the Republic and the Gazette. The Kansas City-Omaha Kings would be in town that weekend, featuring their coach Bob Cousy and Dick Van Arsdale's identical twin brother, Tom.

I thought that the Van Arsdale twins should get the primary promotional focus...but I had only one publicity photo headshot of Dick. So, since they were "identical" twins, I copied the shot I had of Dick, but bumped it up slightly by five percent. I then hand painted the color of the uniform from white to black and overlaid a light screen over one of the photos.

I positioned the original photo and the doctored version side-by-side. The caption said something like: "The Van Arsdale twins will be the featured players at the *Phoenix Gazette* - Phoenix Suns Basketball Clinic scheduled for this Saturday at 10 a.m. at the Coliseum. By the way, that's Tom on the left and Dick on the right...or is it Dick on the left and Tom on the right?"

I thought it was a clever subterfuge which, for the sake of promotion, the *Gazette* editors let slide. Over 6,000 kids attended the clinic that Saturday morning, got tips from Dick and Tom Van Arsdale, and enjoyed a great day of basketball sponsored by *The Phoenix Gazette*. After I got to know them a little better, I found out that Dick and Tom were life-long experts at that sort of twin trickery, often switching caps and uniforms when they were kids. A few years later, they almost did it in the NBA.

BASKETBALL CONGRESS INTERNATIONAL

The Suns were in the basketball business and the newspapers were involved in the promotion of Phoenix through sports and their sports sections. Starting from scratch, a hard-working, local promoter, named Larry Walker, created an organization called Basketball Congress International (BCI). It was an international tournament for youth basketball that would be played in Phoenix. Walker was determined to make it work. Through sheer grit, determination and a few key sponsors, he succeeded.

While still working for Phoenix Newspapers, I was part of a very impressive BCI meeting that brought together pro basketball hall of famer Bob Cousy; Olympic legend Jesse Owens; college basketball legend Hot Rod Hundley; former Brooklyn Dodger great Joe Black; Manny Jackson of the Harlem Globetrotters; Suns GM, Jerry Colangelo and other community leaders.

The meeting was held in the VIP Room at Hundley's *Clown's Den*, a central Phoenix restaurant. I tried not to show my awe of being in such legendary athletic company... after all, it was an awfully impressive group. BCI enjoyed a long and successful run and I was happy to be involved with the effort, first with Phoenix Newspapers and later, while doing community relations work with the Phoenix Suns.

VAN VS. SLOAN

In 1972 the Suns were scheduled to play their traditional Christmas Day game in Phoenix against the Chicago Bulls. One of the NBA's most physical match-ups at the time was the Suns' Dick Van Arsdale going head-to-head against the Bulls' Jerry Sloan. It wasn't exactly the type of marquee match-up that future generations of NBA fans would enjoy...like the rivalries between Magic Johnson and Larry Bird, or Kobe Bryant and LeBron James. It was much more basic than that. More like... "immovable object meets irresistible force," or "high-speed freight train collides with mountain."

Working for the newspaper's PR department, I was looking for ways to promote ticket sales for the Christmas Day game because proceeds would go to benefit *The Phoenix Gazette Youth Fund*. The Suns and Bulls were scheduled to play a game in Phoenix early in the season, so I took advantage of that to get some shots of Van Arsdale and Sloan in the classic "nose-to-nose" boxer pose... trying to set a tone for this game and the rivalry.

Interestingly, just as Van Arsdale was known as "The Original Sun," picked first by the Suns in the 1968 expansion draft, Sloan was "The Original Bull," selected first by Chicago when that team was assembled in 1966. Both were NBA rookies in 1965 and both played their college basketball in the southern end of the "Hoosier" state, Sloan at Evansville and "Van" at Indiana University.

One thing I quickly came to understand and appreciate was that these two guys really respected one another as competitors. They did the "take-no-prisoners" shot for me, but it was clear that they enjoyed the challenge of playing against each another. These were two guys who went hard every minute they were on the floor, played fundamentally sound basketball, didn't "showboat" and they respected their opponents. Not surprisingly, they both enjoyed long and productive careers in the NBA, well beyond their playing days.

Today, the game is all about high-flying highlights, but I kind of miss that NBA era when hard-working, blue-collar guys like Dick Van Arsdale and Jerry Sloan would grind out some solid, physical basketball. They were both my kind of "originals."

FIGHT NIGHT

Comedian Rodney Dangerfield once joked, "I went to a fight the other night...and a hockey game broke out!"

Traditionally, basketball doesn't have the same type of reputation for fisticuffs as our hockey brethren...although, over the years, basketball has demonstrated that it does have its pugilistic moments. A bunch of those moments came during the Suns second season in 1969-70 when fights broke out during a string of six or seven games in a row. The Suns lost most of the fights, but there was a happy outcome... home attendance started to pick up for the "Battling Suns!"

The fight that everyone seems to remember was a confrontation between Chicago's Bob Kauffman and the Suns' Neil Johnson, who came to the defense of his teammate Gail Goodrich. Kauffman, no matter what uniform he was wearing, just seemed to really enjoy pummeling the Suns... with his fists! The year before, the Suns Dave "Big Daddy" Lattin actually broke his hand when he hit Kauffman's iron-like jaw.

This time it was Neil Johnson's turn. Reporter Dave Hicks once described the incident to a curious fan:

"It was early March, the fourth period vs. Chicago," Hicks explained. "As we all know, playoff races are an invitation to practice shove-inism in the NBA, and Goodrich got the baseline treatment from the Bulls' Bob Kauffman. So Gail promptly did what any 6'1," 170-pounder would do: He challenged the 6'8," 240-pounder!"

"Wasn't that courting disaster?" the fan asked.

> **"The Suns lost most of the fights... but home attendance started to pick up."**

"No. The Suns were once again in the 'Goodrich Shift.' Gail was involved in several scuffles during the playoff drive, but paid meticulous attention to the proximity of the Suns bench. He instigated or collaborated in no fight which Neil Johnson couldn't reach within 2.7 seconds coming off the bench."

"So Johnson saved the day?"

"What he did on this occasion was bash Kauffman on and about the fists with his face and suffered a broken nose."

Kauffman had a 20-pound weight advantage over Johnson, which he used with terrible efficiency, not just breaking Johnson's nose but splattering it and causing him to miss a significant number of games.

Suspensions? Fines? An investigation by the league office? Ha! Those are for sissies! N-a-a-a...we're talking about a time when REAL men played NBA basketball! There's another game tomorrow night... just tape it up and play!

MENDY TALKS

Just before the opening of the 1969-70 season, Neal Walk's rookie year, the NBA held its annual referee seminar for the teams. Typically, one of the referees comes in and discusses rule changes, interpretations and game-related items with each team. Comments and questions would follow.

That year head referee Mendy Rudolph had convened four teams in a Southern California hotel ballroom to hear his season-opening remarks. The teams included the Suns, Rockets, Warriors and Lakers.

> **❝There is not one game, one play or one season where an NBA referee will carry over a grudge against any player. ❞**
> **- Mendy Rudolph**

At some point during his presentation, Rudolph said, "I'm here to tell you that there is not one game, one play or one season where an NBA referee will carry over a grudge against any player!"

Suddenly, a huge, hulking figure, sitting in the front row, slowly rose to his full 7'1" height, blotting out the view for all those sitting behind him. Then in a deep, baritone voice, Wilt Chamberlain gave a brief but poignant assessment of Mendy's statement and the meeting in general.

"BULL S_ _T!" he proclaimed.

Big Wilt then stomped out of the room.

NEAL WALKS

For many reasons, among them basketball and fashion, this story describes a "statement" game for Neal Walk... one of his finest nights in the NBA.

The Suns and Bucks had come into the league as expansion franchises in 1968. Both teams had suffered through miserable inaugural seasons, but there was hope at the end of that tunnel. UCLA's talented, 7'2" center, Lewis Alcindor would undoubtedly be the first pick in the 1969 NBA draft. The only question was... who would pick him, the Suns or the Bucks? Milwaukee prevailed in a coin flip and of course, picked Alcindor. The Suns picked next and went with the next-best big man available, Florida's 6'10" Neal Walk.

So there was a natural, ready-made rivalry between the two expansion teams and a healthy competition between the two big men. After three-and-a-half seasons, the Suns had not been able to defeat the Bucks in Milwaukee. But on this cold, snowy January night in Brew City, Neal Walk was unstoppable, scoring a career high 42 points and dominating Alcindor inside. Dick Van Arsdale, fouled by Oscar Robertson in the final seconds, decided the game by drilling two free throws to give the Suns a hard-fought 115-114 victory at the Milwaukee Arena.

Naturally, Walk's performance earned him a spot on the Suns post-game show, as well as the attention of all the media covering the game. The interviews went long and by the time Neal showered, dressed and strapped on a funky pair of purple platform shoes (it was 1972), the locker room was quiet and empty, except for a couple of ball boys cleaning up. Wearing a long leather coat and snapping the brim of a purple hat straight out of the Temptations' song *Psychedelic Shack,* Neal proudly walked out to the arena's staging area to join his teammates in celebration on the team bus… except the bus was gone! Apparently, the team didn't want to wait and they returned to the hotel without their hero!

At first, Neal thought he'd just catch a cab, but this was Milwaukee, not New York City. There were no cabs in sight and it was already a little past 11 o'clock. A slightly steamed Neal thought, "What the heck, the hotel's not that far…I'll walk!"

Walk cut an impressive figure. With the platform shoes and the hat he probably topped out at about seven-foot, four. The Pfister Hotel was a little less than a mile away, but it seemed much farther as Neal began trudging through the dark, cold and snowy night.

With every step Neal was mumbling and grumbling to himself… "How could they do this to me…after the night I had…it's an outrage!"

By the time he reached the bridge that spanned the Milwaukee River, he realized that his feet were absolutely killing him. The purple platforms were designed for style, not long walks through the snow. So, leaning against the bridge railing, he took off the platforms, opened up his gym bag and took out his basketball shoes. Somehow, the Suns' 6'10" center managed to change his footwear right there on the cold, wind-whipped bridge. He then made his way across the span and walked the final quarter mile to the hotel in relative comfort.

We don't know the precise wording of the "statement" Neal uttered to Suns trainer Joe Proski, who had made the decision to leave Walk behind at the arena, but it couldn't have been good.

We do know however, that buried somewhere in the silt in the middle of the Milwaukee River, is a snazzy pair of purple, size 16 platform shoes, exactly where Neal threw them. For Neal, it was a forgettable end to one unforgettable night.

NO SOTTO VOCE

When Jerry Colangelo was in his first stint as coach of the Suns, he was ejected from a game by referee Mendy Rudolph, but J.C. had no idea why.

A ball had sailed out of bounds and was declared "Suns ball!" by Rudolph's referee partner. But Mendy, completely out of position on the other side of the court from the play, thought he saw it differently, reversed the call and the Suns lost possession.

Colangelo protested and then called a timeout. He was kneeling on the floor, designing a play and surrounded by his players, when Rudolph strutted by. Suns trainer, Joe Proski, standing at the edge of the team huddle with his head down, covering his mouth and blocked from Rudolph's view by Neal Walk, said loud enough for Rudolph to hear, "You blew it!"

Rudolph whipped around and, thinking that it was Colangelo who had challenged his judgment, immediately gave two quick tweets on his whistle and with great theatrical gesticulation, ejected the Suns coach from the game.

Colangelo was outraged! He jumped up and began chasing after Rudolph.

"What?! What did I do?!" Colangelo pleaded. He never got an answer. He was gone... ejected!

Meanwhile, Proski and Walk were standing innocently near the bench, biting down on towels to keep from laughing out loud and blowing their little secret. It was a secret they kept from Colangelo until now, almost four decades later.

CHAPTER 2

DAWN OF THE SUNDIOLITHIC EPOCH

THE SUNS CALL

On a Saturday morning in early October, 1973, my wife Alice and I were in the process of moving from a rental apartment into our own condo in east Phoenix. We were homeowners at last! The phone rang and it was Bob Machen, the business manager for the Suns. Bob and I had worked together that summer, putting on the American Legion Baseball Championship Tournament, so we knew each other well. But he surprised me when he said, "Our PR guy, Jim Brochu, just resigned to join the Memphis Tams of the ABA. Jerry called Bill Shover to ask for permission to talk to you about the job and Bill said 'OK.' If you are interested, let's set up a meeting."

I said, "Hold on!" Covering the phone's mouthpiece with my hand, I said to Alice, "Am I interested in a job with the Phoenix Suns?!" She nodded her very excited approval and approximately one nanosecond later I responded to Bob, "Absolutely! Let's do it!"

That night, there was a party for some key Suns sponsors, season ticket holders and Suns management at a North Central Phoenix restaurant called *Rod Hundley's Cornucopia*. I sat down in a booth with Jerry Colangelo and he laid it out for me. He wanted me to be his PR director. The salary was $10,000 a year and I'd have the use of a car from one of our automobile sponsors. I didn't hear anything else. It didn't matter. I was the new public relations director for the Phoenix Suns of the National Basketball Association!

PHILOSOPHY

As a franchise, the Suns can trace their core values back to one day, early in franchise history, and one phrase delivered by Jerry Colangelo.

It was the summer of 1968. The Suns' offices were located on the grounds of the Arizona State Fair, underneath the rodeo arena grandstands. When they weren't grousing about the oppressive heat and the spartan office space, some of the new Suns ticket salesmen were complaining about the fact that the citizens of Phoenix were not exactly turning out in droves to buy tickets and support their new NBA franchise. Jerry stopped them in mid-grumble and said:

"This community owes us nothing... It is up to us to go out and earn their respect!"

I believe those words were at the root of everything the Suns organization achieved, both on and of the basketball court, for the next 40+ years. I know that it became a vital point of focus that guided my decision-making throughout my career with the Suns.

FIRST DAY

It was October 10, 1973, my first day on the job with the Suns. I checked in with Colangelo at the Suns offices on North Central Avenue and he told me that the day before he made a deal with the Atlanta Hawks for a player named Bob Christian. The newest Sun would be arriving at Sky Harbor Airport that morning and Jerry wanted me to go pick him up...my very first assignment. I was eager and ready to go! The only problem was... I had absolutely no idea who Bob Christian was...if he was black or white...5'7" or 7'5."

"Uh, Jerry, how will I know who this guy is?" I asked.

"You shouldn't have too much trouble picking him out of a crowd," Jerry said. "He's black, seven feet tall and weighs about 260 pounds!"

I nodded my understanding.

Thank goodness the Suns had presented me with the keys to a company car that morning...a gently used 1972 Chevy Monte Carlo, on loan from Lou Grubb Chevrolet. Bob Christian would have never fit into my little VW bug, although we would have definitely scored points for creative use of a sunroof!

I arrived at the airport and parked my new-to-me company car in the pay lot in front of the terminal. I walked inside and waited for the flight to show. It was then that I realized that I had absolutely no cash. I mean zip, zilch, zero, nada. Those who know me will not be terribly surprised by this. I had fully intended to stop by the bank that morning and cash a check but, in the excitement of my first day, I just forgot. Since I didn't own a credit card and ATMs had not yet been invented, I needed to figure out how to bail my car out of the pay parking lot, not embarrass my new employer, while staying cool and confident at the same time.

> **❝❝I realized that I had absolutely no cash. I mean zip, zilch, zero, nada. ❞❞**

Just then, this giant of a man comes sauntering into the baggage claim area...Mr. Christian, I presume! He easily fit the description Jerry had given me, literally standing head and shoulders above every other passenger in the terminal. If this guy *wasn't* Bob Christian, I was going to bring him back to the office too!

I went up to him, introduced myself and welcomed him to Phoenix. While we waited for his bags, I made some small talk about how this was the first day working for the Suns... for both of us! Once I had established a little rapport with him, I just decided to ignore my financial embarrassment and said, "Hey Bob, I don't have any small bills (or any large ones either, I thought), so while you wait for your bags, give me a dollar and I'll bail the car out of the parking lot and pull it around front." He just nodded, reached in his pocket and pulled out a dollar. That was enough to get us out of the lot without driving over curbs, backing the wrong way over tire traps, crashing through barricades or having the airport authority invoice the Suns for 75 cents!

Bob Christian played the entire 1973-74 season for the Suns, but was waived by the team the following July. He had a five-year pro career but Phoenix was his last stop in the NBA. I feel bad that I never did pay him back that dollar.

FIRST NIGHT

That evening was my first official game night with the Suns. It was the opening night of the 1973-74 season, the Suns vs. the Seattle SuperSonics at the Arizona Veterans Memorial Coliseum in Phoenix. Sure, I had attended several Suns games over the previous two seasons, but this was different. I don't remember having any type of credential, I just walked in the Coliseum press entrance, told the security guard there that I was the new PR guy and I was directed to go to the courtside press table and find someone named Stan Richards who would set me up.

Stan worked on the game-night stat crew as the "paddle boy." There is little doubt that college fraternities and select bordellos probably have unique job descriptions for the position of "paddle boy," but the NBA had a different definition. Once a referee whistled a foul, it was the job of the "paddle boy" to hold up a pair of 8"x 8" wooden paddles that indicated the number of team and personal fouls and, whether or not the foul created a penalty situation. Additionally, the Suns paddle boy, Stan, was no boy. He was about five foot six, mostly bald, and close to 40 years old at the time. Stan bore a striking resemblance to the character "Boss Hogg" from the old TV show, *The Dukes of Hazzard*.

Stan sized me up and says, "Do you know what the hell you're doing?"

I looked at him, shook my head and said, "Honestly Stan, I don't have a clue."

His response was direct, "OK. Well just sit down here, be quiet and stay out of the way. We'll take care of everything."

I did...and they did... and I thoroughly enjoyed my very first game as the Suns new PR guy sitting at center court in one of the best seats in the house. Just a few years later, the job of "paddle boy" disappeared, as electronic scoreboards took over that task, but Stan Richards didn't disappear. He became our public address announcer and one of my closest friends for the next 25 years.

HAWK HUNTING

The scoreboard clock showed less than a minute to go and the Suns had this game, my first as PR director, in the bag! It would be an opening night win over the Sonics and their new coach, Bill Russell. Just then, our color commentator Rod Hundley, sitting just a couple of seats to my right, waves and gets my attention.

He covers his microphone with his hand and says, "Tom! We want Hawk! Get the Hawk!"

I nodded as though I knew what he was talking about, and then turned to Stan, the Paddle Boy, on my left.

"Why does he want Hawk?"

"For the post-game show."

"How do I do that?"

"Just go back in the locker room and get him."

At that moment, the final buzzer sounded. With Suns fans roaring their approval, the team ran off the court and into the Coliseum's labyrinth of backstage concourses and hallways. Since I had missed the opportunity to grab Hawk before he left the bench, and unwittingly compounded the problem by not following the team off the floor, I thought, "How tough can it be to find the Suns locker room?" I was fully expecting there to be a big sign that said "SUNS LOCKER ROOM" over the door, with a couple of armed security guards standing on either side. I was wrong on both counts. There was nothing that even hinted at what direction I should go.

After aimlessly wandering the back hallways for a couple of minutes, looking around corners and unsuccessfully trying a few locked doors, I was about to give up when a local radio reporter I knew, H.G. Listiak, came bopping around a corner. Figuring that he had probably just come from the locker room, I said, "Hey, 'H,' where's the locker room?"

He hiked his thumb over his shoulder and said, "Around the corner and all the way back."

I followed his directions but still no sign, no guards, no clue.

I went through what appeared to be a promising door. Nope. That one led to the parking lot. I had one final door to try before

I ran out of possibilities. I pulled it open and, at last, stepped into the muggy, smoky sanctuary of the Suns locker room! It was a boisterous scene with players, coaches, trainers, ball-boys and reporters moving around and everyone talking at once.

Having played high school sports, I was shocked to see three or four of the players enjoying a post game cigarette! The smokers included Connie Hawkins, the objective of my current mission. There he was, sitting on a little wooden stool in the middle of the rather small locker room, wearing just his game jersey and contentedly puffing on a cigarette.

Heady with the success of actually finding the locker room, I had a new-found confidence that surprised even me.

"Hawk!" I commanded. "Rod wants you for the post game show!"

"When?"

"Now!" I implored, knowing how much time I'd already wasted looking for the locker room.

> **❝I...stepped into the muggy, smoky sanctuary of the Suns locker room. ❞**

Hawk took one last drag on his cigarette and exhaled a long stream of smoke into a locker room atmosphere that was rapidly becoming toxic. He pulled on a pair of warm-up pants and stepped into a pair of flip-flops. So much for dressing up to meet your public! I shadowed Hawk as he shuffled back to the court for the interview. Now that I found him, I wasn't going to lose him!

I had survived my first day and my first game. Damn! Once I figured out what I was doing, this was going to be fun!

HOT WHEELS

It was already a very warm spring morning in Phoenix when J.C. came into my office.

"I need to borrow your car," he said.

Since my 1973 Monte Carlo was part of the Suns sponsorship arrangement with Lou Grubb Chevrolet, the car really didn't belong to me anyway. So my response was immediately compliant.

"Of course," I said, "But I have a speaking engagement out in Mesa today. How do I get out there?"

"Take my Jag!" Jerry said without hesitation.

He didn't have to say anything more. I was a huge fan of English sports cars: MG, Triumph, Jaguar, and Austin-Healey. I even owned a Sunbeam Alpine in college. When Jerry tossed me his keys, I got goose bumps thinking about taking a long, leisurely drive out to East Mesa in his awesome, blue, hardtop XKE V-12, 2+2...what the Brits call a "fixed head coupe."

A few minutes later, with excited anticipation, I loaded my projector, film and other necessary materials in the XKE's trunk (the Brits call that the "boot"). I jumped behind the wheel and fired it up. The Jaguar responded with the type of throaty roar that befit its name. As I sat there warming up the engine in the Suns parking lot, I did a quick scan of the gauges and started fiddling with the radio and air-conditioner. Quickly feeling comfortable and in control, I pulled out of the Suns parking lot to begin my 30 mile journey to the far East Valley. This was 1974. The modern freeways and multi-lane highways, that would make this a trip of 25 minutes or less today, did not yet exist. My journey would be over local streets, winding through Phoenix, Tempe and Mesa. The one-way trip would take about an hour. But, hey, no problem...I'm riding in style in Jerry Colangelo's XKE!

> **"I'm riding in style in Jerry Colangelo's XKE!"**

I was feeling really cool, until, after driving a few miles, I realized that I wasn't very cool at all. The air-conditioner didn't seem to be working! It was approaching 11 a.m. and the day had already warmed up to nearly 100 degrees, so opening the windows on the E-Type had about the same effect as opening the door to a blast furnace. I know, I know...it's a "dry heat" in Arizona, but I'm wearing a shirt and tie and sitting on a hot leather seat!

I constantly fiddled with the air-conditioning controls but nothing worked. In addition to bad air-conditioners, XKEs are also notorious for throwing off a lot of engine heat, so as the temperature in the foot-wells began to rise, I started to believe that I was inside some kind of rolling convection oven that featured inside-out baking. Just then, it occurred to me why Jerry Colangelo wanted to borrow my car!

I don't remember how many dozen traffic lights there were between downtown Phoenix and East Mesa, but I think they were all red that day and I hit every single one of them. As I waited at light after light, I could feel the perspiration trickling down my spine.

By the time I arrived at the restaurant to make my presentation, my face was flushed, my hair was matted and I was completely drenched in perspiration. My light blue dress shirt looked like someone had doused it with a five-gallon bucket of water. In a feeble attempt to look presentable, I spent 15 minutes in the restaurant men's room, actually removing my shirt and trying to dry it with the air-blowing hand dryer.

Eventually, I made my presentation, drank about 15 glasses of water, and then climbed back in the XKE to make the return trip to Phoenix during the hottest part of the day. I made it back to the Suns office, but I never got into that car again. In retrospect I suppose it could have been Jerry's idea of a "baptism by fire" for his rookie PR guy. I was definitely singed, but not burned. Now you know why Jerry wanted to borrow my car and why he would become a four-time NBA Executive of the Year!

AN EXPLOSIVE SITUATION

A few blocks from the Suns downtown office, there was a major scare one morning when a driver discovered a bomb planted in his car. The device was rigged to explode the instant the key was turned in the car's ignition. Fortunately, when the intended victim got in the car, he noticed two odd looking wires coming out of the glove box, so he immediately jumped out and called the police.

Emergency crews and the Phoenix Police Bomb Squad responded. Of course, one of the first things the police do in situations like this is to check the car's registration. When they ran the plates, they found the car was registered to none other than… Jerry Colangelo!

It turns out that Jerry had traded-in this car, an Audi 100LS sedan, several months before, but the paperwork never caught up with the Arizona Department of Motor Vehicles. Meanwhile, the car had been sold to a new owner. Nevertheless, the media thought they had a bombshell of a story and we spent the rest of the day denying that Jerry Colangelo was the target, or had anything whatsoever to do with the incident.

At the end of the day, Suns business manager Bob Machen and I retreated to one of our favorite watering holes to have a beer and talk things over. The television was on in the bar and on comes the six o'clock news. We watched as an enterprising young reporter from Channel 3, did a live shot standing right in front of the Suns offices, using our big Suns logo as a backdrop.

Normally a lead story would take about a minute, but this one lasted close to five minutes and it seemed like an hour to us. Without the benefit of any real facts, the reporter attempted to tie Colangelo to the incident in every way possible. Bob and I watched, stunned, knowing that this was going to make for very long days ahead. I turned to Bob and said facetiously, "Well...at least he soft-peddled it!"

> **❝Mossad should have warned him... ❞**

Overall, reports of the incident seemed to adhere to one of the tenets of modern journalism, that is, "never let facts stand in the way of a good story."

In fact, the new owner of Jerry's old car turned out to be both a newcomer to Phoenix and an Israeli agent, who was being targeted by persons unknown. Mossad should have warned him... never buy a used car that once belonged to Jerry Colangelo... it could be hazardous to your health!

BE SURE TO TUNE IN

My excitement and enthusiasm naturally remained high through the first few months of the season, but I can't say that Suns fans, or even the team itself, always maintained theirs. We were on our way to a 30-52 record. There was one weeknight game when the Coliseum crowd was even smaller than usual, and the quality of play was less than inspirational. Suns guard Gary Melchionni, who stood about 6'1" and weighed 165 pounds (when soaking wet), slowly walked the ball up out of backcourt. At that moment, the

Coliseum was so quiet that you could clearly hear Melchionni's dribble thudding against the floor.

Suddenly, one of our favorite courtside fans shattered the silence with a loud, exaggerated yawn, quickly followed by an even louder..."Does anybody know what time *Kojak* comes on?!"

There was little doubt that every person in the building heard him. Team management, often referred to as "the suits," sitting in the front row behind the press table, tried to maintain their decorum, but we had a tough time keeping a straight face on that one.

SMALL WORLD

As my career progressed with the Suns, one of the things that always amazed me was how closely interwoven the basketball fraternity can be. As freshmen and junior varsity basketball players at Iona Prep, John Borgia and I had the opportunity to play in a junior varsity practice game down in New York City against Power Memorial High School and their budding super-star, Lewis Alcindor. The big guy was already in the neighborhood of seven-feet and was slated to play varsity that season. My first impression of Alcindor was, "Man, is he skinny!"

During that practice-game there was one play when a shot went up and the 5'11" J-Bo crouched low and spread himself to block out for a rebound. The next thing he knew, he was looking directly at Alcindor's butt. The big guy had simply stepped over him!

I guess our little JV team from the 'burbs wasn't giving Alcindor much of a workout, because after the first quarter, they pulled him out of the game to go to the other side of the gym for some one-on-one coaching with one of their assistants. Whenever I could, I'd glance over to watch as the coach patiently worked with Alcindor on entry passes, his drop-step and a shot that would later gain notoriety as the "sky hook."

Some fifteen years later, I was preparing biographical information on one of our Suns scouts, a soft-spoken, East Coast gentleman named Dick Percudani. Amidst all of his impressive basketball credentials as a player and a coach, I noticed that "Perc" had been a long-time coach at Power Memorial. So the next time we had a chance to visit, I told him the story of my brief on-court exposure to

Alcindor and then asked him, "Perc, were you the coach working with Alcindor that day?" He responded, "Yep. That was me."

The world of basketball is small indeed.

SPEAKING OF SPEAKING

During my first year with the Suns, I found out that one of my duties was to go out and speak to the numerous Kiwanis, Rotary and Exchange Clubs throughout the Phoenix area. I'd load up a bulky 16mm projector along with our current Suns highlight film, toss in a bunch of Suns pocket schedules, a couple of tickets to give away and I'd venture out to be the featured speaker for a club's breakfast, lunch or dinner meeting. Following my introduction I'd usually show the film to get everyone in a basketball frame of mind. After the film I would talk a little bit about the progress of the Suns that season, answer a few questions from the audience and finally I'd ask a quiz question about the team, with a pair of tickets to a future Suns game going to the winner. It was a 30-minute formula that worked pretty well.

I remember my very first speaking engagement for the Suns. It came early in that 1973-74 season and it was to the Deer Valley Optimist Club. The Suns were already in deep trouble that season and there wasn't a lot of hope for them to improve. The club I spoke to that day was, without a doubt, the most pessimistic group of Optimists I have ever encountered. I tried to give them a glimmer of hope for the future, but they weren't buying it.

At the end of my presentation, the chapter president asked me to return to the podium to receive a token of appreciation from the club. With a great flourish, he presented me with a gift box and said, "Tom, thank you for your presentation today. It is my honor to present you with this official Optimist Club letter opener, which you can use to open the one or two pieces of fan mail your team might get this year. Or, if things don't go well for you this season, at the end of the year, you can always use it to commit Hare-Kari!"

And these guys were the OPTIMISTS!

I hadn't done much public speaking before and I was a little uneasy about it when I first started. But after that initial experience, I didn't think it could ever get much worse, so I quickly embraced the many opportunities to improve my speaking skills. There were some years when I did well over 100 club presentations. I also learned to love chicken.

SPIN DOCTOR AT WORK

THE HECKLER

Twenty-five years and hundreds of presentations later, I received an invitation to speak at an evening meeting of the Sun City Lecture Club. I had talked to many of Sun City's civic and fraternal clubs over the years. With the exception of a few old-timers getting a head start on their afternoon naps during my presentations, it was always fun and a great experience. Without a doubt, the Suns have some wonderful fans in Sun City, the nation's preeminent retirement community.

Over the phone, I was told by the club chairman that I could speak on any topic I wished and that he hoped I would be able to attend a VIP reception, just prior to my remarks. I invited Connie Hawkins to join me because everyone loved the "Hawk" and I thought many of the retirees would remember him from his playing days. In addition, I expected my talk to go a little longer than usual, maybe 45 minutes, so involving Hawk in my lecture might afford me the luxury of an occasional break.

Hawk and I made the one hour drive west from Phoenix to Sun City and found the facility dedicated to the Lecture Club. The reception started at 6:30 in the lobby and we chatted with about a dozen people who were involved with the club. Then we moved into a modern, beautifully appointed lecture hall at 7 p.m. Hawk and I were directed to the stage that looked up at the 200-seat hall, set up in a sloping, 180 degree configuration. The same 12 people who attended the VIP event shuffled into the lecture hall. Four of those folks joined Hawk and me on stage because they were the officers of the club. The other four couples took up seats in the center of the hall about midway up. I thought we might want to wait for the rest of the crowd to show up, but the club president assured me that "this was probably it." I then quietly asked him how long he expected me to speak. His response was that he thought that

> **❝❝I was somewhere between the dominance of George Mikan and the invention of the 24 second clock... ❞❞**

two hours would be sufficient. My first thought was, "What?!!!!" My second thought was, "Run!" My third thought was, "OK, how am I going to get through this?"

Thinking quickly, I decided to go with a "History of Basketball" theme, starting in the Stone Age and moving forward...slowly. I had no notes to refer to, just a career in basketball and a mind that served as a storehouse of generally useless basketball facts that could finally be put to productive use.

During the first 50 minutes or so, I successfully navigated my way from the first appearance of homo sapiens on planet Earth, through the Mayan sports culture, where losers were beheaded. Then it was onto James A. Naismith's invention of basketball. I wheeled through basketball's barnstorming era of the 1920s and 1930s and then laid out the foundation of what would become the National Basketball Association. I think I was somewhere between the dominance of George Mikan and the invention of the 24-second shot clock, when I encountered something I had never experienced in all my years with the Suns...a heckler!

"You don't know the players!!!" he shouted.

I stopped, "What?!"

One of the eight people in the audience stood up and, wagging a boney index finger at me, he repeated, "You don't know the players!!"

"I'm sorry," I responded. "If you mean that I don't know these players personally, you're right. But I've followed the NBA since the 1950s and I've met..."

"YOU DON'T KNOW THE PLAYERS!!!" he interrupted.

Exasperated, I looked over at my buddy, Connie Hawkins. His head was down on the table in front of him, buried in the crook of his right arm. His left hand was balled in a fist and he was rhythmically banging it up and down on the table. He was laughing his butt off! I wasn't going to get much help from him.

I leaned over and whispered to the club president, "What should I do?"

"Oh, that's just Morris," he said. "He's 84 and has Alzheimer's. Don't worry about him."

"YOU DON'T KNOW THE PLAYERS!!!" Morris screamed again. "You don't even know who I am!"

Suddenly, Hawk regained his composure, sat up and spoke directly to the heckler, "I know who you are!"

The heckler was stunned, "You do?!"

"Yeah," Connie said, "You're Mo! And you played for the Knicks!"

Well, a visibly stunned Morris sat down immediately and didn't say another word. When we took a short break, Morris and his wife left the event.

We wrapped things up a little while later, but as we were walking out I said to Hawk, "How did you know that guy?"

"I talked to him for 15 minutes at the reception." Hawkins said, "He told me everything. I guess he didn't remember that he even talked to me."

I was the target of an 84 year-old heckler from Sun City. God help me, I love this job!

DUCK

Lamar Green, a Suns player from the franchise's early years, has always kept in touch. I was flattered when he once described me as "kind of like a duck. When you see him smoothly gliding across the surface of a lake, he looks calm, cool, and everything is OK. What you don't see is that, beneath the surface, his feet are paddling like crazy!"

HAWK SWOOPS

After I was with the Suns for a grand total of two weeks, Colangelo decided to trade Connie Hawkins to the Lakers for Keith Erickson in late October of 1973. Because Hawkins had put Phoenix on the NBA map and onto league highlight reels with his spectacular swoops to the hoop, the trade was the story of the year in the local media.

Hawkins would stay with the Lakers until the end of the 1974-75 season when he was traded to the Atlanta Hawks for what would be his last year in the NBA. It would also be an opportunity for him to reunite with his old Suns coach, Cotton Fitzsimmons, who was now the coach in Atlanta. Connie always called Fitzsimmons, "Whitey."

Once during that final season with the Hawks, Connie got the ball on a break-away. Gripping the ball like a grapefruit in one of those giant hands of his, Hawk sailed toward the basket for one of his patented slam dunks. But he mistimed things a bit and the ball slammed off the back of the rim and caromed out to center court. Cotton called time out.

As Hawkins walked to the bench shaking his head, he said to his coach, "Whitey, they've either got to lower the basket or raise the floor, because the Hawk can't swoop no more!"

HARRY THE HAT

He could have stepped out of a Damon Runyon story. Actually, I wouldn't have been the least bit surprised to find out that he was a personal acquaintance of Runyon's from the 1930's. We called him "Harry the Hat," because that's just what you call somebody named Harry. During his years in Phoenix I don't think I ever saw him actually wearing a hat. His real name was Harry Caplan. At least that's what his by-line once read in the *Brooklyn Eagle* and other New York newspapers.

When the Suns opened for business in 1968, Harry, already an old-timer, stopped by to wish the new team good luck and to see if there was something he could do to help. Originally from New York City, he was a retired sportswriter, who had covered some of the greatest games and athletes of the 20th Century. And he had the stories to prove it.

The Suns didn't have a national clipping service back then, but they subscribed to dozens of major newspapers from around the country. Jerry Colangelo put Harry to work part-time, reading those papers and cutting out the stories that related to the Suns or the NBA. Harry loved the feel of the newsprint and everyday the ink on those papers would leave black stains on his fingertips. I remember him in a back room at the Suns office, sitting behind a folding table that was covered with stacks of newspapers, often two feet high. Even though it was virtually impossible for Harry to keep up with the avalanche of papers that came in every day, he gave it one heck of a try.

Colangelo once asked Harry to join the team on a trip to New York. When the two of them walked into the press room at Madison Square Garden, Harry was greeted like a long-lost colleague and treated like visiting royalty. The young GM of the Suns could only smile in appreciation at the outpouring of respect for the venerable Harry Caplan.

Harry would often sit in my office and pass the time with story after story about his life in the newspaper business in New York City. As Harry got older, he would sometimes nod off in mid-story, only to awaken 15 minutes later and pick up his story exactly where he left off. It was amazing!

I intended it to be only an honorary position when I put Harry in charge of the Coliseum press room. At first Harry would just hand out the press releases, game notes, statistics, lineups and other information prepared by the Suns PR office, but after a while he got very possessive of those notes. One night a local radio guy came in and tried to grab a set of notes from Harry, who at this stage, was well into his 80's. Harry quickly pulled the notes against his chest and wrapped his arms around them like he was protecting a baby. When the reporter grabbed for the notes again, Harry hauled off and belted him in the arm! After that, the media guys learned that all they had to say was "please" and Harry would give them anything they wanted.

"Harry the Hat" had a nickname for me too. He called me "Tin Box Tom" after a turn-of-the-century Brooklyn alderman who never "touched" a bribe. This shady city official placed a tin box on the floor in front of his office desk. People would come into his office seeking his help to cut through city bureaucracy and resolve their problems. People knew that a generous cash gift, placed in the tin box, would often help speed up the process. In my case however, "Tin Box Tom" was simply a nickname... really.

> **❝Tin Box Tom... a turn-of-the-century Brooklyn alderman who never 'touched' a bribe. ❞**

Harry passed away quietly one night in his sleep, in July, 1984. When we tried to locate surviving relatives, we found no one. That's when we all realized that the Suns were Harry's family. In his honor, we renamed the Coliseum press room "Harry's Place," because it was.

NO ORDINARY JOE

Phoenix Gazette columnist Joe Gilmartin covered the Suns with wit, and a creative perspective, for more than 30 years. As a columnist, Gilmartin would always take a slightly different approach from the rest of the media. But in order to sit down and discuss his unique observations with Suns coaches, management or players, in a one-on-one environment, Joe would wait patiently. He would wait until post-game emotions had calmed down, until the crush of reporters and cameramen had swept through the locker rooms and the other media people had gone off to file their stories. Invariably, Joe would kill a few minutes of his waiting time with me in the Suns Press Room.

Gilmartin was a keen observer of the NBA and I learned a great deal from him in those post-game chats, including the style and synergy of the game. In the NBA, a first-half lead or deficit of ten, or even twenty points, meant almost nothing, because it's a game of surge and counter-surge; point and counter-point; give and take; ebb and flow, high-tide and low-tide; hot and cold; attack and counter-attack; inside-out and outside-in. Gilmartin also might have mentioned ying and yang. When one team goes up by 20 points in the first half...bet the farm (used here only as a figure of speech, Commissioner Stern) that the other team will claw its way back and will, at the very least, get to within five points before the game ends. It is just the nature of the game. But perhaps the most important lesson Joe taught me... in the NBA, the first team to 100 points will win 99% of the time!

But I was not alone when it comes to people who have been positively influenced by Joe Gilmartin, as Connie Hawkins once reflected:

"The guy who influenced me the most was Joe Gilmartin. We used to sit and talk for hours on airplanes and in hotels and I learned a lot from him. We had a great relationship. Hindsight being 20/20, when I look back on it, he was always teaching me something. He was so smart, a genius. He was always coming up with different angles for stories. He once wrote a great line about me. He said I was like 'a work of art—sometimes poetry in motion and sometimes still life.' He was hard on me sometimes, like that, but he was trying to bring the best out in me."

GOOD SAVE

During the 1976 NBA Finals in Boston, the league had their head-quarters at the Sheraton Hotel, which is also where the Suns and their media entourage were staying. Nick Curran, the NBA's PR director and his wife, had just welcomed their first baby into their lives and the kid was making his first road trip with mom and dad. At 3 a.m., a distressed Curran called Gilmartin for some parenting advice. Nick knew that Joe had two kids and he also knew that sportswriters have a reputation of knowing everything, or at least pretending that they do.

In spite of the fact that Joe had been out late with some of the other scribes, he went down to Nick's room. Their little guy is crying …make that screaming. He is genuinely not a happy kid. Joe's initial diagnosis was nothing short of brilliant. "This baby is really pissed off!"

But then he offered the new parents some good advice, "I think if you change him, feed him, hold him for a while and calm him down, he should be OK."

The next day, Joe ran into the Curran family in the lobby of the hotel. The baby was sleeping peacefully in his stroller. The parents were nearly delirious in their gratitude for everything that Joe had done the night before. Joe just kind of shrugged it off at first, but they continued to be so over-the-top and effusive in their praise of Joe that he began to believe that maybe he had indeed saved the baby's life!

Writer, counselor, dispenser of sage wisdom, unlicensed pediatrician …Gilmartin was definitely no ordinary Joe.

SINGLE STEP

Neal Walk had been traded from the Suns to the New Orleans Jazz where he teamed up with "Pistol" Pete Maravich and Coach Scotty Robertson to open the 1974-75 season. The Jazz got off to an abysmal start, losing 14 games in a row, before Maravich hit a long fade-away jumper at the buzzer for their first win.

In the post-game locker room a new, young reporter asked Neal the significance of the win for the Jazz.

Neal responded with a quote.

"A journey of a thousand miles, begins with a single step."

"That's great!" the reporter said, "Who said that?

"Lao-tzu," Neal said, properly crediting the ancient Chinese Taoist philosopher.

But the fledgling reporter had one last follow-up question about Lao-tzu.

"Where did *he* coach?"

BAH! POLITICS!

I think I've always tried to be someone who plays well with others. When I joined the Suns in 1973, I stepped into a situation where the staff and the game-night operations were already set up for the season. The stat crew was very capably headed by John Olson and Jerry Olsen; the paddle boy and press table coordinator was Stan Richards and the public address announcer (the PA man) was Bob Cowen. All of them were experienced and knowledgeable. I was planning to just stay out of their way. Cowen, in addition to having a great set of "pipes," also had a strong personality that had not always endeared him to Suns management.

I was not aware of the politics when I stepped into the job and all these folks suddenly fell under my purview. So, when it was suggested to me by some of the other Suns executives that perhaps I should develop a back-up plan to cover the public address announcer's position in the event that Bob Cowen became ill or was otherwise unable to perform his duties. It seemed to me a very smart thing to do. I just didn't realize that I was being "played."

Cowen, I learned later, could be cantankerous and difficult and there was a desire by some in the Suns front office to make a change at that position. In real life, our paddle boy, Stan Richards, had been an on-air radio personality for several decades and he too had a smooth, professional delivery behind the PA microphone. I thought he would be the perfect back-up. He knew the NBA game and he was there every night sitting right next to Cowen.

When I suggested to Cowen and Richards that we give Stan an opportunity to do the pre-game announcements at an upcoming game, as preparation for him being a "back-up," there wasn't any protest. After that game was in the books and Stan got good marks, I suggested that we let Richards do the entire first half of another game a week or two later. No problems or complaints surfaced as Stan did the first half and Cowen did the second half.

Not too long after that, at the urging of other Suns executives, I suggested that we let Bob take an entire night off and we let Stan do a full game, from start to finish, completing his "back-up" training. I floated that idea immediately following a game as the three of us, Stan, Bob and I, stood right behind the press table.

I thought the development of a back-up PA man was going extremely well, but I guess Cowen had a different view, perceiving it as a threat to his position. He let me know, in no uncertain terms that he didn't like it, and then he said, "Why don't you just let him do the whole season!?"

I was taken aback by his attitude and he left me with only one possible response, which was simply to say, "OK!"

"Wait! What are you saying? I'm fired!?" an irate Cowen shot back.

"I didn't say it, Bob. You did," I responded. "I'm going to let Stan do the rest of the season."

The conversation was beginning to get a little heated and some fans were sitting nearby waiting for the post game show to begin, so our official scorer, John Olson, said, "Hey guys... this isn't the place." So we all walked back toward the locker room. Cowen immediately sought out Ted Podleski, the team's director of marketing, to plead his case. Ted listened, then just shook his head and told Cowen, "Sorry, Tom's in charge. It's his decision. There's nothing I can do."

That was the moment I knew I had been played as a pawn in a game of personalities and organizational politics.

OF MICS AND MEN

As the public relations (PR) guy, I sat at the courtside press table next to the paddle boy and the public address announcer. I had a phone in front of me that connected directly to the Coliseum switch board. When calls came in during a game, the Coliseum switchboard operator would transfer them directly to me.

The procedure was a little cumbersome but we were usually able to avoid the sophomoric pranks that some people wanted to inflict upon us. There was one night however, when someone came down from the seats while our PA man Stan was busy, and cunningly slipped a note in front of him. When Stan finally saw the note, he just picked it up, switched open the microphone and announced, "Dr. Jack Mehoff, please call your directory!"

It might have slipped by unnoticed, except Stan then proceeded to repeat it... THREE TIMES!!! "Dr. Jack Mehoff... Dr. Jack Mehoff... Dr. Jack Mehoff!" Suddenly, Stan realized he'd been duped and his bald head turned a bright shade of crimson while everyone else at the press table collapsed in hysterical laughter and some of our more conservative fans nearly went into cardiac arrest!

PA MAN STAN RICHARDS AND REFEREE JAKE O'DONNELL

CALL YOUR DIRECTORY

Our Coliseum paging system worked well most of the time but some doctors proved to be problematic. Remember, this took place in the B.T. years...that's "Before Technology." Cellular phones and pagers had yet to become the all-pervasive, intrusive annoyances we know so well today.

When a doctor came to a Suns game he was supposed to register with the Coliseum switchboard and be assigned a number.

When an emergency call came into the switchboard, the operator would note the doctor's name but relay only the doctor's number to me at courtside. The actual PA announcement would sound something like, "Dr. 247, please call your directory!"

> **❝Dr. 247, please call your directory. ❞**

But sometimes doctors wouldn't register at the switchboard, and, when the emergency calls came in, we'd have to use their names (as in the previously described case of Dr. Jack M). There was one doctor who never seemed to have a number and he would be paged, by name, at every game. Dutifully, we made the announcement, game after game, until one night Bob Machen said to me, "Tom, stop announcing his name, he's just trying to get free publicity!"

"But Bob," I replied, "he's a doctor. We could be liable. It could be a matter of life and death!"

"That may be true," Bob deadpanned, "but the guy's a veterinarian."

POWER TO THE PA MAN

One of the most popular promotions in any NBA arena is "Ball Night." Giving away a full-sized or a mini-sized basketball to kids is a sure fire way to pump up ticket sales when attendance figures are down or a "lesser" opponent is coming to town. During a season when Cotton Fitzsimmons was coaching a struggling Kansas City Kings team, he once quipped, "Everyplace we go...it's 'Ball Night!'"

For the struggling Suns in the 1970's, "Ball Night" was becoming a way of life. It was not unusual for the team to schedule two or three of these give-away nights per season. Consequently, they had developed a certain expertise in how and when you could distribute the balls to kids and not impact the enjoyment of the game for the other fans.

Designed as a multi-purpose facility for the Arizona State Fair, the Arizona Veterans Memorial Coliseum had thousands of square feet of exhibit space adjacent to the arena seating area and the basketball court on the floor level. The idea was to hand out a coupon for a free basketball to the first 5,000 kids coming to the game that night. During the game, we would make an announcement out-lining when and where they could claim their basketballs. Also, during the game, we'd have crews working to inflate the 5,000 basketballs.

We set up the process and redemption area in one of the exhi-bition halls where there was plenty of room for people to line up and there was even more room for frisky kids to start bounc-ing their new basketballs. The plan was to finish blowing up the balls and begin redeeming the coupons at the end of the third quarter. The first announcement, outlining the procedure, would come in the second quarter.

At the first time out of the second quarter, PA man Stan Richards announced, in his usual mellow and measured tone, "Ladies and gentlemen, you can redeem your basketball coupons in the Coliseum's North Exhibit Hall beginning at the end of the third quarter."

Suddenly, we heard a rumbling, almost like an earthquake. It was a stampede of little feet. Stan looked up to see thousands of kids leave their seats near the top of the Coliseum and stream down the aisles, determined to be first in line for their free basketball.

Stan flipped on the microphone and in his deepest, sternest, most authoritative voice, boomed out, "STOP!!!"

The kids stopped so suddenly it was almost like they had run into an invisible wall.

"GO BACK TO YOUR SEATS!" Stan demanded.

To the kids, I'm sure it sounded like the voice of God command-ing them. And, all at once, every one of those kids turned around and ran back to their seats.

"YOU CAN LINE UP AT THE <u>END</u> OF THE <u>THIRD</u> QUARTER!!!" Stan thundered in a final admonishment of the retreating youngsters.

We all sat there at the press table, chuckling, in a state of bemused shock, before somebody behind us commented; "Now *that* was amazing!"

TRY IT AGAIN

In 1988, Phoenix was playing Houston at the Coliseum and the Suns' Jeff Hornacek got into a major scuffle with the Rockets' Sleepy Floyd.

Everybody…players, coaches, trainers, security guards, referees and even a few fans out of the stands started charging toward the fight.

Stan quickly opened up his microphone and in that same stern voice, that once halted the kids, commanded, "GET BACK IN YOUR SEATS, IMMEDIATELY!!" Amazingly, the fight paused as everyone stopped, at least momentarily. They all looked back at Stan and then seemed to say, "To hell with him!" and the fight immediately resumed. That night offered definitive proof that history does NOT always repeat itself.

NOT SO SUPER SUB

Most fans think that the public address announcer's job is easy. Take it from somebody who had to fill in once, in an emergency, it's not. No matter how many games you sit there and watch or listen, it is very different once you pull up your chair and open that microphone. Stan Richards was a rock. He was calm, experienced and as reliable as a PA man could be. Stan passed away in 1992 at age 60…way too early and much too young. He once wrote about this episode in my career, so I will let Stan's words tell the story.

"A few years ago, when we were playing the Utah Jazz, I got really sick. That had never happened to me before. It was about the third quarter and I turned to Tom Ambrose, the Suns VP of Public Relations who was sitting next to me and said 'Tom, you are going to have to take over. I've got to go to the bathroom!"

"I was virtually running out of the Coliseum, but as I left, Alvan Adams committed a foul, and I heard Ambrose say, 'Offensive foul on Alvan Adams, his third personal.' And I thought, 'Oh, he sounds fine!'

"Well as I came back in through the East staging area about 15 minutes later, I heard Tom say in a voice so high that he sounded like a young girl with adenoid problems, 'Time out! Jazz!'

"What had happened was, the longer he sat there, the more he thought about it and the more he thought about it, the more nervous he got. Of course, what happens when you get nervous is your voice starts climbing because your throat closes. By the time I got back, Tom was a nervous wreck.

"When people saw me coming back they started to applaud because they thought it was funny. By the time I got to the table I had a standing ovation. Tom saw me coming and when I got to the table he stood up, put his arms around me and whispered in my ear, 'Don't you EVER do that to me again!'"

ANOTHER FINE MESS

While working at an NBA press table, the stat crew, staff and media are supposed to maintain a detached professionalism about the game. NBA public address announcers especially, are supposed to remain absolutely neutral when it comes to officials' calls, no matter how many of those calls seem biased, one-sided or driven by some unexplainable hidden agenda or conspiracy theory.

The Suns public address guy, Stan Richards was a consummate pro who knew the rules, but there were some nights when he just couldn't help himself and his facial expressions would give away his opinions on some calls that went against the Suns. Sometimes the offended NBA referee would come over during a time out and very subtly deliver the message that he didn't need that kind of _____ (please insert your favorite expletive here) from any member of the stat crew. Usually, that was the end of it.

> **❝Any more histrionics from YOU and YOU will be history. ❞**
> **- Earl Strom**

But sometimes the referees aren't so subtle. Bill Straus, who served as a volunteer on the Suns game night staff in the early days of the franchise, remembers referee Earl Strom coming over to his seat at the press table, leaning over to get directly in his face, and, very calmly, threatening, "Any more histrionics from YOU, and YOU will be history!"

At other times, the refs would just mentally note a PA man's negative reaction and then write him up after the game in the refs' report to the league office. That was the case during one hotly contested game at the Coliseum when Stan let his emotions get the better of him and he rolled his eyes back after a particularly egregious (in his mind) call that went against the Suns. The ref didn't have time to berate Stan during the game so he simply reported the incident to the league afterwards, for disposition.

A couple of weeks later, I received a letter from the NBA, mildly chastising Stan for his behavior, but that was it...no sanctions to invoke...no fines...no suspensions...no mandatory counseling sessions. I shared the letter with Jerry Colangelo and told him that I would talk to Stan and that I was confident that it would not happen again. Jerry contemplated for a few seconds, before he grinned and said, "Let's have some fun with this. Let's fine him!"

So I went to work crafting an absolutely scathing letter from Jerry to Stan, admonishing Stan for his total lack of professionalism, how his behavior was an embarrassment to the franchise and how further incidents of this nature would not be tolerated! We also told him that we were going to fine him $25 per game for the next ten games and take the money out of his check. I think Stan was making about $75 per game at the time. Jerry signed it and we sent the letter over to KTAR Radio, our flagship station, where Stan worked and where we had plenty of friends who could report on Stan's reaction.

Later, we heard that Stan stormed around the station, waving Jerry's letter high over his head, screaming, "Fifteen years! Fifteen years I give them and this is what I get?! This is unconscionable!"

We were just about to cave-in and call Stan to tell him it was all a joke, when our marketing guy, Harvey Shank, had a stroke of brilliance. We weren't done yet!

There was a local radio personality whose "shtick" could be best described as Candid Camera for radio. Kids today might call it "getting punked." We set up this radio personality to play the role of Jack Joyce, head of NBA Security, who would call Stan to "investigate" the incident and get his side of the story. Everything was recorded to be aired later.

Stan started out the "official" NBA phone call by being very defensive and blustery about the whole situation. He claimed that the incident was blown completely out of proportion and that what the referee perceived as Stan rolling his eyes back, was actually due to a little uncontrollable twitch that Stan had in his eyelid. That was a total fabrication. But Stan's bluster and bravado quickly collapsed and by the end of the interview he was a quivering mass of protoplasm, groveling for another chance.

Mercifully, "Jack Joyce" then revealed his true identity and the whole scam. Stan's reaction to the "reveal" made for a perfect ending that had to be edited for radio.

"What?!...You ass (BLEEP)! ...You son of a (BLEEP)!"

When re-telling the tale a few seasons later, Stan said, "Jerry, Harvey and Tom put that together and one of these days, yeah, one of these days, I'll return the favor. I've been working on it for years!"

Stan passed away before he could execute a retaliatory practical joke, but I wouldn't put it past him to somehow reach out from the great beyond and exact his revenge.

IT'S NOT WHAT YOU SAY...YEAH IT IS

There was a game in the 1980s when the Suns were taking on one of those power-house Lakers teams with Magic, Kareem, Worthy, et al, at the Coliseum. The Lakers didn't need much help in those days but on this particular night, in the first quarter, the Suns were whistled for eight, count 'em, EIGHT team fouls in the period, while the Lakers were called for exactly zero. Colangelo, furious, was sitting courtside with "the suits," just behind the announcer's position.

Through clenched teeth he said to Stan Richards, "Announce the team fouls!"

Stan turned around and said, "Jerry I can't do that! We'll get fined!"

Jerry was insistent, "Just do it! I'll pay the fine!"

So Stan got on the microphone and shaking his head the entire time, said, "In the first quarter, the team foul situation was Phoenix Suns eight... Lakers zero!"

The Coliseum crowd exploded. Frustrated Suns fans booed long and hard. The referees, who had been sharing a quiet moment on the other side of the court, as far away as they could get from Suns team officials, came sprinting over to the press table and to Stan in particular.

"What the hell do you think you're doing?! Who told you to say that?!" the refs screamed at Stan, as the boo decibels rose to eardrum-shattering levels.

Stan just hiked his thumb over his shoulder at "the suits."

The refs looked up at J.C., wagged their fingers at him and said, "You're gonna hear about this!"

Jerry's response was, "Just open your eyes and call the game!"

J.C. paid the fine.

STATS THE WAY IT IS

One of the more tedious aspects of an NBA PR job is keeping the statistics. Once a game was played, and the game box score compiled and distributed to the media, it was then the responsibility of the team PR person to make sure that all information was immediately reported to the NBA's official statistical agency, the Elias Sports Bureau, in New York City. After that, it was their further responsibility to update season and career statistics for each player.

In addition, back in those early days, as a courtesy, the home team PR director would update the stats of that night's visiting team and relay them to the PR office of next team on their road trip. This was all done manually; the computer age had not yet arrived in the NBA. I quickly realized that this part of the PR function really needed someone to focus on it full time...a statistician.

It was about that time that a young man named Barry Ringel gave me a call. He wanted to talk to me about doing statistics for the Suns, and, when we set up a time to meet, I promised him that he would have my undivided attention. I desperately wanted to delegate the stat function, but I had no budget to do so. After we got to know each other Barry offered to do the statistics for free... so I could see first-hand what he could do. Once I realized what a remarkable statistical talent he was, coupled with a great, analytical, basketball mind, I had to have him on my team. We had a deal. I figured out a way to pay him.

"Rings," who was a fellow New Yorker, proved to be an outstanding statistician and became a close friend. No question, he made us a better PR operation, producing incisive game notes and more accurate stats for the media. He was one of the first statisticians to develop a performance index, measuring a player's on-court effectiveness for every minute he played. He dubbed it the "Ringel-dex." Once the coaching staff realized its value and implications they couldn't get enough. For many years now, Barry has been a successful basketball coach for the girls program at Thunderbird High School.

As I think about my early "modus operandi," when it came to stats, Barry Ringel was truly a gift, directly from the Almighty. Typically, a 7:30 p.m. Suns game would end by 10:30. Post game interviews, statistical work, locker room sessions with the players, press room work along with equipment breakdown and storage would take us until about 11:00 p.m. Even beyond that, it was not unusual for a visiting writer or two to still be banging out a game story, doing a preview, or writing a follow-up column.

Once we made sure that the visiting writers had transportation back to their hotel, we'd select one of the local watering holes for a game "debriefing," which usually included a bucket of steamed clams washed down with a couple of Jack Daniels. Following the debriefing, I'd arrive home at about 1:30 a.m. and sit down to begin the process of updating the stats, usually wrapping up about 2:30 a.m. Under these often-blurry circumstances, I guaranteed all stats to be within 40 percent accuracy. Barry, thankfully, pushed that percentage up to 99.99%.

Barry's car, a vintage Barracuda had a custom Arizona license plate that read "STATS." He earned that plate.

For my own personal reference, I always kept a series of unofficial, "sidebar" statistics. These "everyday" stats included attendance records, along with what officiating crews did vs. the Suns at home or on the road. Frequently, Colangelo would ask for this kind of background information and I always wanted to be ready. Let's just say that with certain refs, there were noticeable "trends." You know, things that make you go "h-m-m-m-m."

SIMPLE SURGERY

When a team is struggling like the Suns did in 1973-74, the PR guy is looking for anything...and I mean anything...that will net his team a few positive column inches in the daily newspaper. Just about any story idea is a good idea. So, when I learned that one of our prized young forwards, Corky Calhoun, would undergo knee surgery, I thought that perhaps *Arizona Republic* sports columnist Dave Hicks might want to sit in on the operation and get a behind the scenes view of something very few people ever get to witness. Dave was the kind of writer who could see the humor and find an angle in just about anything. I got the OK from Colangelo and from the doctors who, of course, welcomed the thought of any publicity at all.

The morning of the surgery arrived early...very early. I was at the hospital at 5:30 a.m. Hicks was supposed to be there at 6 and the surgery was scheduled to begin at 6:30 a.m. Why do all surgeries need to be done so early? On top of that, Hicks seemed to be running late...6:10...6:15, 6:20. It seemed like my great idea for a story was beginning to fade. Our team physician, Dr. Paul Steingard, came out to say that if Hicks wasn't there by now, he was probably a no-show. So, doc invited me to put on some scrubs and come into the operating room to watch. "It'll be fun," he said.

"Why not?" I thought. I'm here anyway...it'll be a new adventure. If anything really good happens I'll just relay it to Hicks and maybe he'll turn it into a column. I quickly changed into scrubs and put on a cap and mask. The operating theatre was really cold...I mean "meat locker" cold... and I was shivering as I stood and looked over the shoulders of the surgeon, Dr. Jim Nichols, and Dr. Steingard, who was assisting. They were going to give me a step by step primer in how a knee surgery was performed. Cool.

Meanwhile, Corky was more than cool...he was out cold. He'd been under anesthesia and was sleeping peacefully even before I walked into the operating room. He was on his back on the operating table, but his left calf and leg were braced in such a way that his knee was flexed at a 90 degree angle and elevated to give the doctors total access. This was a basic knee cartilage surgery, but back in 1974 that meant a fairly large incision, six inches or so in length. The minimally invasive arthroscopic procedure that is so familiar today had not yet been fully developed.

Dr. Nichols explained that Corky's leg was wrapped in several layers of a surgical compression bandage designed to drive the blood from the knee area. So, with the wrapped leg elevated, when the incision was made, there would be very little blood. As

I stood there and watched, Dr. Nichols used some surgical scissors to carefully cut away the layers of the white surgical wrap around the knee area, exposing Corky's dark skin underneath. Dr. Nichols then pointed out to me exactly where, alongside the knee cap, he was going to make his incision. I nodded my approval, although I don't think he was waiting for it.

Then he took his scalpel and in one swift motion, deftly drew it down alongside the knee cap. He was right. There was virtually no blood! The doctor then took the skin on either side of the incision and pulled it back. Underneath, he explained, was muscle tissue. Because of the lack of blood in the area of the incision, the muscle tissue was entirely white. I remember thinking, "Wait a minute…Corky is *white* on the inside?!"

Actually, that is also the *last* thing I remember thinking before I collapsed and passed out on the floor. I had absolutely no control. It was like somebody flipped the switch to my brain, the lights went out and the next thing I remember was sniffing the pungent ammonia-based odor of smelling salts that one of the operating room nurses was kind enough to administer.

The Corky Calhoun surgery was successful and it did result in a Dave Hicks column in *The Arizona Republic.* My role in the story was that of "comic foil."

But Hicks was just approaching the starting line.

Years later, when we started publishing *Phoenix Suns Fastbreak Magazine,* Dave became one of our contributing writers, and took the occasion to revisit the Calhoun story and nail me once again.

It was about 1990 when Dave Hicks wrote this *Fastbreak* story, which he called:

The Ambrose Factor

As it approaches a centennial celebration, basketball is widely heralded as one of the most exciting sports of our time (Mountain Standard).

But what of the second hundred years? What will the game be like? Will its rules change? Will its structure change? Will it finally feel the impact of the Ambrose Factor?

The Ambrose Factor?

Today, Thomas P. Ambrose is the handsome, clean-cut, intelligent, Notre Dame educated, charismatic, creative, articulate, productive, industrious, fair-minded, all-around nice guy who is the Phoenix Suns' Vice President in charge of public relations. One of his functions is remunerating writers who contribute to this magazine.

But in the early '70s, Ambrose was a relative newcomer on the job when one of the team's players, Corky Calhoun, faced knee surgery.

A PR possibility loomed, so Ambrose opportunistically invited a reporter to join him in witnessing the early-morning operation. Unfortunately, the reporter he invited—the Fifth Amendment is invoked here – was one who had difficulty detecting anything before noon, including the slightest evidence of his own pulse.

But never mind the sleep-in no-show. Ambrose would go solo. He went through the proper procedures and entered the operating room.

Surgery on Calhoun began.

Within minutes, a crisis had developed. Anxiety engulfed the place. The gravity of the moment was punctuated by all that esoteric medical jargon used by surgeons under pressure. Like: "You still a 20 handicap?"

There was undivided concern, however, after an alert nurse exclaimed: "He looks! Terrible!" Agreed. "He's lost his color!" Agreed. "We might lose him!" Agreed.

None of this involved Calhoun, whose surgery was progressing nicely. The focus was on Ambrose, who had turned woozy and appeared ready to demonstrate how one could pass out without benefit of anesthetic.

A nurse suggested that Ambrose put his head between his legs. He complied, noting at the time: "It's difficult to watch an operation from this angle."

It should be noted that basketball historically has not always progressed on a fast-forward mode. During the game's infancy, it took several years for someone to think of cutting the bottom out of the old baskets. And legend insists that the perspective

Ambrose developed by keeping his head between his legs for an unspecified length of time, made him a management "natural."

What's the painfully elusive point of all this, you ask? Well, success invited emulation, and after the Suns achieved success, others considered scavenging for their slightest secret.

Persistent rumors linked a "top level" Sun to an unspecified operation. Had a player been subjected to revolutionary technology that enabled doctors to implant specified assets such as speed, brawn and brains?

But, while the Suns had enjoyed enviable success, they had not reached the pinnacle of the league championship. So the Ambrose Factor was not investigated and never flourished.

Not until the Suns have won a string of NBA titles will the Ambrose Factor emerge anew, with all its awesome potential. By then, the league will be international, and the game's thinkers and shapers will be as far flung as the franchises – among them the Brussels Sprouts, the London Derrieres, the Accra Bats, the Bolivia Newton-Johns and the Manila Folders.

One of those thinkers and shapers will be overly ambitious. His quest for an advantage will lead to renewed scrutiny of the Ambrose Factor. He will actually keep his head between his legs for several weeks, and soon others will join him. Anything to keep up.

Unfortunately, there are always those who go too far. In this case they will ultimately achieve notoriety for having their heads in a position that symbolizes ineptitude.

Properly harnessed, the Ambrose Factor is a positive. But the wrong heads will precipitate intriguing moments. To wit:

2010 A.D. – The NBA announces that one of its franchises has discovered a talent hotbed that should increase the number of white jumpers available. The plan was stymied however, when Toyota files suit against the NBA for tampering.

2025 A.D. – Noting that the only shot players have left in their repertoires is a slam-dunk some coaches propose a bold revamping of the sport. Rims as we know them would disappear. Rim-sized holes would be cut into the floor, and a goal would be scored by depositing the ball in the hole.

The plan is implemented. To gain an edge around the new baskets, teams sign as many Munchkin types as possible. The little guys soon dominate. They rule the game (particularly the low post). They become idols.

But the retooled game encounters fatal disfavor after ambitious parents all over the country are found to be admonishing their offspring: Son, how do you expect to grow down to be a pro if you don't smoke and stunt your growth?"

CRIPPLED

All NBA teams and probably all professional sports teams, receive hundreds of letters every month from individuals, schools and non-profit organizations, requesting autographed auction items or some type of sports memorabilia that they can turn into cash to support their charitable endeavors.

One of the letters was from a non-profit organization that we'll call the "Crippled Children's Home of Elmira, New York." The letter requested autographed memorabilia so that they could raffle it off to raise funds for the children who were served by the home. The request was not unusual, but the letterhead was. The letter was typed on a black and white facsimile copy of the organizational letterhead and was signed by a Jim Smith, who requested that we send the items to his home instead of the office, because some items had recently been pilfered from their office mailbox. The whole thing struck me as odd, so I called the phone number on the letterhead.

"Crippled Children's Home of Elmira."

"Can I speak to Jim Smith please?"

"Um, well, Jim Smith doesn't exactly work here."

"Really? Is he on your board or affiliated with your organization?"

"Well, no. But he is a very close friend of our executive director, Brian Johnson."

"Is Brian available?"

"Hold on. I'll connect you."

I talked to their E.D. and read him the letter from Jim Smith requesting the autographed items. There was dead silence on the other end of the phone.

"Everything OK?" I inquired.

"I am so sorry. My friend Jim is a great guy, but his one weakness is that he is an absolutely crazed collector of sports memorabilia. He would do just about anything to expand his collection. It's really sad because now I know just how low he is willing to go. Obviously, don't send anything. We don't have any events scheduled. Now, I've got to confront him about this. Who knows what else he's done...?"

A sad but true story.

AN ARM OF THE MILITARY

Arizona in general, and the Phoenix area in particular, became one of the fastest growing areas in the country as a result of the many military training bases established here during World War II. At that time, virtually the entire state of Arizona was an armed camp. Naturally, because of that military heritage, the Suns have always featured lots of promotional activities related to the armed forces.

“There was lots of slapping, stabbing, punching and bodies flying around... ”

Once, the U.S. Army Rangers put on an incredible demonstration at half-time of a Suns pre-season game...first, a dozen Rangers in full gear rappelled down from the Coliseum ceiling on ropes, covering the 60 feet to the floor in about a second and a half. Once they took command of the court, they proceeded to put on an exhibition of hand-to-hand combat. There was lots of slapping, stabbing, punching and bodies flying around... all of it staged and carefully choreographed to demonstrate to the audience how well-trained and well-conditioned our U.S. Army Rangers were.

And then, as if they needed to further demonstrate their absolute toughness, they ripped off one soldier's arm!!! OK. That was staged too, with a prosthetic arm and the clever use of Velcro, but the effect was amazing. A collective gasp went up from the crowd and then total shock set in. The fans could not believe what they just saw! One of the visiting writers, who had been sitting at the courtside press table, ran up to me, wide-eyed with horror at what he had just witnessed, and said, "Tom, what is this?! Are these guys from this planet!!??"

I could not have been more proud that the U.S. Army Rangers were on our side!

SORRY, WE'RE CLOSED

In September of 1974 the Suns acquired Dave Stallworth, a 6'7" forward from the Washington Bullets, along with a second round pick, in exchange for guard Clem Haskins. The Suns held their training camp in Prescott, Arizona at the time. The coaching staff quickly realized that Stallworth would not be able to earn a spot on the team. So, just a few days after camp opened, they waived him.

Stallworth was an NBA veteran of seven seasons and the coaches wanted to give him a chance to catch on with another NBA team. Additionally, they did not want him to suffer the indignity of riding back to Phoenix on a Greyhound bus, so I was recruited to drive him "down the hill" to Phoenix. I remembered him as Dave "The Rave" Stallworth, an enthusiastic young Knicks' rookie out of Wichita State in 1965. But now, here was a guy who was staring, point blank, at the end of his career in professional basketball. I could sense that there was no "Plan B."

It was a difficult and very quiet ride. The gas gauge looked pretty low to me, so I started looking for a place to pull off and get some petrol. This was on a stretch of Interstate 17 near New River, Arizona, about halfway between Prescott and Phoenix, where there were no large, freeway service areas, only tiny towns with local facilities. I noticed a sign that said "GAS," so I pulled off the interstate.

It was about 10 in the morning on a Monday, but there were no signs of life...not in the small gas station, or in the nearby trailer. The property lines were neatly defined by white-painted rocks and some half-buried tires that were also painted white, but the gas pumps were chained and locked. It was only then that I noticed that the place had a name. Hanging over the entrance to the driveway was a crudely painted sign that said, "JACKASS ACRES." We both laughed out loud.

"Well, Dave," I said. "Now you can tell your grandkids that you once visited a place in Arizona called "JACKASS ACRES"...but it was CLOSED!"

Stallworth got one last shot in New York, where he began his NBA career. He played only seven games for the Knicks that season, before retiring. But at least we shared a laugh at Jackass Acres.

IT'S IN THE FABRIC

Long-time Suns fan and friend Emmit Klienschmitt had been divorced for about a year and was starting to date once again. Emmitt had a reputation for being a total "clothes horse" ... always dressed impeccably. On the rebound, he began dating a girl who I guess you could describe as being "pretty, but a little unstable." Emmitt quickly figured out this wasn't a relationship he wanted to continue, so he broke things off. Although the parting seemed amicable, he forgot that she still had a key to his place.

One day he was shocked to come home to find that all of his designer-label clothes had been removed from his closet, dumped out into his back yard, doused with lighter fluid and set on fire. Everybody in the Suns office had heard the story and thought, "Wow, that's just insane!"

A few days later, just before a home game, I was sitting with Al McCoy at the Coliseum press table talking about the incendiary incident and how horrible it all was, when in walks Emmitt, absolutely dressed "to the nines." He was wearing a brilliantly starched white shirt, set off by gold cuff links, and framed by an immaculately tailored, double-breasted suit and accented with a beautiful silk tie.

Al and I looked at each other, shocked.

Then McCoy leaned toward me and whispered, "You know, it's absolutely amazing what they can do these days with fire-proof fabrics!"

SOCK NIGHT

The Phoenix Press Box Association had a weekly meeting where coaches and front office personnel from local college and professional teams were invited to offer insight, previews or make special announcements. The fact that these weekly meetings were held in the hospitality room of one of the local breweries did not usually hurt attendance.

Toward the end of the 1973-74 season, I took the podium to announce that Phoenix Suns "Sock Night" was being cancelled because the truck carrying the custom-made Suns socks from Denver had crashed and burned en route to Phoenix.

Suddenly, a voice from the audience blurted out, "Kinda' like the Suns' season!"

It took emcee Ted Brown five minutes to stop the laughing and restore order.

STATISTICAL PADDING

My first NBA PR meeting took place in Seattle during the 1974 All-Star weekend. The Suns sent a large contingent to the Seattle game because Phoenix was going to host the All-Stars the following year. The NBA also took the opportunity to bring in team executives for PR and marketing meetings as well as meetings for the coaches and general managers. The discussions would cover common problems and possible solutions, minimum standards, best practices and new ideas.

As a newly minted PR guy, I was there to learn from the best, absorb knowledge from the top people in my new profession and develop some working relationships. At least that's what I thought we were supposed to be doing. In the case of the PR director's meetings however, I was an observer of an animated shout down between PR guys that I thought might actually come to blows.

When exactly did I know the meeting was really getting out of hand? I believe it was when Bill Russell, coach and GM of the Sonics, came in from the GMs-Coaches meeting next door and said with more than a little animation of his own, "Will you guys, please shut the F@#$ up?!" That was only the second time I had ever seen the legendary Bill Russell in person, and I'm part of a group that he scolds like we were misbehaving kindergarteners... great!

The shouting match in the PR meeting was between Rudy Martzke of the Buffalo Braves and Harvey Pollack of the Philadelphia 76ers. Harvey had built an amazing reputation as a statistician. He was clearly the best in the world of NBA stats and probably beyond. Rudy had been involved with the St. Louis Spirits of the American Basketball Association, even ascending to the position of team GM for a short time. Like many who had come through the ABA experience, Rudy was glib, free-wheeling and high-spirited.

Their conflict was over Buffalo's rookie sensation, Ernie DiGregorio, whose assist statistics, Pollack claimed, were being "padded" whenever the Braves played at home. Usually Ernie D would average about 12 assists per game at home but substantially fewer on the road. Remember, TV coverage was sparse back then and video tape was just in its infancy. Most games were filmed in 16mm black and white, but just for coaching analysis. So the only way to really check this stuff was through the box scores which every team mailed to every other team immediately following every NBA game. Harvey would pour over those daily box score returns and play-by-play sheets with a zeal that bordered on obsession. To Harvey, statistics are the way, the truth and the life. For as long as I have been in the NBA, Harvey Pollack has kept the league office, the team PR people and even the league's "official" agency, the Elias Sports Bureau, on the statistical straight and narrow.

For the record, Ernie D led the league in assists with 8.2 per game and was named NBA Rookie of the Year for the 1973-74 season.

JUST A THOUGHT

For me, my entire experience at that first NBA PR director's meeting made me think, "We've got to be more professional, or no one in this league will ever take us seriously." So, within a year or two, I moved for the formation of the National Basketball Association Public Relations Directors' Association, more simply known as the NBAPRDA.

We created a Code of Ethical Standards along the lines of the Public Relations Society of America, and we were on our way. The overwhelming majority of the PR directors felt the same way I did because we voted in the standards and structure without opposition. By default, I became the organization's first president. The overriding hope was that perhaps, as a professional group, we could become part of the NBA's pension plan.

But we were summarily dismissed with a condescending pat on the head and a derisive "Not a chance!" from the then deputy-commissioner of the NBA, Gary Bettman. That's the same Gary Bettman who is now the commissioner of the National Hockey League.

I am pleased to report that the NBAPRDA is still in operation and one of their projects is to financially support former members who have fallen on difficult times. You can't ask for more than that as a legacy, although being part of the league's pension plan would have been really nice.

THE STREAKER

It was the final month of my first NBA season. I had learned much, made hundreds of new friends and had incalculable amounts of fun. The future looked great, but a piece of the counter-culture past was about to sprint through Suns history.

"Streaking," loosely defined, is the act of taking off one's clothes and running nude through a public place. It is considered a light-hearted form of public nudity that is not intended to shock, but to amuse potential spectators. The origins of the activity can be traced back as far as 1799 in London. The first documented "streak" on an American college campus took place a few years later, in 1803 at Washington College. By the 1960's the activity was well-established on many college campuses, shamefully including my alma mater, Notre Dame.

Streaking probably began as some kind of a bet or a joke, maybe even as a rite of passage, but at some point in the sixties, it became an expression of freedom. I suppose it evolved into a way for the "protest generation" to thumb their noses (and possibly some other body parts) at the "establishment." Whatever...

I will leave that for pop-culturalists and anthropologists to sort out. I just remember guys, and sometimes girls, running naked across college campuses and often right through the middle of large public rallies, ceremonies or sporting events.

Though the activity had faded somewhat by 1974, streaking was still going on around the country. Sometimes it manifested itself as large "group streaks" but mostly it was a single perpetrator in his or her birthday suit. They would be running on adrenaline and who knows what else, frantically trying to escape the local security forces that were generally in hot pursuit... if they weren't just standing around laughing.

Typically, Arizona is a couple of years behind the curve when it comes to national trends. So, it made perfect sense to us when we got a tip that somebody wanted to "streak" a Suns game at the Coliseum. We didn't have much to go on. We didn't know who was behind it, or when they would strike. We only knew they wouldn't be wearing anything when they did it.

> **❝Typically, Arizona is a couple of years behind the curve when it comes to national trends. ❞**

It was April of 1974...the Suns' season was winding down with just three home games left and no hope of making the playoffs. The Suns organization prided itself on being a "G-Rated," family oriented, sports and entertainment option. The last thing Suns management wanted was some crazy, naked person running through the middle of a home game. My goodness, there are always lots of impressionable kids in attendance! We simply could not let this happen. So, with just a few games left on the schedule, we beefed up security on game nights at the Coliseum, especially around the basketball court itself.

Sometime during the third quarter of that first game, with security on full alert, we spotted a very suspicious couple, way overdressed for a warm spring night in Phoenix. They were wearing long coats, hats, and sunglasses while trying to surreptitiously move into a couple of seats about three rows off the court. Immediately, we dispatched several security guards to monitor the situation. One stood in the aisle behind them, while a second rather burly guard, knelt in the aisle directly in front of our two suspects and stared directly at them. It was pretty clear that any attempt to "streak" the floor that night would be stopped. It worked. They didn't try.

A few days later, I thought we had come through a second home game without incident. But after the game was over, I was in the coaches' office, breathing a sigh of relief that we had not only won the game, but that there had been no streaker. Just then, our marketing guy, Harvey Shank, came in.

"We caught the streaker!" he said excitedly.

"Really!?" I responded. "That's great but...where...who...how did you know?!?!?!"

"It was a woman. They caught her up on the concourse. She was wearing a hat, some bedroom slippers and an old raincoat..."

"Yeah...but...how did you know that *she* was the streaker?" I asked.

Harvey responded, "Easy...it wasn't raining."

That was just the beginning, but the incident that night helped reveal some additional "intel."

Apparently, the guys behind the plot were members of a local civic-fraternal organization that met once a week for lunch and also served as a quasi-fraternity for young guys starting out in the business world. The woman in the raincoat, we learned, was a local dancer of the "exotic" variety, hired by members of this club to make an unencumbered dash through the crowd and across the basketball court. The "perps" were all Suns fans and this was their idea of spicing up the Suns late season doldrums, as the team, without any playoff hopes, played out the last few games. But now, there was only one game left and time was running out for their prank.

The final home game was against the Golden State Warriors. We knew that the conspirators would pull out all stops to accomplish their mission and they knew we would do everything we could to stop them. One of the club members who I happened to know, called to say there would be no hard feelings, no matter what happened. I didn't agree and pleaded with him not to do it. The game, most decidedly, was "on."

We got through the first quarter without incident and, when the horn blew to end the period, the teams retreated to their benches. The quarter break was only a few seconds old when a thin, long-haired and mustachioed man, sitting in the first row under the basket, jumped up, ripped off his shirt, stepped out of his pants and ran, butt-naked, out onto the basketball court. The crowd reaction was one of total shock and surprise. His best move would have been to run at top speed from baseline to baseline and then directly out the exit at the other end. But what may have seemed like a hilarious idea after a few beers the night before was suddenly a stark (naked) reality for this guy. From the baseline he raced out to the free throw line, before he suddenly put on the brakes and veered toward one of the near corners and hopefully, freedom.

The Coliseum security guards had been staking out the court's perimeter, looking up into the stands with their backs to the court, never expecting the streaker to be sitting in the front row and *inside* their ring of security. Now they were ready to redeem themselves. As the naked man sprinted toward the corner, one of the uniformed guards, who moved laterally like a former line-backer, followed the streaker's every stride, reminiscent of a lion stalking its kill. The streaker suddenly changed speeds and made his move, bolting for the corner aisle. The guard lunged, attempting a thigh-high tackle, trying to bring him down. I don't remember if the security guard used the proper tackling technique, but the streaker, his adrenaline pumping, somehow shook off the hit and sprinted through the exit.

The crowd reaction morphed into a sort of mirthful buzz. The players on both teams had enjoyed a first-hand, close up view of the incident and, as they returned to the floor for the second quarter, there were smiles and laughter all around.

This was back in the days when a jump ball started every quarter. But just as the referee got ready to toss the ball up to begin the second quarter, Warriors' center George Johnson just put his big mitt on top of the ball, shook his head "no," and staggered backward, overcome with laughter. The refs were also laughing and gave big George a few seconds to compose himself. The image had obviously lingered.

Meanwhile, just a few yards away, out on the Coliseum's lower concourse, it did not take long for other security guards to identify and apprehend the perpetrator. Since the streaker wasn't carrying a wallet, he was unable to produce any identification. And since the "collar" was made quite some distance from the Coliseum's security holding cell, the guards decided to handcuff the suspect until a supervisor could be summoned.

Well, they handcuffed the guy all right...with his arms pulled forward and wrapped around a support pillar in one of the Coliseum's unused "exhibition" halls (they really called them that). He stood there, hugging the pillar, still naked as a jay-bird, through most of the second quarter. There was public access to the area, so a lot of Suns fans and their families came by to gawk until security finally hauled the streaker off to the holding cell. It was, as I think back on it, a nearly perfect finish to my first year with the Suns!

RENDEZVOUS WITH SHU

Apparently I did such a great job of delivering Bob Christian to the Suns office, on my first day on the job in 1973 that Colangelo trusted me to re-engage *Amby's Airport Shuttle Service* to pick up one of the players we were considering for our top pick in the 1974 NBA Draft. We were bringing him in about a week early for a face-to-face meeting with the coaching staff...not a bad idea considering what would surely be a major financial investment in the fourth pick. But, at the same time, Colangelo liked to maintain a high degree of secrecy when it came to our selections. He didn't want to tip our hand to other teams or the media, just in case there was an opportunity for a draft-day trade of our pick. The player under consideration in 1974 was John Shumate of Notre Dame. Shumate had earned All-America honors and was coming off a season when the Irish knocked off UCLA, and their star, Bill Walton, ending college basketball's longest winning streak at 88.

This time, supplied with sufficient cash reserves, I went to the airport gate to meet Shumate when he got off the flight. Like Bob Christian, Shumate was not hard to pick out in a crowd. He was a chiseled 6'9" and weighed 245 pounds. On top of that he was wearing a t-shirt that screamed, "GOD MADE NOTRE DAME NO. 1!" OK, So much for a discrete arrival. The closely guarded secret of who we were considering for our top draft pick was officially blown.

Shumate did indeed become the player selected fourth by the Suns. He came into Phoenix early to get his contract finalized and begin informal summer workouts with some of the pro players who live in the Phoenix area.

Because Shumate had suffered from a blood-clotting disorder, early in his college career, Suns management thought it would be a good idea to take out a "salary protection" policy on Shumate's contract. This was a regular thing in pro sports at the time, protecting the franchise against a debilitating injury to a key player. An insurance deal was struck with Lloyd's of London. But within a month of the policy going into effect, Shumate's blood condition, phlebitis, resurfaced. The condition caused excessive blood clotting in his legs. If not aggressively treated with a regimen of blood thinners, it could not only end his NBA career, but possibly his life.

The medical verdict was in…Shumate would have to sit out the season. The Suns were not happy, Shumate was disappointed, but because they had to eat Shumate's salary, Lloyd's of London was nearly apoplectic. Because of the Shumate payout and a few other bad experiences with pro sports, eventually Lloyd's stopped doing business in that sector.

Jerry Colangelo did not want Shumate to become distant and disconnected from the team, so he slotted him in as a color commentator with Al McCoy on the Suns radio and TV broadcasts. "Shu" is a talker, so that was not a problem, but he did, at times, get a little creative with the English language. There were occasions when reinforcing a point made by McCoy, Shu would add, "It's un-doubtable, Al… un-doubtable!"

Shumate would come back to play the next season and post some solid numbers for the Suns, before he was traded to the Buffalo Braves at the All-Star break, in exchange for Garfield Heard.

Since his NBA playing career ended in 1981, Shumate has coached and scouted at both the college and professional levels. That includes stints at Notre Dame, Grand Canyon College, Southern Methodist University, the Toronto Raptors, the Phoenix Mercury and the Suns.

KUNG FU SUMMER

Sports psychologists, off-season programs to improve strength and agility, even a ballet instructor...you name it... Jerry Colangelo was always looking to gain a physical or mental edge for his team.

Not many people knew Gus Hoffling well, but Suns Trainer Joe Proski's description of him pretty well sums it up.

"You just knew that Gus could rip your heart out with his hand!" Proski once said.

That seemed to get everyone's attention...if not their total respect.

Gus Hoffling was a kung fu instructor who the Suns hired during the summer of 1974 to run their off-season conditioning program.

On a Suns road trip to Philadelphia the previous season, Proski and Keith Erickson had gone to observe one of Hoffling's brutal conditioning sessions. They liked the discipline and Gus' no-nonsense, drill instructor, approach. Proski convinced Colangelo to bring Hoffling in for summer workouts.

As Gus began working with the Suns, there quickly developed a long list of players who wanted to swear at him. But there was already an equally long list of famous athletes who had gone through Hoffling's ultra-tough program and consistently would swear *by* him.

> **❝You just knew that Gus could rip your heart out with his hand. ❞**
> **- Joe Proski**

Hoffling was credited with extending the NFL career of the Philadelphia Eagles quarterback, Roman Gabriel. Hall of Fame pitcher Steve Carlton of the Phillies was another who said, "Gus saved my career."

Hoffling was physically and verbally tough on everyone, but the Suns top draft pick that year, John Shumate, seemed to get the brunt of it. During a particularly tough workout, Gus would pick on Shumate, saying, "Now, don't go crying to your daddy, Jerry Colangelo!"

The players were terrified of Gus but, not wanting to show their fear, they did some amazing things at his command. As they were doing crunches, Hoffling might stand on their stomachs or walk on their chests. As they stood, knees flexed in a "ready" position, Hoffling might put his hands on their shoulders and stand on the back of their legs. In a personal demonstration of strength and focus, Gus would press the ends of wooden chopsticks against his own throat and press hard until the chopsticks snapped in two.

Dick Van Arsdale and Joe Proski were the only two guys to complete every workout...six days a week for six grueling weeks. It was the summer of 1974, and for Shumate, Charlie Scott, Neal Walk, Dick Van Arsdale and the rest of the Suns, it was a summer that they will never forget.

THE TWIRL

He was drafted out of Winston-Salem and his name was Earl. But a few years earlier, another Earl from the same school had laid claim to the moniker, Earl "The Pearl." So this later Earl became Earl "The Twirl." I don't think it had anything to do with his game... it just rhymed. Earl Williams, a 6'7" 235-pound forward, was a third round Suns draft selection in 1974, the 49th overall pick.

As Williams was getting ready to sign his first pro contract at the Suns offices, he wanted to confer with his college coach, the legendary Clarence "Big House" Gaines. He was on the phone in a tiny waiting area, just outside my office, and I couldn't help overhearing the conversation...at least Earl's side of it.

"Yeah...yeah...I don't care 'bout dat... *(pause)*... I know...but I don't care 'bout dat. All I want to know is... am I gonna have fi' taw-san dolla cash money in my pocket? *(pause)*... I don't care 'bout dat. *(pause)* Am I gonna have fi' taw-san dolla cash money in my pocket? I will?! OK, I'll sign!"

"The Twirl" would appear in 79 games as a Suns rookie, averaging 13.2 minutes, 4.7 points and a rather solid 5.8 rebounds per game on that limited playing time. Earl could rebound and play some defense but he proved to be a poor free throw shooter and an offensive liability.

Shortly after the season was over, Williams was traded to Detroit for a second round pick. Suns coach John MacLeod called Williams to inform him of the trade.

"Earl, I've got great news for you," MacLeod said optimistically, trying to soften the blow. "You've just been traded to the Detroit Pistons!"

"The Detroit Pistons!?" Earl responded, "*In* Detroit?"

Later that day, Williams came into the office to talk to Suns GM Jerry Colangelo. Once again, Earl made a couple of calls from the waiting area outside my office which had yet to be fitted with a "cone of silence." One of the calls was to an out-of-town friend whom Earl informed about the trade. Again I could only hear Earl's side of the conversation, but I imagine it went something like this:

Earl: "Hey man, I've just been traded to the Detroit Pistons."

Friend: "No! Who told you that?"

Earl: "Jerry Colangelo."

Friend: "Who's Jerry Colangelo?"

Earl: "Who's Jerry Colangelo?! Man, he da head m_____ f____ what is!"

Personally, I would love to have a business card that said that!

FILM TO TAPE

When I took over the production of the highlight films, it coincided with the advent of video tape, so we suddenly had greater flexibility in our shooting schedule and at less expense. We used a production company called GENESIS, headed by Pat and Tim McGuire. Not only did they work with us on new concepts for our highlight films, they also aided us in the set up of a video tape system for coaching analysis and the cataloguing of all of our games.

This was a huge change for Coach John MacLeod, who had used 16 mm film throughout his college and professional coaching career. MacLeod would typically wear out two or three "pickle" switches each season, with his constant back-and-forth, start and stop, rewind and replay, action on the screen.

It was remarkable how quickly John adapted to video tape. We got him a new, battery-powered remote control and, like a kid with new technology, he adjusted almost immediately. We also hired a young man named Todd Quinter, who had played basketball at Lebanon Valley College, to break down the video tapes for easy analysis by the coaches. For more than 30 years, Todd was an integral part of the Suns' player personnel and scouting departments.

THE EMMY

I wanted to make the Suns highlight films a little more interesting, more creative and more entertaining. And I'd be damned if I was going to let a lousy season or two stand in the way of an entertaining highlight film! Typically we would debut the film sometime during the pre-season, at a team dinner for all major Suns sponsors. I figured that the Suns team itself, by virtue of their on-court performance, offered the serious, substantive side of basketball. But our highlight films should be all about fun and entertainment and maybe even a little fantasy. The players, coaches and even Jerry Colangelo, were always willing to play along.

Here are the films with a brief plot (and we use that term loosely) summary of each:

The Dream Season- Based on the age-old plot device known as "...and then I woke up," Coach MacLeod is in his office late one night when he hears a voice from on high. It's an angel who happens to be a Suns fan. The angel takes the earthly form of the Suns Gorilla and suddenly, with backing from "upstairs," the team catches fire. We pulled some great basketball–themed music from the movie, *The Fish That Saved Pittsburgh*. At the end of the film, Walter Davis is at the line for two free throws that would win the NBA Championship for the Suns and then...

The Dream Season won a Rocky Mountain Emmy Award in 1982 in the Sports category.

Mission: Very, Very Difficult - More than loosely based on the popular television series, *MISSION: Impossible*, the assignment for Coach MacLeod was to defeat the evil Lakers' empire. It was *MISSION: Very, Very Difficult* ...but not "impossible." The film also "unmasked" the Suns Gorilla.

The Sunlight Zone – This was a slightly twisted look at the Suns, taking off on the classic sci-fi TV series, *The Twilight Zone*. Joe Proski suddenly is transformed from a hard-working Suns trainer to the team's successful, long-time coach. He doesn't know how it happened, but he rolls with it until everything suddenly changes back.

The History of Basketball - Beginning in 1,000,000 B.S. (Before Suns), the film progressed from gorilla games to Stone Age "rock ball" and then moved forward in history to feature the entire Suns team as Dr. James A. Naismith's original class at the Springfield, Massachusetts YMCA. They figured out that the game moved faster once the bottom fell out of the peach basket. Stan Richards starred as Dr. Naismith. The film culminated in the modern era with some fast-moving Suns highlights.

During the shooting of *History*, our director, Pat McGuire, was very nervous about working with the team and the shooting schedule was falling behind. During one of the breaks between scene set-ups, Suns guard Jay Humphries approached McGuire, who was holding a large cup of Coca-Cola in his left hand.

"How much longer do we have to stay?" Humphries demanded, "I've got things I've got to do!"

McGuire nervously turned over his wrist to look at his wristwatch and in the process, poured his entire Coke down the front of his pants! It was a shame the cameras weren't rolling. It would have been the funniest scene in the movie!

A Night in the Sun - The Suns Gorilla sleeps-in as the rest of the organization gets ready for the big game. In this one we stole a hot, new formula of quick cuts with great music from the popular TV series *Miami Vice*. We went behind the scenes to look at all the preparation that goes into the presentation of an NBA game and finished with a fast-paced flourish of great plays.

Top Sun - We used the sensational music from the movie *Top Gun* as the basis for this one. There were also some cool shots featuring new, paint-box technology.

"Scoop" HairySun – This video starred the Phoenix Suns Gorilla as the intrepid reporter, "Scoop" HairySun. Featuring a Walter Winchell style narration, it had a 1920's "feel," with some hard-hitting journalism from "Scoop." It featured a wonderful script, written and narrated by long-time Phoenix advertising exec, George Jett.

The Old Mascot's Home - We collaborated with GO Media for the production work on this piece. The Suns Gorilla has long-retired from basketball and is living with other broken-down sports mascots at the Old Mascots Home. A gray-haired Jerry Colangelo comes to visit his old buddy and they spend time looking through the Gorilla's furry scrapbook, which leads to lots of memories and lots of Suns highlight footage.

FROM THE WACKO! FILE – MORE THAN LOOSE LACES

Gentlemen:

I would like to render a service for all the NBA basketball players. Most of them are millionaires and they have never learned to tie their shoes. It seems as if they would feel embarrassed. Of course we all sometimes act like kids. My proposition is to teach anyone in the NBA, trainers or all the players that have this problem. My shoe strings have never come loose since I was a little grasshopper. I would like, in exchange, a new Camry Nissan auto, everything paid…I'm on Social Insecurity. I have a Honda Accord 14 years old and really need a car and these basketball players need my services. It's dangerous for any sport for shoestrings to come loose and this is rampant in all sports. I guarantee I will stop this. If you think my service is not needed, you don't have to respond.

Thank you.

HOPE

Some people think that the NBA Draft in June signals the beginning of summer. For most NBA teams and their fans, it signals only one thing…hope for a new beginning. The NBA champion has been crowned, but everyone else is looking toward next season.

In preparation for the draft, NBA franchises make a tremendous investment in scouting and player evaluations. In addition to the in-person scouting teams that literally spread across the planet looking for talent or its potential, teams also invest heavily in technology. Satellite TV helps teams retrieve and analyze almost every high school, college, and professional game played on six of the earth's seven continents. And you can be sure that as soon as the first basketball game is played in Antarctica, there will be a legion of scouts and coaches watching it the next day.

You would think that with all that experience, expertise and technology working it would be relatively easy to make the right picks. Unfortunately, no draft pick comes with a guarantee of success... never has... never will.

For a team like the Suns in the early 1970s, "hope" was just about all you had to sell, so we tried to make the draft an "insiders" event for our fans. Once restricted to general managers, coaches and NBA personnel, we opened up our end of this formerly "closed" activity to Suns fans. In the 1970s the 10-round draft was conducted by conference call. Phoenix was in the perfect time-zone location to allow 1500 people to gather for lunch at the Hyatt Regency in downtown Phoenix and listen to an amplified telephone call.

During those calls the Celtic's Red Auerbach was often the impromptu entertainment, making off-the-cuff remarks that were not always politically correct (but that was before "political correctness" had been invented, so nobody cared). Once a pick was made, you might hear Auerbach say in the background, "He's a stiff!" Another time, on another pick, Red might blurt out, "Who???" The eavesdropping Phoenix crowd loved it!

In 1975, the Suns had the fourth pick in the draft and were as sure as they could be that a young center from Oklahoma would be their pick. The hotel audience of close to 1,000 fans was amazed when we announced that the Suns' selection was Alvan Adams of Oklahoma...and then Adams walked into the ballroom and up onto the stage. Nobody believed me when I told them that it was purely coincidence that the downtown Phoenix hotel hosting the draft that year was...the Adams Hotel.

PHOENIX SUNS ROOKIE CAMP

JUNE 25-28, 1974 VETERANS MEMORIAL COLISEUM

MORNING SESSION 11 AM - 1 PM   **MORNING**
EVENING SESSION 6:30 PM - 8:30 PM   DATE _____ **EVENING**

NAME	POS	HT	WT	COLLEGE	SCORING / COMMENTS	RATING FORM				
						SHOOTING	REB	PASS	DEF	COMPOSITE
Randy Allen	G	6-0	165	Indiana of Pennsylvania						
Ralph Bobik	G	6-7	200	Creighton University						
Mike Contreras	G	6-2	180	Arizona State University						
Clyde Dickey	G	6-3	190	Boise State						
Ted Evans	F	6-9	225	University of Oklahoma						
Tom Holland	F	6-8	215	University of Oklahoma						
Steve Mitchell	C	6-9	238	Kansas State University						
Fred Saunders	F	6-7	210	Syracuse University						
John Shumate	F-C	6-9	235	University of Notre Dame						
Collis Temple	F	6-7	208	Louisiana State University						
Mark Wasley	F	6-9	230	Arizona State University						
Earl Williams	F	6-7	230	Winston-Salem						
Mike Bantom	F	6-9	210	St. Joseph's College						
Bill Chamberlain	F	6-6	200	North Carolina						
Gary Melchionni	G	6-2	187	Duke University						
Jim Owens	G	6-5	200	Arizona State University						

GENERAL MANAGER — Jerry Colangelo

HEAD COACH — John MacLeod

ASSISTANT COACH — Dennis Price

TRAINER — Joe Proski

RATING SYSTEM
4   **Excellent Pro Prospect**
3   **Above Average Pro Prospect**
2   **Average Pro Prospect**
1   **Below Average Pro Prospect**
Rating Forms May Be Turned In At The Coliseum Press Table or At The Suns Ticket Office.

Additional Comments

A YEAR OF OPPORTUNITY FOR SUNS SEASON TICKETHOLDERS!

☆ TICKET DISCOUNT — $1 Per Game Per Seat

☆ FREE PARKING — A Savings Of $41

☆ FREE STADIUM CLUB MEMBERSHIP

☆ FIRST CHOICE OF AVAILABLE TICKETS FOR JANUARY 14 ALL STAR GAME HERE IN PHOENIX

There's never been a better time to own Suns Season Seats. Call or visit the Suns Office (2303 N. Central / 258-5753) soon about season tickets for your family or your busines.

ROOKIE CAMP

In late June of 1974, following the NBA draft (a 10-round affair), the Suns brought together all of their draft picks and a few of their young players for three days of double-session workouts at the Coliseum. Suns brass simply wanted to see what kind of talent they had picked up in the draft and how it would stack up against a few Suns players with NBA experience. All of the practices were open to the public.

With the possible exception of top Suns draft pick John Shumate, you really couldn't tell the players without a scorecard. So the Suns PR Department (me) worked with local printer, Thom Meaker, to create one. But instead of providing just the player names, heights and weights, we turned the card into a player evaluation sheet. We'd let the fans tell us what *they* thought of our young prospects. We did it as a way to try to get the fans involved, but we totally underestimated how popular the idea would become.

> **❝You really couldn't tell the players without a scorecard. ❞**

After the first day, we realized that we needed to print more forms. The coaching staff, consisting of John MacLeod and Dennis Price, along with GM Jerry Colangelo, poured over the filled out and turned-in forms like returned ballots in a contested election. Some of the comments were hilarious, others fairly blunt. But the fans had their say.

From that rookie camp, three players... Earl Williams, John Shumate and Fred Saunders, would eventually earn spots on the Suns roster.

FROM THE WACKO! FILE – DREAMIN' BIG

To whom it may concern,

Hello, my name is Kelvin J. Collins. I am 25 years old, 6'1" and 220 pounds. I am writing this letter from Rio, Illinois. I am writing you to inquire about the upcoming NBA Draft. I have always had a passion for the game of basketball. I play the position of a forward or a guard. I am quick on my feet and a great shooter. I love to play the game. In high school I played all four years. I just knew that once I get to college I was going to be at a D list school and enter into the draft. It was unfortunate that my dreams did not come true.

I attended a community college and graduated with my associate's degree in physical education. I did not play basketball for the school. The coach did not hold tryouts. He already had his team. But that did not discourage me. I played in summer leagues and with churches. I love basketball and this is my career goal. I will do whatever has to be done to enter into the draft. I am willing and able to prove myself skilled and worthy enough to be in the league. I believe hard work pays off. If it is possible to go to a training camp to prepare and watch players, I would be interested in this also. I have been trying different things to get seen but I guess I am at the wrong place at the wrong time. I wish I had a video to send but I do not. But I can, upon request, send some clips along with pictures.

I am a working man with a big dream of taking care of my family and doing the one thing I love…playing ball. I would love a one-on-one interview or at least enter a camp for the league. I want my talent to be seen. And there is always room for improvement. Please give me a response back if possible.

Thank you for your time
and attention.

Sincerely,

KC

MISTAKEN IDENTITY

I used to think that it was just Los Angeles and that city's total obsession with celebrity. Now I believe that the whole country is nuts.

In the 1980s, on a Suns road trip to LA, somebody thought I was the actor, Alan Alda. After I made several polite denials, the guy finally said, "It's OK. I understand. You want your privacy. Not a problem. It was an honor to meet you, Mr. Alda!"

Giving up, I said it was nice to meet him too, shook his hand and thanked him for his discretion.

More recently, the Suns were in LA for a playoff game and a young man came down to my seat in the lower level and asked me if I was James Cameron. Again, I denied it, but the young man clearly wasn't convinced, thinking that he had just met the director of the movie, *Titanic*.

Then there was the time at an NBA All-Star Weekend in San Antonio when Connie Hawkins and I went to a big public event that featured the NBA Legends -- the super-stars of yesteryear. Connie was talking to a few of his old acquaintances and I was standing nearby when a couple of young guys came up to me and said, "Excuse me, but can you tell us who that guy is over there?"

They pointed at Hawkins.

"Sure," I said, "That's Connie Hawkins."

"And who's he talking to?"

"Oh, that's Jo Jo White from the Celtics."

I proceeded to identify several more of the NBA legends for them, but then one of the young guys turned to me and looking at my mostly white hair, said, "Hey! Wait a minute! You used to play too. You were that guy that played for...the Knicks! Yeah! You played for the Knicks!"

"No," I said politely. "I'm not a player. I work for the Suns. I'm not who you think I am."

We went back and forth a few more times before one of them said, "Would you autograph my book for me?" And he held out a small book that he no doubt kept exclusively for special auto-graphs.

"I'll sign it," I said, "But I'm not who you think I am."

"That's OK," he said.

So I took the book and pen he handed to me. But I paused just as I was about to sign.

I looked at him sincerely and asked, "How do you spell DeBusschere?"

HOT AIR

One of the things I liked best about working for Jerry Colangelo was that he encouraged innovation and "out of the box" think-ing. So, after doing my due diligence, I was prepared to sell Jerry on the idea of the Phoenix Suns having their own hot air balloon.

The winter months in Phoenix are perfect for hot-air ballooning and innovative marketers all over the Southwest were coming up with attention-grabbing balloon designs that were extending their product branding.

In consultation with Gregg Ostro of Go Media, we came up with the concept of creating the "world's largest basketball." I thought it was a great idea, but I've had great ideas shot down before, so when I gave JC my best sales pitch...something like... "You don't want to buy a hot air balloon do you?" and automati-cally started retreating from his office, his response brought me back. "Wait a minute! Let me see that drawing!"

Within a few months, we had a Suns hot air balloon, custom designed and manufactured in North Carolina. It did indeed look like the world's largest basketball, about to be stuffed into a hoop and net, with our Phoenix Suns logo plastered all over it. We had an enthusiastic balloon captain named Walker Ross and a hard-driving chase crew.

Our "aviation" team flew the balloon constantly in competitions, at air shows and over big public events. Once, with wind and temperature conditions absolutely perfect, the Suns balloon hov-ered just a hundred feet over the final holes of the Phoenix Open golf tournament, on the final afternoon of play, with over 100,000 spectators walking the course below. You couldn't get better exposure than that.

We had a great time taking up VIPs and visitors, but eventually the Suns hired some in-house lawyers and the fun was over. While evaluating our overall risk-management they said "You have a hot-air what? And you take people up for rides?" They didn't really see the benefit. All they could see was the potential liability. So we divested ourselves of the balloon. But it was a high-flying chapter and great fun while it lasted.

THE WORLD'S LARGEST BASKETBALL

GETTING PHYSICAL

One of the great benefits offered to Suns executives was an annual physical exam. As players report for training camp each year, it's a league requirement that they undergo a thorough physical examination. In order to eliminate any questions regarding the health and condition of the players, the team physician assembles a team of medical specialists from ophthalmologists to proctologists. Jerry Colangelo and Suns team physician, Dr. Paul Steingard, generously offered the annual exam to the coaching staff and to members of the Suns executive team. Sometimes this "dream team" of doctors would be assembled in a medical office complex. Lately, the exams have been conducted at the US Airways Center.

Each person going through the physical would start out with a blood and urine test and then be handed a chart listing all of the specialists they'd have to see. After the blood test there was always a nice spread of juices, doughnuts and bagels. You worked your way from station to station, each doctor usually in a private office or examining room. As you completed each exam, the physician would sign off on your chart. I would tell you that one rookie stayed up all night studying for his blood test, but I don't know that for a fact.

The PR man-doctor-patient privilege prevents me from naming names, but there were more than a few stories coming out of these physicals. One Suns rookie big man was so needle-phobic that he had to be held down by four burly weightlifters just so the medical staff could draw some blood. He was so opposed to the needles, he said, "I'd rather not play in the NBA, than have my blood drawn!" Ultimately, he would get his wish.

FICKLE FINGER OF FATE

For just about any guy, the most uncomfortable part of a full physical exam is the visit to the urologist for the "digital" prostate exam. So onerous was the thought of this exam to one star Suns player that he looked at the charts of some of his fellow players who had already done the exam and then forged the urologist's signature on his own chart. His star status notwithstanding, the player was busted when the doctors compared notes at the end of the day. He still refused the test.

One year, while I was waiting for an examining room to open up, one of the medical assistants told me that the urologist was available. So thinking, "Let's get this over with," I took a deep breath, opened the door and stepped into the room.

> **"This is unnatural!"**
> - Unidentified Suns player

Well, it turns out, the doctor was not free. One of our players was already in there and they were in the middle of their exam. The player was facing me, leaning over the examining table, with the doctor barely visible behind him. Before I could say "Oops," excuse myself and bow out of the room, the player proclaimed, "This is unnatural!" That was a perfectly understandable thing for him to say. But to me, the really "unnatural" part was not that he was in the middle of his digital prostate exam, but that while it was going on, he was eating a jelly doughnut!

MUST NOT BE JEWISH

Then there was one first-round pick who was asked if he liked the food that had been served at the physical. He responded, "It was OK but I thought the doughnuts were a little hard."

He'd been eating a bagel!

IF IT'S FREE, IT'S FOR ME

If you worked for the Suns in the early years, one of the other "perks" was a sponsor related tie-in with McDonalds. It doesn't get any better than free food! All that Suns players or Suns front office people had to do was just show their special Suns card at the McDonald's counter, then order whatever they wanted...no charge! Harvey Shank confided that he simply could not have made it as a young sales guy, in 1971, without this benefit. Bon appétit!

THE SUNS TWO MILLIONTH FAN

We almost missed it, but one day, as I was adding up some attendance statistics, I realized that we were closing in on a team attendance milestone... two million fans through the Coliseum turnstiles! Based on our average attendance, I roughly calculated the game when we'd pass this milestone so we planned some special things to honor whoever was destined to become the Suns' two millionth fan.

On the projected night I waited with our Suns marketing guy, Harvey Shank, on the Coliseum's upper concourse for the Suns' two millionth fan to make his, or her, appearance. There are a couple of different approaches you can take in order to do this. You could pick a single turnstile and say, "when the 53rd person walks through that turnstile, whoever it turns out to be, we'll declare them the winner." Or you could do what we ultimately decided... go with a "gut feel" and just pick a fan at random.

HARVEY SHANK

So, we focused on one entrance and waited for a fan that "looked right." TV cameras from several local stations were nearby and waiting, but they'd keep their lights off until we gave them the cue. We didn't have to wait too long before we spotted a family of three that looked like true "Suns fans" with all the right stuff. The couple had a little boy in tow and he was wearing a Suns t-shirt. We gave the cameramen the high sign. This was it! Let's go!

The cameras came swooping in with lights ablaze ready to capture the excitement and surprise reaction. Everything was going great, that is, until Harvey closed in and tried to shake the father's hand. The guy reacted like we had just blown his cover in the witness protection program! For a moment we thought that we had accidentally uncovered Richard Kimball from *The Fugitive*!

Understand that Harvey Shank is a big man, a former athlete who stands about 6'5", so as he moved into this guy's personal space to offer congratulations, for a split second I actually thought the guy was going to haul off and belt Harv right in the chops. Turns out the dad was just startled by all the sudden attention and was a little intimidated by the attack of the giant marketing man. He was also painfully camera shy. But later on we had good interviews with the boy and his mom. Eventually they all joined us at center court and accepted tickets to future games and other Suns gifts for their good luck in being selected as our two millionth fan!

Jeez, Louise! So much for the "gut feel" technique!

FROM THE WACKO! File – NO MAIL ORDER BRIDE

Dear Mr. Colangelo,

My name is Eldon Presser and I live in Southern Nevada. For a while, I lived in Arizona and nobody in the whole world was more devoted to your Phoenix Suns. I used to see them play all the time.

My reason for writing is the following. I have a wonderful girlfriend in the Philippine Islands. We have writtened to each other for over 5 yrs, over that period of time we have become best friends and now we have fallen deeply in love with each other we want to be together and I want to make her my wife.

Now, my problem is this: I do not meet the guidelines of the U.S. State Department. I need a sponsor that can get my beloved here. The sponsor is one who can show the State Dept that my girl doesn't end up on welfare.

My woman is not a mail-order bride. I got in touch with her through my church.

I ask you Mr. Colangelo, can you help me find a sponsor for my wonderful Maria, I have ask your help I plan on living in Arizona I want to see the Suns play.

Mr. C any help or advice you can give me will be so appreciated.

Sincerely,

Eldon Presser

NO CONTEST

When Alvan Adams was a rookie, we scheduled him for an autograph session at one of our sponsors. In this case, the sponsor was Jack in the Box™ and Alvan was going to meet fans and sign autographs for two hours one evening. Alvan's first response to the request was, "I don't think I can eat for two straight hours!"

My response to him was, "Alvan, this is just a meet and greet session and maybe signing some autographs. It is not an eating contest!"

So, on the appointed day, at the appointed hour, Alvan sat down in a booth at the Jack in the Box location. Then, in between autographs, he proceeded to spend the next two hours sampling everything on the Jack in the Box menu...burgers, tacos, fries, deep-fried apple pie. You name it... Alvan ate it. If he seemed to enjoy it, the staff would bring him another order...and another... and another.

It was an impressive, well-mannered and very methodical performance. If it *had* been an eating contest, there is little doubt that Alvan would have chewed up the competition.

SNL

Connie Hawkins' reputation as a New York City schoolyard legend was without peer. So it only made sense, in 1975, when New York City music legend Paul Simon wanted to do a music video for his guest-host appearance on *Saturday Night Live*, that he selected Connie Hawkins to be part of it. The song Simon picked for the soundtrack of the Hawkins skit? ... *Me and Julio Down by the Schoolyard*... of course!

NBC sports reporter Marv Albert got involved with the sketch as well, conducting pre-game and post-game interviews with the two combatants.

Hawkins was playing for the Atlanta Hawks at the time and the SNL producers flew him into New York City to film the segment.

The location was an outdoor court near Columbia University in Harlem. When Hawk asked how the one-on-one game was supposed to come out, the film crew told him that they were shooting with three possible outcomes in mind: Hawk wins... Simon wins... or it's a tie. The editors would later decide which outcome would be best for the show.

During a pre-game interview, Hawkins told Albert, "Well actually, I'm probably known as one of the best one-on-one basketball players in the schoolyards, and I found out through the grapevine that he's probably one of the best basketball players in the schoolyard, so I challenged him to see who's the best."

Since Simon was a vastly more talented musician than he was a basketball player, the 6'9" Hawk had to make up moves to avoid hurting the diminutive, 5'5" Simon. Once he actually had to jump completely over Simon's head. Connie remembered the final score as being 21-6 in his favor, but other reports list the final outcome as 14-0 in favor of Simon. Apparently, the editors played some aggressive "D" and made sure that all of Connie's baskets wound up on the cutting room floor.

"You let Paul Simon beat you?!"

In the post-game interview with Albert, a clearly exhausted Simon, wearing uniform number **.02**, indicated that in spite of his on-court success, he was going to return to singing and songwriting. I'm sure that was a great relief to music fans... and basketball fans... everywhere.

The show aired October 18, 1975. It was the second episode of the first season of *Saturday Night Live!*

There were subsequent repercussions for Hawk. For many months, perhaps years afterwards, Connie got plenty of abuse from his friends and teammates... "You let Paul Simon beat you?!"

But on the positive side, through the Screen Actors Guild (SAG), Connie was able to cash a couple of talent-fee checks for his appearance.

1975 NBA ALL STAR GAME

When the NBA All-Star Game first came to Phoenix in 1975, the host team was in charge of just about everything. Today, the event has not only grown to consume an entire weekend, but the NBA has taken full control of... well... just about everything. Local fans and sponsors are fortunate if they can get tickets.

The 1975 Phoenix All-Star Game was played on January 14th, a Tuesday night, because no NBA teams wanted to give up their cherished weekend playing dates. The game was televised nationally on CBS, but because it was not sold out until the last minute, it was blacked out in the Phoenix area.

NBA Commissioner Walter Kennedy was presiding over his last All-Star Game prior to his retirement. At the banquet on the eve of the game, Kennedy was joined by celebrities like recording star Andy Williams, comedian Foster Brooks and television star McLean Stevenson, who entertained a then-record crowd of 1,500 people at the Phoenix Civic Plaza.

The next night the East All-Stars beat the West All-Stars 108-102, in front of 12,885 fans. The East was led by Walt Frazier of the Knicks who tallied 30 points and earned Most Valuable Player honors.

DRIVING MR. KENNEDY

J. Walter Kennedy was an inspiration to me. Like me, he was a Notre Dame graduate and a PR guy. He served as the sports information director at Notre Dame, before becoming the public relations director for the Basketball Association of America. Eventually the BAA merged with the National Basketball League to become the National Basketball Association. He also toured with the Harlem Globetrotters as their publicity director. He then found the time to become mayor of Stamford, Connecticut, before the NBA owners tapped him to be their president in 1963. His title changed to "commissioner" in 1967.

By the time he was ready to step down as commissioner in 1975, the NBA had grown substantially under his leadership, expanding to 18 teams, landing a lucrative national television contract, increasing attendance considerably and solidifying the league's overall financial condition.

The 1975 NBA All-Star Game in Phoenix was the Suns' first and Kennedy's last as commissioner. I had tremendous respect for the commissioner and wanted to make this a very special time for Walter and his wife Marion. I solicited my good friend, and car-buff, Bob Coffman to secure a special vehicle in which we could squire the Kennedy's around Phoenix during the All-Star festivities. Bob outdid himself, commandeering a vintage, white Rolls Royce Silver Cloud from a local collector named John Sullivan. Coffman then volunteered to wear a dark suit, a chauffer's cap and white gloves and serve as the Kennedys' driver for all of the official All-Star events. Ever humble, the Kennedys were actually a little embarrassed about all the special treatment that the Suns franchise showed them.

TOM AMBROSE AND NBA COMMISSIONER KENNEDY

Another thing that endeared me to J. Walter Kennedy was his extensive involvement in social causes. When Kennedy passed away, in 1977, the NBA selected the perfect way to honor his memory. Today, the *J. Walter Kennedy Citizenship Award* is presented annually to an NBA player or coach for outstanding service and dedication to their community. Here is a poem that Walter Kennedy always carried with him. I pass it on to you.

Today, my hands are strong, so let me help you.

Tomorrow they may be weak or old or sick,

And you will have to lighten my load.

But today, my hands are strong, so let me share your burden.

For why do we exist if we cannot care for our fellow man?

Walk in his path.

Know his sorrow.

Today my hands are strong. Let me help you.

CHAPTER 3

ONE SEASON IN TIME

MASKED MAN

Just before the Suns made their fabulous stretch run to the play-offs in 1976, starting forward Curtis Perry took a hard shot to the face that resulted in a broken bone in his upper jaw and a mouthful of loose teeth. Medical definition: broken Aveolar ridge of the maxilla. Street definition: broken face.

The broken bone was just below his nose and just above his upper lip. The perpetrator was Kansas City's 6'10, 220-pound center Sam Lacey, who had a well earned reputation for sharp elbows and physical play. It was an accident, but that didn't make Curtis hurt any less.

The Suns desperately needed Curtis' rebounding and "C.P." desperately wanted to play, but the possibility of re-injury was high, so trainer Joe Proski and the Suns medical team had to figure out a way to protect the injury. After the Suns doctors' had wired the fracture, they went to work molding a plastic mask for the lower portion of Perry's face. C.P. didn't feel comfortable wearing the mask because it was too restrictive. So, Proski tried a couple of different hockey goalie masks that gave Perry plenty of protection but tended to limit his vision, especially overhead.

Although the hockey mask offered maximum protection with just minor irritation, Curtis wore the mask only a short time. After putting up with jokes from his teammates and catcalls from the stands, Curtis dumped the mask idea after just two games. Today, some NBA players wear custom-molded full-face, protective masks for entire seasons at a time.

The injury took more than six weeks to heal. During that period, Curtis had a mouthful of wires, chewed food with his back teeth and suffered through a 10-pound weight loss. He claimed that the wires in his jaw enabled him to pick up radio stations from as far away as Australia.

When Curtis retired from basketball, a couple of years later, he quipped, "I looked in the mirror after my last elbow to the face and decided that there must be an easier way to meet congenial people of my own age."

FAMILY

❝Hundreds of Suns fans raced to the Suns office...with blankets, sleeping bags and lawn chairs.❞

Unquestionably, times have changed. Although technology has brought more efficiency and greater convenience, it has also resulted in less personal contact with our fans. That's not always for the better.

Toward the end of the 1975-76 season, the Suns were about to win a critical game and clinch a spot in the playoffs. We had to announce that playoff tickets would go on sale at the Suns ticket office, on North Central Avenue, the next morning at 9 a.m.

So, our public address announcer, Stan Richards, opened his microphone and announced to the sellout crowd at the Coliseum, "Ladies and gentlemen...Suns playoff tickets will go on sale..." That was it. The rest of his message was completely drowned out as the crowd exploded in a deafening roar of delirious euphoria.

Immediately following the game that night, hundreds of Suns fans raced to the Suns office on North Central with blankets, sleeping bags and lawn chairs. After five frustrating years out of post-season play, they were vying to be first in line for tickets, when the Suns opened their doors and playoff tickets went on sale the next morning.

It's sad that, with the introduction of the Internet, *ticketmaster*™, StubHub, ticket brokers and telephone credit card sales, camping out for tickets just doesn't happen much anymore. But back then, when the sun came up the next morning, Jerry Colangelo was on hand to say hello and offer coffee and doughnuts to all the fans who had camped out overnight in the Suns parking lot. That's just what you did back then. They were family.

EULA AND WHITEY

Eula and Whitey Dillman were two of the Suns most loyal fans. They rarely missed a game. They were retired and already in their 70s when the Suns made the playoffs in 1976. Eula had some mobility issues so she had to use one of those little motorized scooters to get around. She was able to take a step or two to get into her seat on the baseline in the front row, but even that was a struggle.

The first playoff series for the Suns that year was against the Seattle Super Sonics who featured a 7'2," 230-pound center from North Carolina State named Tom Burleson. The Suns frequently countered with their own big guy, 6'10," 250-pound Dennis Awtrey from Santa Clara. The match-up didn't produce many points but it did result in a lot of pushing, shoving and hard fouls. The confrontation finally exploded into a full-blown fight during one of the games at the Coliseum. As the two giant players grappled along the baseline, Awtrey, with a clear advantage in both weight and strength, just picked up Burleson and literally threw him into the front row of seats...right onto Eula Dillman's lap! With the weight and impact of Burleson, all four of the legs on Eula's folding chair snapped and they both went crashing to the floor. Burleson got up but Eula didn't.

The game was delayed as emergency medical crews quickly came to Eula's aid, extracting her from the collapsed and broken chair. They strapped her onto a gurney, put her in an ambulance and raced off to the emergency room. We feared the worst and thought that might be the last we'd ever see Eula Dillman. Imagine my total shock and surprise when, just two days later, I'm walking the corridors of the Coliseum, getting ready for another playoff game, when here comes Eula, buzzing down the hallway on her little electric scooter. I stopped her to say hello.

"Eula, I'm really surprised to see you here tonight," I said. "Are you okay?"

Her response spoke to her loyalty and determination. She said, "Tom, if I stayed home every time I didn't feel good... I'd never leave the house!"

I'm not sure they make fans like that anymore.

MR. DEPENDABLE

During the first half of the 1975-76 season, the Suns were getting some solid play from three rookie first-round picks: Alvan Adams, John Shumate and Ricky Sobers. Shumate was coming back after a year on the shelf due to his blood-clotting, phlebitis condition and he was making a strong contribution off the bench. Adams' consistent all-around game earned him an All-Star Game spot and the league's Rookie of the Year Award. Sobers, picked 16th in the first round of the 1975 draft, was a rookie who simply played like a veteran. The future looked bright for the Suns, but heading into the All-Star break, their record was a disappointing 18-27.

Colangelo and MacLeod knew that they needed to shake things up to make a run at the playoffs. MacLeod had his eye on one of his former Oklahoma University players, 6'6" Garfield Heard, who had proven himself to be a dependable forward for Seattle, Chicago and Buffalo over five seasons.

I learned about the trade as I was traveling to the NBA All-Star game in frigid Philadelphia. The Suns would get Heard and a second round pick, in exchange for Shumate. I was saddened to hear the news because "Shu" was a fellow "Domer" and we had become buddies during his time in Phoenix. Additionally, he had been playing well in his comeback bid. Outside of his stats, I really didn't know much about Gar Heard.

A few days later, when the opportunity presented itself, I asked MacLeod to tell me about the decision and a little bit about Gar Heard. John described Heard as one of the most loyal and dependable people he had ever had the pleasure of coaching ...or knowing.

"If you made a pact with Gar Heard today, to meet ten years from now, on a particular street corner, at a specific time and date," MacLeod explained. "You'd better show up, because I guarantee that Garfield will be there waiting for you."

Perhaps it was the addition of Heard... or his experience... or his confidence... or the team chemistry his addition produced... whatever it was... it worked! The Suns stormed out of the All-Star break, going 24-13 to push their final, regular season record up to 42-40. That was good enough to squeak into the playoffs.

Time and time again during those 1976 playoffs, Heard would demonstrate why MacLeod had such faith in him.

SLO MO

In the Western Conference Finals, against the defending NBA Champion Golden State Warriors, the Suns trailed 3-2 going into the sixth game in Phoenix. The Suns were fighting for their playoff lives and the game came down to the final seconds. Phoenix had forged a one point lead, 105-104, but the Warriors had the ball. The Suns played a frantic, scrambling defense as the final seconds ticked away and the Warriors moved the ball around the perimeter. With just two seconds left, the ball went to the corner and into the hands of one of the finest shooters in the NBA, Jamaal Wilkes.

Thirteen thousand Suns fans suddenly thought their team was doomed, because they knew that a Wilkes' jumper from 22 feet was absolute "money!"

Wilkes had a slightly unorthodox shooting style, cocking the ball back behind his head before launching a high-arching shot that rarely missed.

Those two seconds on the clock seemed to take forever. It was as though everything...the game...the fans... even the sound... went into super-slow motion.

Wilkes lined up the shot and smoothly brought the ball behind his head. Faces of Suns fans were twisted with emotion as they started to scream a primeval, "N-o-o-o-o-o-o-o-o-o-o-o-o-o-o!!!!!!!" ...trying to collectively "will" his shot to miss.

Suddenly...from nowhere...a white jersey streaked toward Wilkes...it was Heard! But Wilkes, totally focused on the rim, was already into his shooting motion.

The entire Coliseum thought, "We're done!"

But Heard wasn't! As Wilkes released the shot, Heard, his right arm extended, launched himself toward the spinning shot. Up… up…up he went.

No way… he can't get it…not that shot…not Wilkes' shot!

But somehow, seemingly in defiance of gravity, Heard continued to climb and with just a fingertip, he clipped the shot, knocking it straight up. Miraculously, the final buzzer sounded, the ball came down and landed in the waiting arms of… who else? … "Mr. Dependable," Garfield Heard! Game over! Suns win!

What immediately followed was the loudest explosion of cheering that I have ever heard. As the Suns raced off the floor, having forced a deciding seventh game with the Warriors, the 13,000 Suns fans in the Coliseum, often referred to as "The Mean 13," roared…and I mean ROARED their approval. The acoustics in the Coliseum made it so loud that, after a few seconds, I thought my eardrums were going to burst and I actually had to cover my ears with my hands. In 37 years of watching Suns basketball and dozens of fantastic finishes, that's the ONLY time that's ever happened to me.

Gar Heard would have more great nights in the NBA, and more amazing plays in the playoffs, but that was one frantic finish I will never forget!

Uh… sorry…I didn't hear you…did you say something?

HOT NIGHT

A few days later, the Suns pulled off an amazing, 94-86 road win over the Warriors in the decisive seventh game, stunning the basketball world by knocking off the defending NBA champs and earning the right to meet the Celtics for the NBA title. Having watched it all on TV, Suns fans wanted to share their excitement. They needed an outlet for their bottled up emotion. They had to DO something. So they headed for the airport.

The Suns' commercial flight from Oakland was scheduled to touch down in Phoenix, just a few minutes before midnight. When it did, the fans would be there waiting to greet their triumphant "Purple Gang." But their sudden, spontaneous, late-night "invasion" of the airport absolutely overwhelmed the system. They paralyzed street traffic, filled up parking lots and actually caused the cancellation of some flights. Sky Harbor International Airport was effectively shut down by Suns fans.

On the flight down from Oakland, the pilot informed the team that a "welcoming party" would be waiting for us at the airport. But even that advance warning couldn't possibly have prepared us for what we confronted when we got off the plane. Thousands upon thousands of delirious Suns fans had jammed themselves, shoulder-to-shoulder, into the lobby of Sky Harbor's Terminal 2.

Everyone getting off the flight literally had to run a gauntlet of cheering fans, who were reaching out to touch and high-five anyone who had anything to do with the Suns entourage. We fought our way through the clinging crowd to the terminal's main lobby. Airport security personnel directed the Suns' travel-ling party up some stairs to a balcony that overlooked the lobby and the chanting, screaming, cheering thousands. Players and coaches shouted down their thanks to the assembled masses, but it was so loud nobody could really hear anything. That night, in that sweaty terminal, the

> **ɪɪThey had to DO something. So they headed for the airport. ɪɪ**

excitement, emotion and the anticipation of the coming NBA Finals, was palpable.

There was one major casualty from the Terminal 2 celebration. One of the local Phoenix car dealers had a new model car parked on display in the terminal lobby. That night, the car was alternately used as a viewing platform, a drum, a trampoline and who knows what else. Rumor at the time said that the next day, the dealer pushed the car out of the terminal, loaded it onto a flatbed truck and took it directly to a salvage yard.

BIG SHOES

The Suns headed to Boston to face the Celtics in the first two games of the Championship Finals. The first game was slated for Sunday, May 23rd. The team and coaching staff left Phoenix on a commercial flight on Thursday. I stayed in Phoenix to finish up some of the media work and wrap-up my media guide for the finals. My plan was to join the team late the following day in Boston. The next day I got an early-morning call from Boston. It was our back-up center, Dennis Awtrey. He asked me if I could please drive by his house and pick something up for him and bring it with me to Boston.

Apparently, in his excitement and hasty preparation for the Boston trip, he had, of course, packed a pair of his basketball shoes. Unfortunately, with a closet full of sneakers, he'd accidentally grabbed two "lefts!" My job was to go pick up a couple of "rights!"

Although I don't think that the injury had anything to do with his basketball shoes, Dennis played the entire NBA Championship Series with a broken bone in his foot.

Consider that a "footnote."

TRAGEDY

The Suns' thrilling dash through the playoffs and into the NBA Finals, against the lordly Celtics, dominated Arizona news coverage until the tragic events of June 2, 1976. That was the day Don Bolles, an investigative reporter for *The Arizona Republic*, was scheduled to meet an informant at the Hotel Clarendon in Phoenix. That hotel was located just a block from the Celtics' hotel headquarters, the Del Webb Towne House. However, Bolles' informant in a land fraud investigation never showed up, so Bolles left the hotel and returned to his vehicle. As he began to pull away, a powerful bomb was detonated under his car.

It was just hours before the tip-off for Game 4 and several members of the Celtic traveling party were in the pool area of the Del Webb Towne House. They clearly heard and felt the concussion from the nearby explosion. Bolles was critically wounded, but clung to life for 11 days before succumbing. Although two men went to prison for the murder, the motive for the crime and the identities of those who ordered the "hit," remain a mystery.

GAME FIVE AT BOSTON GARDEN

The Celtics won the first two games in Boston, but the Suns bounced back with two big wins at the Coliseum in Phoenix. So the series was squared at 2-2 going back to Boston for the pivotal fifth game. The Warriors' Rick Barry joined the CBS TV crew to help with color commentary, along with Mendy Rudolph, the former NBA referee. CBS's play-by-play man was the now-legendary Brent Musburger who, in 1976, was merely a broadcasting "boy wonder."

Game Five, because of the CBS broadcasting schedule, started at 9:00 p.m., Boston time. It was a Friday night. Al McCoy and I speculated as to where all those Bostonians went between the time they got off work at five o'clock and four hours later when the game started. Let's just say that there was a real "buzz" in the building at tip-off time.

The broadcast position for Suns radio was in a little press box on the leading edge of the upper deck of the old Boston Garden. It was a great vantage point except you couldn't hear some of the referee's calls or see things that were going on close to the court. In order to get in and out of this little press box there was a step or two that led up into the regular seats and then back up the aisle to the exit.

> **❝There was a real 'buzz' in the building at tip-off time. 🎧**

A couple of young Celtic fans, looking for a place to sit down, wound up sitting on the press box steps right next to Al and me. They continued what they had no doubt started at five o'clock that afternoon and were drinking pretty heavily throughout the whole game. At one point I think they offered McCoy a drink...naturally, he refused. The Suns went down by 22 in the first half and it looked like it was pretty well over for Phoenix, but give thanks to an unheralded back-up Suns point guard named Phil Lumpkin. He came into the game, got the team settled down and the Suns slowly, inexorably, mounted a comeback. By the end of regulation, the game was tied.

Just before the end of regulation, McCoy realized that these guys sitting on the steps were getting a little unruly, so, he learned over and whispered to me, "Get these guys out of here!" So, I climbed back up 10 rows or so and found a security guard standing there yakking to an usher about the game. I said, "Hey, guys, we've got a couple of people sitting in the press box, and we'd like to get them out of there." The guard looked at me and said, "What!?

Are they bothering you?" I said, "No...not exactly. But, they're not supposed to be there. It could be a problem." He just kind of waved me off ... "Yeah, yeah, yeah, we'll take care of it."

So I went back to my duties of keeping score and doing the occasional on-air scoring summaries for Al and our Phoenix audience, but that was it. Security never got around to "taking care of it." The game went to overtime...and then came the amazing finish to the second overtime.

With just seconds to go, John Havlicek hit a leaping-leaner to put the Celtics up by one point as time ran out. Game over. Or was it? The crowd stormed the floor and a fight broke out between referee Richie Powers and one of the Boston fans. Apparently, the Boston fans were a little unhappy with the officiating that night. A couple of Suns players, Curtis Perry and Dennis Awtrey were trying to break up the fight and the scene on the court below us was absolute bedlam!

But time had not run out. Powers judged that there was still one second left in the game. Eventually, order was restored and it was Suns' ball with one tick remaining on the game clock. Paul Westphal, realizing that the odds of the Suns going the length of the court and scoring, was less than nil, convinced Coach MacLeod to call a time out even though the Suns had no time outs left. That resulted in technical foul which the Celtics' Jo Jo White converted, but the strategic maneuver gave the ball to the Suns at half court, now down by two points with one second left to play. It was brilliant strategy, but it was still a long-shot.

Curtis Perry inbounded the ball to Gar Heard at the top of the key. In one motion, Heard caught the ball and launched a high arching jumper – the "shot **Heard** 'round the world" – it seemed to take forever to come down, but the ball swished through the net cleanly, as the buzzer sounded! At that moment, one of the two inebriates sitting next to McCoy and me passed out, right onto Al's lap! So, as Al is calling what is arguably the most exciting play in Phoenix Suns history, there's a drunk passed out in his lap! Without missing a word, McCoy deftly slid the drunk off his leg and down into a heap at the foot of the press box steps. There was mass confusion down on the basketball floor as well. Did the shot count? YES!!

We were headed for a third, amazing, overtime period!

AL McCOY

RICKY RECONSIDERS

In the excitement and exuberance of the moment immediately after Heard's shot swished through the net, Suns guard Ricky Sobers grabbed the basketball and heaved it toward the Boston Garden ceiling. Suddenly, thinking of the many strange things and strange calls that had already happened that night, Sobers realized that flinging the ball as he did, might not be such a great idea. By this time though, the ball had reached its apex, nearly grazing the rafters before it began its return trip. Sobers, suddenly determined not to let the ball hit the floor, moved into position like a catcher drifting under a foul pop-up. He caught the descending sphere. Then, carefully avoiding any eye contact with the referees, he very gently placed the basketball on the floor before running over to the Suns bench. The whole scene just took a couple of seconds, but it was just one more bizarre, little vignette during a very strange night.

MY FIVE SECONDS

Somewhere in this world there's an old Magnavox 33 1/3 RPM vinyl record album (or maybe an eight-track tape) of that exciting play-by-play from late in the second overtime. Al McCoy's breathless description is, all of a sudden, interrupted by this high-pitched, squeaky voice that says, "There's a fight out on the floor! A fan is going after referee Richie Powers! Curtis Perry is trying to pull them apart!" Because McCoy was looking for the clock and trying to figure out what was going on with the time, he was looking down at the official timer and then up at the scoreboard clock. He did not immediately see the fight going on down on the floor. So, I had an open microphone and I just jumped in, helping myself to five seconds of fame. My brief but unaccredited "play-by-play" is on that commemorative record album. I'm sure that over the years, when people listen to the recording and hear that "other" voice, they say, "Who the heck is that?"

TEAMWORK

Game Five ended just after midnight. The clock finally struck 12 for the "Sunderella Suns." The Celtics had beaten back a fierce

Suns rally and barely escaped with a narrow, 128-126, triple-overtime win. Many basketball fans still say that Game Five might have been the most exciting NBA game ever played.

Everyone in Boston Garden that night had been through an emotional wringer. But no matter how personally disappointing the loss may have been, I still had a job to do and the obligation to do it professionally. I came down from our broadcasting perch to pick up the final box score and other post game stats from the Celtics' press room. It was there that I ran into *Arizona Republic* reporter Dave Hicks.

Because of the time zone differences, Hicks still had some time to file his story, but he didn't want to do it from the Boston Garden press room, which was already jammed with media and was a virtual madhouse. So I agreed to accompany him back to our hotel and help him file the story.

We jumped in a cab, which, somewhat miraculously, immediately broke free of the gridlock around Boston Garden. Boston fans were everywhere and, following the Celtics' dramatic win, they were justifiably dancing in the streets. It had already been a long night and I was really beginning to hate all things green.

When we arrived at the hotel, Hicks and I had a plan. Dave would immediately retreat to his room and craft the first pages of his report on the epic Game Five. Meanwhile, I would stop by the hotel bar to rustle up some beer and supplies for the hours ahead.

By the time I got to Hicks' room with the provisions, he had finished his first page. I got on the phone and called the *Republic* sports desk. We'd be transmitting the story via remote portable telecopier, a device which could send one page of copy at a time when coupled to a standard telephone receiver.

When compared to today's technology, the telecopier was just a little faster than chipping the story onto a stone tablet. But, in the mid-1970s, the telecopier was a godsend to reporters and PR people alike. You attached the page of copy to a cylinder inside the telecopier. As the cylinder spun, a sensor would move across the page "reading" the bits of copy and turning them into pulse signals. Those signals were then sent over phone lines to an identical machine at the other end that would decode the pulse signals and burn a duplicate image onto a special type of paper that was spinning on the receiving machine's cylinder. Simple... right? I have to laugh when I think of the volumes of information that can be sent instantly over the Internet today. Back then, using the telecopier, each page took six minutes to transmit!

So as Hicks banged out his story on a tiny, manual, portable typewriter, I manned the telecopier. We proved to be a pretty efficient team, because Dave could bang out a page of copy in about five minutes. I could send and confirm the receipt of one page and he'd be ready to give me the next page to send and we never had to break the connection with the *Republic* sports desk. I think Hicks did about 10 pages on the game and we got them all in under deadline.

The next morning, I was very proud when I spoke to my wife by phone and she assured me that there was indeed a game story by Dave Hicks that appeared in the morning editions of *The Arizona Republic*.

Hicks' opening paragraph said it all:

"Somewhere in the hallowed halls of musty, championship-steeped Boston Garden this morning, the Phoenix Suns probably are still scrambling and plotting and searching for a victory. These guys just don't quit."

DINERS CLUB

PR guys remember great things that happened to their team on the court. Of course, they'll remember their own great ideas and their suggestions that made it into print or on the air. But quite often, their best memories are of the gastronomic variety...the good company, the great stories, the fine dining and the occasional libation enjoyed during a season or a long playoff run.

For the Suns, the 1976 playoffs went through some of the best restaurant cities in the country: Seattle, San Francisco and Boston. I had an expense account and some well-experienced guides when it came to finding the best dining experiences those cities had to offer. Dr. Paul Steingard was the Suns' team physician and the unofficial team gourmand. At breakfast, Dr. S would plan lunch. At lunch he'd map out plans for dinner unless it was

a game night. Then there were dinners with the media, dinners with folks
from the travelling party, as well as
assorted meals with other teams' PR
people.

*"Der poundin'
da veal!"*
\- Vito

One particularly memorable night
was set up by assistant coach Al
Bianchi, at Vito's Restaurant in Seattle. The Suns coaching staff
and executive team took over Vito's back room. We were joined
by Vito himself for what would be a 12-course Italian meal. At
about 9:30, already over-served in every way possible, we heard
this loud banging and hammering coming from the next room. I
said to Vito, "It's a little late to be doing remodeling isn't it?" He
laughed and in a very Italian, god-fatherly way said, "Der poundin' da veal!" A short while later a delicious veal scaloppini was
served.

The playoffs ran from mid-April through the first week in June. During that time I went from a svelte, in-shape, 195-pound running
machine, to a wheezing, lumpy, 220-pound PR potato!

SURF N' TURF

It was during the NBA Championship series with the Celtics,
that I had a chance to take our newly crowned Rookie of the
Year, Alvan Adams, out to dinner in Boston. We selected a restaurant in Quincy Market called Durgin Park, known for its traditional home cooking, red and white checkered table cloths
and huge portions. The restaurant was unaware, but they
were about to be tested by Alvan's legendary appetite. People who meet Alvan for the first time, think of him as "slender,"
maybe even "skinny." Officially, he was 6'9" and weighed 220
pounds, but the "Oklahoma Kid" could really pack away the
groceries!

For openers, Durgin Park served some rich, buttery and great-
tasting cornbread. I had one piece that settled in my stomach
like a five-pound brick. But Alvan consumed the remainder of
that basket and then asked for and devoured another. We had
some deep-fried mushrooms for an appetizer and then it was
time to order. Alvan asked about "surf and turf." When he was

told that the restaurant didn't offer a combination "surf and turf" entree, Alvan proceeded to order a full steak platter as well as a full lobster entre with all the accompanying side dishes.

I was shocked to see one man consume that volume of food. But he wasn't quite done. Once the entrées were gone, it was time for dessert...deep dish apple pie a-la-mode! Alvan polished that off and I somehow had the impression that he was still hungry while I was looking around for a wheelbarrow to roll me out to the curb. On my expense report, I listed that night as "dinner for three."

When I recounted the story to Alvan recently, he seemed to reflect enviously, almost hungrily, on those times, before he added; "Now I'm splitting entrées with my wife!" Nevertheless, Alvan is still within a few pounds of his playing weight of 25 years ago! Amazing!

YABBA DABBA DO

It was Al Bianchi who brought this to my attention. After Tommy Heinsohn retired from playing and coaching, he did what nearly all former Celtics do...he went into broadcasting. He worked for the Celtics, but he also did some national TV games during the playoffs.

Heinsohn was originally from Jersey City, New Jersey and, as a commentator, his street-tough Jersey accent came through with a certain gritty realism. Bianchi told me, "the next time you listen to him on a broadcast...just close your eyes and tell me who you hear."

I did as Al suggested...closed my eyes and focused my listening solely on Heinsohn's voice. Bianchi was right! It wasn't Tommy Heinsohn at all. The voice sounded just like... Fred Flintstone!

CHAPTER 4

WANDERING IN THE DESERT

FREAKY FRIDAY

It started out like any other game day during the injury-riddled 1976-77 season as the Suns got ready to face "Pistol" Pete Maravich and the New Orleans Jazz. Suns coach John MacLeod used the team shoot-around that morning to work around some injuries and pull together yet another patch-work line-up. But by early afternoon, things got a little strange.

On their way to enjoy some home cooking at Mrs. White's Golden Rule Cafe, five Jazz players were injured when their taxicab collided with another car in a downtown Phoenix intersection. All five players were rushed to a local hospital, treated for assorted bumps, cuts and bruises and then released. Although none of the five were seriously injured, on the advice of doctors (and probably a few of their agents) all five players stayed in their hotel rooms and did not show up at the Coliseum that night. Fortunately for the Jazz, Pete Maravich wasn't in that cab.

New Orleans Coach Elgin Baylor didn't have many options. He had just seven players available to play. League rules required that a minimum of eight players must dress for a game, so special dispensation had to be obtained from NBA headquarters in New York. As the Jazz petitioned the league, at the Suns office we prepared to alert the media and cancel the game. But because of the extenuating circumstances, Commissioner Larry O'Brien gave his OK and the game was a "go."

Things were winding down on a frustrating season for the Suns. Following a trip to the NBA Finals in the spring of 1976, injuries hit hard this season and the Suns would finish 34-48 and out of the playoffs entirely. Even though the Suns were struggling, and New Orleans was on an eight-game losing streak, both clubs had their pride.

A weird side note was that rookie Jazz guard Mo Howard started the game, played six minutes and then did not play again all night. So, for all intents and purposes, the short-handed Jazz played the entire game with just six players. Maravich was the only Jazz player to go the whole 48 minutes and he turned in an amazing performance.

In the first half, it was a duel between Maravich and the Suns Paul Westphal. Maravich scored 10 points in the first quarter but Westphal was on fire, answering with 19 points and putting the Suns up 30-18. By halftime, the Suns led 50-44. Westphal had 23 points and Maravich totaled 24.

> **"Commissioner Larry O'Brien gave his OK and the game was a 'go.'"**

About halfway through the third-quarter, with the Suns still holding the lead, Maravich began to take over the game. He drove the lane...he bombed from long range and the Jazz took the lead. At one point, late in the third quarter, Maravich's shoe came loose and he stayed down by the Jazz basket to lace it up. Sure enough, a Suns fast break misfired and Jazz guard Andy Walker heaved a long pass down to Maravich for an uncontested lay-up. With 11 points in the period, "Pistol" ran his total to 35 for the game. As the fourth quarter opened, Maravich hit four straight jump shots, one of them from at least 28 feet and the Jazz went up by as many as eight.

But then, Westphal came alive, scoring four hoops on three drives and a mid-range jumper and the Suns battled back to within one point with fifteen seconds to go in the game. The out-manned and exhausted Jazz took their final time-out. On their ensuing in-bounds pass, the Suns Alvan Adams stole the ball. He spotted Westphal streaking down court, but Adams' full-court pass sailed past him, out of bounds. Seconds later, when R.C. Coleman of the Jazz missed the second of two free throws, the Suns still had a chance to send the game to overtime. Remember, this was before the NBA adopted the three-point field goal.

But the Suns couldn't get a decent shot and the ball wound up in the hands of Maravich who was fouled at the buzzer by a frustrated Keith Erickson. With no time on the clock and standing alone at the Coliseum's West basket, Maravich hit the first free throw, and then nonchalantly tossed up the second. Before the second shot banked off the backboard and swished through the net, Maravich turned his back and ran toward the Jazz locker room with an improbable 104-100 win. Forty eight minutes, fifty-one points for "Pistol" Pete, while the rest of his his teammates scored a total of 53! It was a remarkable performance...a night to remember...and definitely one freaky Friday in the NBA!

FROM THE WACKO! FILE – QUITE THE OPPORTUNITY
WOMEN'S CAUCUS
North Dakota

Phoenix Suns
Office of Community Relations

Dear Sir,

The Women's Caucus of North Dakota is proud to launch its campaign to establish an endowment fund for our "Educate-a-Youth" program. You have the opportunity to become a charter participant in a unique and innovative plan to raise a minimum of one million dollars for assisting young people in our community.

The plan requests that you or your company lend the Women's Caucus the use of one million dollars for a period of from 1 to 5 years. This amount, less interest, will be returned in full to the lender at the end of the agreed upon period. The interest that occurs from the one million dollars will serve as the base for the endowment fund.

Please review the enclosed fact sheets about our organization and the "Educate-a-Youth" program.

We look forward to hearing from you soon.

Sincerely yours,

Millicent Mackley
President
Women's Caucus

TWIN TEAMMATES

As August, 1976 came down to its final days; Suns GM Jerry Colangelo announced that he had made a deal with the Buffalo Braves that would bring Tom Van Arsdale to Phoenix. For the first time in 11 years, since their college days at Indiana, the Van Arsdale twins, Tom and Dick, would play on the same team.

Unfortunately, it was a long, frustrating season for the Suns and for both of the Van Arsdale boys. After the Suns' wild run through the NBA playoffs the year before, the Suns would not make the playoffs in 1977. As the team approached their final game of the season, Dick tried to persuade Tom into secretly switching uniforms for the last game. It was something they had pulled off successfully several times when they were kids, but this was the NBA. Exhibiting the maturity of an older brother (by 15 minutes), Tom nixed the idea.

On April 10, 1977, Tom announced his retirement as a player. Slightly more than a month later, Dick also called an end to his playing career.

Dick finished his career with 15,079 regular season points, while Tom ended up with 14,232. Their total of 29,311 made them the highest scoring family in NBA history.

RESPECT

One morning during the 1976-77 season, the Lakers, then coached by the legendary Jerry West, were in Phoenix, going through their morning shoot-around at the Coliseum. I had to ask West some questions about the playing status of a couple of his players, so we had a conversation while sitting on the press table, near center court.

At one point, West looked around the arena and saw the huge banner we had recently hoisted to the rafters, honoring Connie Hawkins as the first player enshrined in the Suns Ring of Honor.

No doubt remembering the many one-on-one battles he had over the years against the Suns' Dick Van Arsdale, West said, "I see you just retired Hawkins' number. What are you guys going to do when Van Arsdale retires… give him the building?"

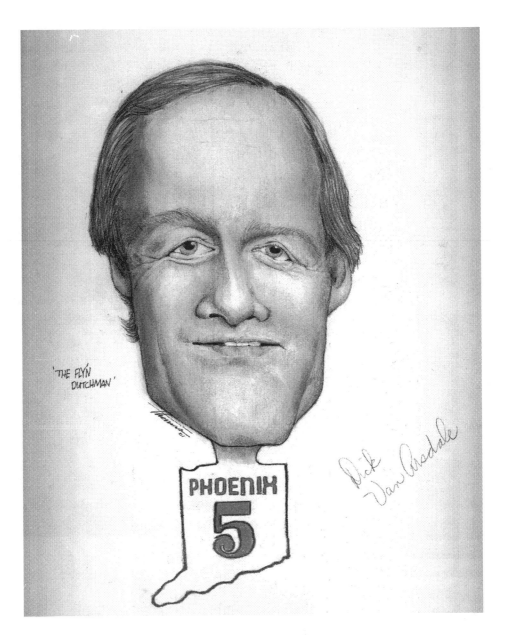

'THE FLYN DUTCHMAN'

PHOENIX 5

DICK VAN ARSDALE

A TRIBUTE TO THE DUTCHMAN

Following the 1976-77 season Dick Van Arsdale, the "Flying Dutchman," announced his retirement. Connie Hawkins had already gained admission into the prestigious "Suns Ring of Honor," but Van was extra special. He was "The Original Sun," the first player selected in the expansion draft as the Suns took shape in 1968. Not to get too biblical, but it was upon this rock of a player that Colangelo built the franchise. Van Arsdale would prove to be a solid foundation.

It was my honor to pull together a fitting ceremony and tribute to salute the life and career of Dick Van Arsdale. I produced a booklet chronicling Van's journey. But when I first sat down to write it, I couldn't get going...the dreaded "writer's block." Perhaps it was because I had so much respect for Van and I knew this had to be good. Then it hit me...write a eulogy...but Van is going to be here to hear it! How cool is that!?

For those who weren't around in 1977, here are some excerpts:

VAN...A TRIBUTE

Since Dick Van Arsdale announced his retirement from professional basketball after 12 years in the NBA, there has been a profound sense of loss among Phoenix fans, a feeling that there will never be another player who embodies all the qualities that set Van a cut above the rest.

Oh, there might be others who come along to score more points, deal more assists, or grab more rebounds than Dick Van Arsdale...and by the statistical measure applied to sport, he will never be regarded as a "superstar"...but attempting to measure Van's contributions to the Suns only by the harsh, cold light of statistics is grossly incomplete...for there is so much more to this man.

Qualities of courage...intelligence...leadership...dedication... and character...those are the true measure of a man.

Dick Van Arsdale has them all.

THE EARLY YEARS

Dick Van Arsdale was born the younger of the identical Van Arsdale twins (15 minutes after his brother Tom) on February 22, 1943, in Indianapolis, Indiana. The only children of Raymond and Hilda Van Arsdale, Dick and Tom were raised in Greenwood, Indiana (population 2,500), eight miles south of Indianapolis.

They grew up in a home that was nestled in the middle of a one-time park, overgrown with trees, expansive lawns and shrubs. It was a scene ideal for kids, with a creek and a pond "just down the road." They had an old dog named "Pal," that was a world-class muskrat hunter. Neighbors can still remember the Van Arsdale boys trying to float rafts on the pond, kicking along the dusty lanes or selling strawberries and vegetables grown in the family garden.

Their love for sports came from their father, a teacher and a track coach, who encouraged, but never forced his boys into athletics. Even as youngsters, the twins wreaked confusion on opponents and coaches alike. Dick remembers a Little League baseball game in Southport, Indiana one summer:

"The only way people could distinguish us was that we wore different colored caps," recalls Dick. "That day, Tom was scheduled to pitch, but his arm was sore. So we switched caps, and I pitched and he played shortstop—and nobody knew the difference—including our parents. It wasn't a Hollywood ending since I didn't pitch a no-hitter... but we won."

When the twins were only five years old, their grandfather tacked up a hoop in the backyard and the Van Arsdales' basketball careers were underway.

HIGH SCHOOL

As the Van Arsdale twins grew, so did their basketball skills. At Manual High School in Indianapolis, they came under the influence of basketball coach Dick Cummins.

"Coach Cummins was a definite force in our development as players," Dick remembers. "He was a good coach and a gentleman, who took a genuine interest in us as players, as students, and as young men. We always felt that he had our best interests at heart."

The twins further improved their game against some of the top basketball talent in the Indianapolis area. They would travel to the Falls Creek YMCA to play against performers like Hallie Bryant of Indiana University, who later enjoyed a long career with the Harlem Globetrotters; long-time NBA pro Bob Boozer, and Bobby Edmonds, who later played with the ABA Indiana Pacers.

At Manual High School the twins each won three letters in basketball, three letters in track and two each in baseball. With his dad's track team, Dick threw the shot put, was a high jumper, ran both the high and low hurdles, and was member of the relay team.

Only those who have been in Indiana in the spring can describe the Indiana High School Basketball Tournament...statewide bedlam. In tournament play, the Van Arsdales led Manual High School to two sectional titles. As seniors they led Manual to the regional playoffs, semi-finals and eventually to the state finals. Then, in a dramatic final game, their team lost the 1961 state championship by two points in overtime, to Kokomo High School.

Following that emotion-packed state tournament, the prestigious Trester Award for Sportsmanship was, for the first time, presented to two players, Tom and Dick Van Arsdale. Later, both twins were named "Mr. Basketball" in Indiana, the state's highest honor. Through their high school careers, the Van Arsdales each averaged an identical 16 points per game.

And the college recruiters came knocking on that door in Greenwood, Indiana.

INDIANA UNIVERSITY

Besieged by scholarship offers from major colleges all over the country, the Van Arsdales selected Indiana University in Bloomington, about 45 miles from their home in Greenwood. An important consideration in their selection was their uncle, who had attended the school and had been a teammate of Indiana coach, Branch McCracken. McCracken would be another coach who had a profound influence on the twins.

"He was great at firing a team up." Dick remembers, "The players would do anything to win for him."

Both Dick and Tom were Sigma Alpha Epsilon fraternity brothers and roomed with teammate Jon McGlocklin, who would later star in the NBA. Jon had been identified as the "third twin" because he had been raised in nearby Franklin, Indiana and had played countless hours and games with the Van Arsdales.

Indiana was on NCAA athletic probation and was excluded from tournament play when the Van Arsdales arrived on campus. But that didn't stop the twins from enjoying tremendous college careers. In 72 college games, Dick scored a total of 1240 points, a17.2 points per game average. Tom scored 1252 points for 17.4 per game.

"Tom," Dick recalls, "was the gunner."

After their senior season, both Dick and Tom were named first team Academic All-America and second team All-America. Looking ahead to graduation both had taken their law board exams and had been accepted at Indiana University Law School. But another challenge would come first.

THE NBA

The spring of 1965 brought the National Basketball Association Draft and law school took a back seat. With only nine teams in the NBA at that time, both Vans were selected in the second round of the college draft...Dick by the New York Knicks and Tom by the Detroit Pistons. The twins were separated for the first time in their athletic careers, but that was the way they wanted it.

"When we first started out in the NBA, we knew it would be better if we each went our separate way," recounts Dick, "because we knew that on the same team we'd be fighting for the same job and it was unlikely that a team would keep two players who were the exact same size and who played pretty much the same game. We were happy to be able to prove we could each make it on our own merits.

"I didn't care much about who drafted me. I just wanted to play.

"I didn't know much about the NBA then, because the TV coverage wasn't like it is today. Going into camp, I was frightened to death, but I was determined that nobody was going to work harder than I did."

Dick did work harder than anybody and was voted to the NBA All-Rookie team that year. He settled into his role as the small forward on that Knicks club, averaging double figures in scoring three straight years, with over 30 minutes of playing time per game.

But times were changing. The NBA was in the throes of major expansion and when the Phoenix and Milwaukee franchises came into the league in 1968, the Knicks decided to leave Van Arsdale unprotected in the expansion draft. Phoenix fans would quickly learn that it was the best mistake the Knicks ever made.

THE SUNS

Phoenix was granted a National Basketball Association franchise on January 22, 1968. Less than four months later, on May 6, the NBA Expansion Draft was held to stock the new Phoenix and Milwaukee franchises with veteran players. Suns General Manager Jerry Colangelo selected first and picked Dick Van Arsdale from the roster of the New York Knicks.

Van Arsdale would prove to be exactly what Colangelo said he was at the time, "the ideal player to start an expansion team with."

As a Sun, Van Arsdale quickly emerged as a solid NBA star. In his first three years in Phoenix, Dick averaged 21 points per game and was named to the West All-Star squad three straight seasons.

It was October 18, 1968 when Van Ardale took a pass from Dick Snyder and scored a basket on the type of driving layup that became his trademark. It marked the first basket in Phoenix Suns history. Van went on to score a total of 12,060 points, an average of 17.6 PPG during his nine seasons in Phoenix. Over his 12-year NBA career, Dick tallied 15,079 points vaulting him to the 23rd position on the NBA's all-time scoring list, ahead of such NBA notables as Richie Guerin, Bill Russell, Dave DeBusschere, Jerry Lucas and Billy Cunningham.

In 1975-76, Van courageously came back from a broken wrist to play a key role in the Suns wild dash to the NBA Championship playoffs.

Prior to the 1976-77 season, the Suns made a deal to obtain the services of Tom Van Arsdale. After 11 NBA seasons, the twins were finally reunited, playing on the same team for the first time since their college days. At the conclusion of that season, Tom decided to retire from the game. After wrestling with the decision for another month, Dick also decided to step out of basketball at age 34.

Suns Coach John MacLeod had this observation of Dick Van Arsdale, "He approached his job with personal and professional pride, working as hard in practice as he played in games. You could always depend on him to give his best effort. He was an example to young players and the kind of guy who was a pleasure to coach."

THE LEGACY

For nine years his hustle and attitude were the spirit and the identity of the Phoenix Suns...through good years and bad years with the Suns, he gave his all. Now, whenever fans gather to talk basketball in Phoenix they will measure the heart...the courage... and the character of new players against Dick Van Arsdale.

Superstars came and went from the Suns...but Dick Van Arsdale remained. Superstars are good for stories, soon forgotten, but franchises are built on the backs of men like Dick Van Arsdale...

Phoenix will be forever in his debt.

THE VAN VIDEO

We took the copy from the booklet and with minor revisions created a script for a video that we would show on the Coliseum's big screen on the night we celebrated Van's retirement. Carefully weaving in still photos of Dick with some of the 16 mm footage we had on file, film editor Sonny Stires and I crafted a five-minute video tribute to the "Original Sun" which would be presented on his special night. Al McCoy did a masterful and emotional job on the narration.

I wanted Jerry Colangelo to preview the final product before we showed it to the fans at the Coliseum, so a couple of days beforehand I darkened a conference room and rolled the tape exclusively for J.C. When it was over, I flicked on the lights, turned to Jerry and said, "Well...what did you think?" Jerry didn't say a word, but when I looked a little closer, there were tears streaming down his cheeks. That's the kind of heart that beat throughout the Suns organization back then, and that's how special Van was to everyone.

A KROLL DOWN MEMORY LANE

Always looking to improve strength, stamina, conditioning, balance, coordination and communication, the Suns were constantly bringing in specialists to try new and innovative approaches. In the business world, you'd call them "consultants," but they always seem to come with their own set of eccentricities.

Bill Kroll was brought in to be the team's first strength and conditioning coach. On his first day at practice at the Phoenix Jewish Community Center, he came in and slowly walked around the basketball floor. All the while, he was holding a six-foot long, wooden staff. He didn't say anything. He just absorbed the situation. When Proski introduced him to Coach MacLeod, Johnny Mac said, "What's with the stick?"

Kroll's response was, "That's to kill the snakes!"

MacLeod glanced at Proski, then just shook his head and walked away.

Someone came up with a nickname for him and he became known as "The Human Kroll." It just seemed to fit. Regular, in-season weight training was a relatively new thing in basketball. Many Suns players, most notably Paul Westphal, thought it would hurt, not help, and refused to participate.

Kroll may have been ahead of his time. Today, virtually every team in the NBA has a regular weight training regimen for all their players.

THEY'RE KILLIN' US!

In the late 1970s, in the waning days of Larry O'Brien's reign as NBA commissioner, the league convened their annual meeting at the Hotel del Coronado in San Diego. At the opening session, O'Brien's "state of the league" speech was preceded by a specially prepared slide show.

The league had suffered through several years of drug scandals and player misbehavior. Images of headlines from major newspapers flashed across the screen, interspersed with exploded quotes that were definitely not flattering to the league or its teams. You could hear the murmuring running through the several hundred league and team executives in attendance.

"The media is killing us!" seemed to be the prevailing sentiment in the room.

But we all sat there and endured the embarrassment. Very few teams escaped the stinging criticism. After a solid five-minute, multi-media "beat-down" of the NBA, Commissioner O'Brien took the podium. He had the full attention of the now thoroughly upset coaches and GMs, not to mention the team marketing, management and PR executives. They were upset with the media and they were upset with the league office. But O'Brien would quickly point out that their anger was decidedly off-target.

"As you saw in the presentation, we have been the subject of much criticism in the news media," O'Brien began, "but I want you to know that EVERY negative comment and EVERY negative quote you saw on that screen today...were uttered by people in this room...by coaches, general managers or team executives. If we want the media to stop being negative about the NBA, then we first have to stop criticizing one another!"

O'Brien's message that day was one of unification. There was no question that there were lots of other issues the league needed to address, but to stop the bitter infighting was a great place to start. If we wanted the NBA to be better, we all had to work together to make it happen.

SOMEBODY OPEN A WINDOW

Phoenix Gazette columnist Joe Gilmartin once wrote that NBA Commissioner Larry O'Brien was "one of the great Postmaster Generals of all time." It was a reference to O'Brien's time in that post during the Lyndon Johnson Presidency. During O'Brien's years with the NBA (1975-1984), the league showed tremendous progress.

With a raspy voice that sounded like he gargled with Drano™, O'Brien would often speak of protracted negotiations with powerful people, in "smoke-filled rooms." It all sounded very dramatic but the reality was that O'Brien was usually the only one smoking.

Without a doubt, O'Brien headed many important negotiations. During his tenure: the NBA expanded from 18 to 23 teams, a rich, new television deal was struck and cable television was integrated into the media mix. Also, there were new collective bargaining agreements in 1976 and 1983.

He presided over the ABA-NBA merger, established a free agent system for veteran players and brought the three-point field goal into the NBA. O'Brien also helped negotiate the salary cap and an anti-drug agreement with the NBA Players Association. All in all, his was not a bad reign, if you discount the second-hand smoke.

FROM THE WACKO! FILE – JUST ADD VINEGAR

Dear Suns Trainer,

Sprains usually are better treated with a warm towel soaked in vinegar. Usually because it has to be healed by salt and swimming. I know it helps because I've had a lot of them. Good for sprained ankles, this is true. Takes the fever and pain out.

Thanks.

TAZ

You couldn't help but love Ronnie Lee. A solidly built 6'3" guard drafted by the Suns in the first round in 1976 as the 10th pick overall, he played the game with a reckless abandon. A tremendously gifted athlete, Lee was also drafted by the San Diego Chargers of the NFL and Portland Timbers of the North American Soccer League, as a goalie. That might help to explain the head-long, flat-out dives for loose basketballs that defined his NBA game.

Lee's defensive intensity was non-stop, causing teammate Curtis Perry to nickname him "Taz" after the Warner Brothers' cartoon character, the whippet-quick and totally vicious "Tasmanian Devil."

Yet, Ronnie had a ready smile and an enthusiasm for life that was absolutely contagious. We got a hint of where that came from when, on the Suns first trip to Boston during Ronnie's rookie season, a woman walked through the Garden crowd towards the Suns bench. She wore a big smile and a custom-made t-shirt that boldly stated "I'M RONNIE LEE'S GRANDMA!"

One night at the Coliseum, in 1977, Lee had a simply amazing game against Philadelphia. He was a one-man wrecking crew with 28 points, 15 rebounds, eight assists and a blocked shot. Afterwards, in the locker room, radio reporter H.G. Listiak asked him how it felt to have that kind of game. His response was 100% pure Ronnie Lee. He enthused, "Man, some nights you just feel like you can fly!"

THE KAMIKAZE KID

Typically, Suns players were asked to make a handful of community relations appearances every season, but it was never easy to get them to commit. Then there was Ronnie Lee. If we asked him to make a one-hour appearance at a recreation center, Ronnie would get there an hour early, spend three hours playing with the kids and then sweep up, turn off the lights and lock up the gym on his way out. He would not only make every appearance we asked him to, but then he'd come back to us and ask to do more.

Ronnie was a bundle of nervous energy and might be considered a little "quirky" by some. He was flat-footed and could only jump off of one foot. He loved to squirt gobs and gobs of ketchup on virtually everything he ate. He was also an insomniac who combined that problem with an unusual love of bowling. If Ronnie could find a late-night bowling alley that served hot dogs with lots of ketchup...man, that was heaven!

In spite of what should have been physical limitations, Ronnie nevertheless had some amazing "hops." So much so that we encouraged him to go for a spot in CBS-TV's NBA Slam Dunk Competition that was being pre-taped in arenas around the country. It was the first season following the NBA-ABA merger and the league was looking to showcase its new star power. The unheralded Lee defeated the Lakers' Kareem Abdul-Jabbar, the Pistons' M.L. Carr and the Nuggets' David Thompson before he was forced to withdraw because of a strained knee. The contest was eventually won by Darnell "Dr. Dunk" Hillman of the Indiana Pacers.

The next season the Suns marketing department came up with a unique, performance-based contest for fans to follow the exploits of the hyper-kinetic Lee. It was called *The Ronnie Lee Floor Score Contest*. Fans were asked to guess the number of times that Lee would hit the floor during the course of the season as he dove for loose balls, took charges, and otherwise wreaked havoc on opposing offenses. In 82 regular-season games, Lee hit the floor **over 300 times!**

Long-time Suns fans still cringe when they think of Ronnie Lee's bruised hips and skinned knees, not to mention his perpetually floor-burned elbows. Coming off the bench that season, Lee averaged 12.2 points and ran away with the NBA steals title with 2.7 per game, a remarkable feat for a non-starter. His physical game didn't prevent him from playing in all 82 games during the regular season.

Halfway through 1978-79 the Suns traded Lee along with Marty Byrnes and first round picks in 1979 and 1980 to the New Orleans Jazz in exchange for Truck Robinson.

VERBOTEN!

At one of the Suns' Prescott training camps in the late 1970s, *Phoenix Gazette* reporter Bob Crawford took his son Bobby fishing at one of the nearby lakes. It was a successful outing and they returned to the team motel with a nice stringer of fish. But, not wanting to stink-up their own motel room, they cleaned their fish in the sink of our motel's media hospitality suite! The residual dead fish odor lasted for several days, prompting me to create and post a sign over the hospitality room sink that announced:

> **The cleaning of fish, mollusks, crustaceans, octopods, or other sea creatures on these premises is strictly forbidden!**
>
> **–The Management**

BATHTUB BEER

During our out-of-town training camps, we would always rent an extra room to serve as a hospitality suite. We'd have the hotel replace the beds with some tables and chairs, and "bingo!" we had a place for coaches, staff and media members to gather during camp, for some informal discussions, an occasional card game and perhaps a few adult beverages.

One year in Prescott, in order to keep the beer and wine properly chilled in the hospitality room, we spread out a couple of towels on the floor of the bathtub, filled the tub with ice and chilled down several cases. Late one afternoon, one of the stat crew guys, who was just in town for the day, decided that he wanted to get cleaned up before going out to dinner. So he got the key to the press hospitality room, removed all the beer and ice from the tub, took a shower, and then put everything back in the tub! Later on that night, when I asked him if he had rented a room, he matter-of-factly told me, "Nah, I just used the shower in the hospitality room." I was simultaneously stunned and revolted.

That effectively ended the use of the media hospitality room for the remainder of camp. We gave the beer to the players.

WALTER DAVIS

GOT TO MAKE IT

When Walter Davis came to the Suns as the fifth overall pick in the 1977 NBA draft, you knew he was special. He had a textbook-perfect jump shot that was pure silk. He never wanted to come out of a game or even a practice scrimmage. His talent, effort and perspiration were all measured in buckets.

One day, after a particularly frustrating pre-season practice session, the newly-signed rookie was clearly distraught. His jump shot was off and his confidence was down when Jerry Colangelo approached him.

"Walter," J.C. said, "What's wrong?"

A totally dejected Davis responded, "If I keep playing like this...I don't think I'm gonna' make the team!"

"Walter, don't worry," Jerry soothed... thinking of Davis' multi-year, multi-million dollar, iron-clad contract.

"I can guarantee it... you're gonna' make this team!"

FORE FOR FOUR

Playing golf with Walter Davis on the back nine at Orange Tree Golf Club, we watched him slice a drive toward one of the homes surrounding the course. After a moment or two, we heard the ball clatter off some of the red roof tiles, clearly out of bounds.

"Damn! That's four!" Walter muttered.

"No. Actually Walter, when you tee it up and hit another one, with the penalty, that'll be three strokes."

"No! That's the fourth house I've hit today!"

JUST IN CASE YOU MISSED IT

The Suns and the Portland Trail Blazers, always a great Pacific Division rivalry, had faced off the night before at the Coliseum with the Suns scrapping their way to a hard-fought win. A few of the guys from the Suns organization were scheduled to play golf early the next day at one of our regular courses, Hillcrest Golf Club. Joining us was one of the Portland broadcasters, Mike Rice.

We were the first foursome going off the first tee that morning. We all loosened up a bit and gave Rice the honors. A fine athlete in his day and an excellent golfer, Mike very deliberately went into his pre-shot routine. The chatter on the tee box diminished, then hushed, as Mike waggled a couple of times addressing the ball. He took a breath and slowly drew the club head back. Just as he reached the top of his backswing, the club's PA system thundered through the cool, morning air, "JUST IN CASE YOU MISSED IT...LAST NIGHT'S FINAL SCORE WAS SUNS 109, PORTLAND 102!!! Rice, completely unnerved, lost his focus and hit the ball about ten feet as the rest of us collapsed in laughter. One of the guys in our foursome, Bill Dougall, a lifelong friend of Rice's, had made all the "special" arrangements with the club pro.

ONE WAY TICKET

During a pre-season, "team and staff only," golf outing at Orange Tree, an errant Jeff Cook tee shot nearly bonked Suns coach John MacLeod, who was playing in a foursome on the next hole.

As the ball sailed over MacLeod's head, "Cookie" exclaimed, "Uh oh! That could be a one-way ticket to Cleveland!"

A few months later, it was. Jeff was sent to Cleveland as part of a deal with the Cavaliers for James Edwards.

FROM THE WACKO! FILE – MEET MR. GADGET

Dear PHOENIX SUNS

I am an Italian boy, my name is Giuseppe Milan and I am 26. I am a collector of sport gadgets and, first of all, I am a great PHOENIX SUNS fan (I have made a fans club in Italy!). Unfortunately, in my country I can't find anything about this club. Please, help me!!!

I should be very grateful if you would send me gratuity some little gadgets and souvenirs for my collection (first of all: caps, pennants, plush mascots, sweatbands, car mini kits with club logo, pens, money boxes, etc...). Even if they belong to past seasons merchandise, I will be very grateful if you would send me all the same.

Thanks for your kind and polite availability and I hope to receive some items for my collection. Bye Bye!!

Grazie.

ORIGIN OF SPECIES

The Suns high-flying Gorilla mascot has been a special part of the Suns franchise for more than 30 years. In the fickle world of pro sports, that is true "staying power." I would love to tell you that the concept of a Gorilla mascot was the result of a carefully calculated marketing and public relations plan, based on extensive market research, focus groups, costume design and a psychological analysis by a national panel of experts. I'd love to tell you that...but I can't. The truth is...the Gorilla just showed up at our back door one night and never left.

Back in 1980 there was a local Phoenix company called Eastern Onion, which offered creative, singing telegrams. Customers had a long list of options from which to choose and subsequently embarrass their friends or relatives with the surprise singing telegram. Customers might pick a dance hall girl to sing "Happy Birthday," or they might choose a singing cowboy to belt out "Happy Anniversary." If they really wanted to be silly, they'd hire a singing gorilla to deliver, "I'm in the Mood for Love." Quite frequently, fans would hire these characters to deliver their singing telegrams at Suns games. It was a lot of fun and with hundreds of your closest friends surrounding you, the embarrassment factor was heightened. What could be better?!

Playing Eastern Onion's gorilla character was a young man named Henry Rojas. His costume included a red vest and a red cape with "Eastern Onion" embroidered across the back. He had a little wind-up monkey that also wore a red cape/vest outfit, and rhythmically clashed cymbals together as part of the act...sort of a "monkey metronome." The rubber mask Henry wore muffled his singing a bit, but maybe that was a good thing.

We always let these performers come into the Coliseum, without a ticket, because usually they just did their thing during one of the time-outs and then left to go onto their next gig. But Henry Rojas grew up in Phoenix and was a life-long Suns fan. So, if he did not have another singing "Gorilla-gram" to deliver, he'd hang around the lower level grandstands, still in costume, to sneak a peek at the game.

> **"Where did you guys get that gorilla? He was great!"**

And so it was one night when Kenny Glenn, a member of our game operations crew, suggested to the "off-duty" Gorilla that he step onto the court during a time-out to get the crowd going. When you are wearing a mask and a costume, you are simply not yourself...you are the character. So the normally shy Rojas stepped onto the court, and with the Coliseum sound system belting out some hot music, he broke out into an impromptu "gorilla jig." Waving his arms and shuffling his feet, he finished off his dance with an exaggerated bow. The fans sitting in that corner of the court loved it and they gave the gorilla a big ovation as he ran off the court.

Meanwhile, flash to the other side of the arena where "the suits," were on their feet, wondering "...who the heck is that?!...what does that guy think he's doing?!...get some security over there now!!" But we were too late. The time-out ended and the gorilla was gone!

The next day at the Suns office, we started to receive phone calls from fans who had been entertained by the Gorilla's brief, but highly animated, performance.

"Where did you guys get that gorilla? He was great!"

"That gorilla was fantastic! Is he going to be a regular thing at games?"

We quickly decided that if the fans liked him, why not bring him back? A deal was struck with Eastern Onion. Their gorilla, Rojas, would appear at all remaining Suns games that season. But as we tried to re-negotiate the deal at the end of the 1979-80 season, the discussions broke down and Henry Rojas became an unrestricted free-agent. Mind you, this was eight full years before Tom Chambers would become the NBA's first unrestricted free agent and sign with the Suns. So, who says man can't learn from the apes?!

The Suns worked out a deal with Rojas. The new character would be called "The Phoenix Suns Gorilla," which was then shortened to "The Gorilla." Those who worked with him everyday just called him "Go." It was decided that The Gorilla wouldn't speak. That would keep him out of potential trouble and besides, with the mask, you couldn't really hear him anyway. We also decided that the person inside the gorilla suit would be anonymous. His identity, like those of super-heroes, would be a closely guarded secret. This was done only to preserve the integrity of the character, not necessarily the identity of the person inside.

But first there was the matter of a costume. Eastern Onion had kept theirs, so we had to find something for Rojas to wear. Finding an appropriate furry suit didn't take too long, but full-head gorilla masks were not in bountiful supply in Phoenix. Eventually, I traveled to Hollywood to secure a full-head, rubber, "King Kong" mask from a well-stocked costume shop. They carefully packaged it and presented it to me in a hatbox! As I was flying back to Phoenix with my precious, carry-on cargo securely placed under the seat in front of me. Someone asked, "Hey, what's in the box?"

I wasn't sure that I could adequately explain why I was carrying what would no doubt look like a severed head in a fancy box. So, I just responded, "You really don't want to know."

A year later, Rojas would make his own trip to Hollywood to have a custom mask shaped and fitted by the same people who did all the masks for the movie, *Planet of the Apes.*

Not only could he dance, but Rojas also proved to be a talented comedian who excelled at parody. One of his favorite targets was Portland coach Jack Ramsay, whose personal coaching style included kneeling on a towel on the sideline, while his personal wardrobe leaned toward very loud checkered pants and bright, pastel sport coats. The Gorilla once confided to me that he did the clothes shopping for his skits at local thrift stores. I'm not sure where Ramsay got some of his outfits.

One night at the Coliseum, as the Suns took on the Blazers, the Gorilla came out about halfway through the first quarter. He was wearing an outfit that was virtually identical to coach Ramsay's... plaid trousers and a pastel blazer. Directly across from the Portland bench, the Gorilla carefully placed a folded towel on the sideline and took a knee. He then proceeded to mimic everything Ramsay did. If Ramsay stood, the Gorilla stood. If Ramsay walked down the sidelines, so did the Gorilla. If Ramsay gestured to one of the officials, so did The Gorilla. The fans and the players on the Portland bench loved it!

On another night, the Gorilla came out sporting a curly, salt-and-pepper wig, a pin-striped suit and a silk tie, perfectly mimicking Suns Coach John MacLeod. No one was safe from a Gorilla parody.

Then there was the night when the Suns were playing the Bulls and the Gorilla came onto the court wearing a red Michael Jordan Bulls jersey and with an equally red, 18-inch tongue hanging out of his mouth...a tribute to Jordan...I think.

Many of the great ideas for Gorilla skits came from the fertile mind of the Gorilla's assistant Kenny Glenn, who played the Coliseum's big SunsVision boards like a Stradivarius, bouncing back and forth between live and previously taped monkey business. Kenny reminisced about some of his favorites:

"We dressed the Gorilla up as Evel Knievel and had him ride a bicycle down a ramp and out of the Coliseum. Then we switched to previously filmed video that showed him flying through the air but splashing down into the lake just outside the Coliseum.

"Another was the Gorilla dressed as Batman, arriving at the Coliseum 'on tape' after a long drive in the Batmobile. Then the real Gorilla comes onto the court frantically looking for ... the 'Batroom.'"

OK...I guess you had to be there...but it WAS funny!

AUTHOR (R) COMPARING FUR WITH THE GORILLA

BUNGEE

When bungee-jumping was all the rage. The Gorilla walked onto the Coliseum court during one time-out, wearing a safety helmet and carrying yards and yards of bungee cord looped over one shoulder.

Our public address announcer, Stan Richards, said over the loud-speakers, "Gorilla... are you planning to bungee jump off the roof of the Coliseum?"

The Gorilla excitedly nodded his head up and down.

"I don't know, Mr. Gorilla," Richards added. "That looks like an awfully *LONG* bungee cord!"

The Gorilla shook his head, "no" and hauled what appeared to be hundreds of feet of bungee cord out of the arena. For the next 20 seconds we heard loud, amplified footsteps walking up metal stairs. Then came a cartoon-like sound effect for a falling object...b-e-e-e-e-w-w-w-w-w...BOOM!

Seconds later, a little Gorilla, squished to half-size and still wearing the helmet, staggered back into the arena and out to center court. The crowd howled!

Backstage, our game-ops guys had dressed a little six-year old kid in a full-sized Gorilla suit and bunched up the fabric in the arms, legs and torso in accordion-like fashion, to make it look like the Gorilla had been compressed by the fall. It was a near-perfect skit and another theatre-of-the-mind Gorilla classic.

FROM THE WACKO! FILE – JUST YOUR AVERAGE "WING NUT"

To whom it may concern:

This letter is in regards to the invasion of my privacy. I would appreciate any direct information leading to the explanation of this. Periodically for ten years there have been famous and non-famous strangers watching me in the privacy of my home via wireless technology. Wherever I exist in the world, these strangers stalk me and invade my privacy.

I am constantly surviving interpreting the constant malicious manipulation of my environment by these complete strangers. As I am typing this letter I am being watched by over thirty groups of hostile strangers stationed all around my apartment. For the past several years I have been stalked and my privacy has been invaded every second of every day and night by complete strangers.

People such as Tom Hanks, Bill Gates, Steven Spielberg, Kate Capshaw, Melinda Gates, Eddie Money, Axl Rose, Paul Allen, Tom Petty, Ivanna Trump, Michael Eisner, Kenny Loggins, Jamie Lee Curtis, George Lucas, some members of the Rolling Stones, The Who, The Beatles, Led Zeppelin, to name <u>very</u> <u>few</u> of the people who were and are involved, have added to this hate crime and harassment.

Despite my pleas to ask them to leave me alone, these people keep finding new people to watch me. Sometimes, some of these people gratify themselves or each other sexually while invading my privacy in all arenas in which I choose to live. There is also drug use at times by some of these people while invading my privacy. At times, these people are accompanied by escorts and or somebody's children while brutally intruding on my life.

I am greatly incapacitated by all this and the talk that surrounds such treatment of a human being. Along with the excruciating pain that is ever-present due to this unwanted intrusion of these famous and non-famous strangers, I am not employable because of the false reputation I have been handed by these brutal strangers. While sadistically invading my privacy, people from Microsoft and Warner Brothers Studios, among several other companies have told me I will know only suffering and I will never be able to live without being terrorized by the people they motivate to perpetuate this hate crime for which I am the target.

Before these famous people held charity dinners on behalf of the cause that they fabricated around my life and exploited me in every way imaginable, I had a happy, typical, affluent, conservative, respectable, middle-class life. I had no reputation as did all of my naturally selected peers. I have no idea how any famous person knows that I exist. I have never had the first thing to do with any famous person or anyone who has ever had anything to do with them or anyone they ever knew.

I have been conservatively waiting for ten years for this hate crime and intrusion to end and there is no end in sight. Someone tied to some famous person obstructs the delivery of this letter at times. So, if you receive this letter and are able to shed any light on this, please call or write. The only way I know anything about this exploitation of me is by interpreting the antagonistic manipulation of my environment by complete strangers. I am desperately seeking one human being to shed light on this in person. I look forward to hearing from you.

Sincerely,

JYAWN

ERUPTION

The 1984 USA Men's Basketball Team was coached by Indiana University's volatile coach, Bobby Knight. As he prepared his team for the Olympic Games at the end of that summer, Knight tested his team in a series of games around the country against top NBA players. His plan was designed to "toughen up" his USA squad for the Olympic competition.

Jerry Colangelo wanted one of those pre-Olympic games to be held in Phoenix. So Jerry cobbled together a team consisting of Suns players like Dennis Johnson and stars from other Western Conference teams and the game was set for the Coliseum.

Typically, Knight closed all of the USA team practices to the media, but I was lucky enough to be invited by the USA team PR guy, to watch one of their Coliseum sessions. Since CBS-TV would be televising the game, one of their producers was also invited to attend the practice. This was before the "Dream Team" so the USA team was comprised of college stars. Nevertheless, it was a very impressive group including Michael Jordan, Patrick Ewing, Wayman Tisdale, Alvin Robertson and Chris Mullin, to name just a few. The USA team was so loaded with talent that Knight had cut Charles Barkley from the squad during the early tryouts.

We watched from the first row behind the courtside press table as the talented USA team casually loosened up... at times laughing and joking. Knight however, seemed to be all business as he quietly paced the baseline, head down, brooding, yet taking in everything.

The phone rang at the press table and it was promptly answered by the USA team's PR guy, who spoke for a moment, then handed the phone to the CBS producer. The call was from some of the higher-ups in the USA Olympic Committee and the conversation could not have taken more than a minute. The producer hung up the phone and returned to sit down in the seat beside me.

Suddenly, we were confronted by an angry Bobby Knight who had moved quietly but swiftly from the baseline to our center court location. Knight leaned across the press table and proceeded to direct a red-faced, eye-popping, vein-bulging, spittle-spewing, invective-laced tirade at the CBS producer. We were in absolute shock as Knight raged, alternately wagging his finger at the producer and banging his fist loudly on the metal press table.

"I wanted to be a nice guy! I wanted to cooperate!" Knight screamed at him, punctuating each of his comments with a smack on the press table.

"You said you wanted to come to practice...and against my better judgment...I say okay!

"And what do YOU do? Do you watch practice? No!! All you do is talk on the g__ d__ telephone!!"

At that moment, Knight picked up the entire phone and slammed it down on the table in front of us. Then, he stormed off.

When my heart resumed beating and I took a deep breath, I looked toward the end of the court where the USA team had been warming up. No basketballs were bouncing, in fact not a single player was moving. They stood like statues, all starring in our direction and, like us, clearly in various stages of shock. They had just witnessed a class-A Bobby Knight eruption...probably 8.5 on the Richter scale.

If the whole thing was an act by Knight to get the undivided attention and focus of his team, it was very convincing...and effective! The 1984 USA Men's Basketball Team went on to win the Gold Medal in Los Angeles at the XXIII Olympic Games.

Just a few years later, that CBS producer unfortunately died of heart failure and, fifteen years after that, I had to have a pacemaker implanted. Were those subsequent events merely coincidence? You be the judge.

MEDIA MASTER

Because the USA team practices were closed to the media, Knight reluctantly made himself available to the press afterwards. Both local and national media assembled in the Suns press room at the Coliseum. A microphone and podium was set up in the front of the room and many of the TV and radio stations had added their own microphones to the podium.

Knight came in with a scowl on his face and took up a position behind the podium, but about three or four feet behind it, leaning up against a wall. As he did with almost all of his media sessions, Knight's demeanor and body language said clearly that this was probably the last place on earth he wanted to be. He answered a question or two brusquely and dispassionately, before one of the local TV guys, cameraman Terry Juntti, who was getting poor audio levels, asked, "Coach, could you please stand closer to the microphone?"

It was as though someone had rolled a hand grenade into the middle of the press conference. The question hung in the air and you could sense a fear in the room... a fear that the question might trigger yet another Bobby Knight explosion. Everyone wondered how many seconds it would be before he blew.

But Knight just folded his arms across his chest and made himself comfortable, continuing to lean against the pillar, still well away from the microphones. He stared directly at Terry and said very calmly, "No."

YOU DA MAN!

Kyle Macy of the Kentucky Wildcats was the Suns first round pick in 1979 (the 22nd overall pick in the draft). In high school, Macy was accorded Indiana's highest athletic honor, being named the state's "Mr. Basketball." But after playing his freshman year at Purdue, Macy would shun the Hoosier state to finish his college basketball at Kentucky, where he became consensus All-America.

In order to showcase their prized draft pick, the Suns scheduled a pre-season game against the Chicago Bulls at Rupp Arena in Lexington, Kentucky. It was a homecoming for Macy, who was absolutely revered in Kentucky for his outstanding play as a Wildcat. About 8,000 people were in attendance that night...not a bad crowd for an NBA pre-season game.

Just before the game, as the Suns gathered outside their locker room, just a few feet from the tunnel leading to the court, veteran Paul Westphal spoke earnestly to the team's top rookie, Macy.

"Kyle, this is your place. This is where you earned your reputation. Everyone who's here tonight is here to see you!"

Then, handing him a basketball, Westphal said, "We want YOU to be the guy who leads us out onto the court tonight!"

Macy was honored that his new team would respect him in this way, and with great enthusiasm, he took the ball, turned and led the charge through the tunnel, out onto the court and into the bright lights of Rupp Arena.

The Kentucky crowd cheered loudly when they saw their college hero dribbling out onto the hardwood. Macy made it all the way to center court before he turned around and realized that absolutely no one was following him. The entire Suns team was still in the tunnel, twisted into assorted contortions of laughter. His Suns teammates let Macy die out there for a good minute and a half, before joining him, still laughing, for pre-game warm-ups.

The Suns and Bulls wrapped up their game about 9:30 that night. A few hours later, at one minute past midnight, the University of Kentucky held "Midnight Madness," their first practice of the college basketball season. The attendance was a capacity crowd of 15,000.

THAT'S RICH

We all knew we would love Rich Kelley when, during his Coliseum debut, Suns fans welcomed him to Phoenix with an enthusiastic, standing ovation. It was quite unlike the reception he usually received at his previous NBA stop in New Jersey, where the fans rode him hard.

After the game, Kelley was asked about the warm reception he received from Suns fans.

Kelley said, "Give 'em time...they'll learn."

A BACHELOR'S PERSPECTIVE

In 1981, the Suns wives, players and front office staff collaborated on a cookbook called *Courtside Cuisine -- Favorite Recipes of the Phoenix Suns.* Lisa Cook and Diane Wetzel pulled the project together, with help from Ann Mulchay and Lynn Morrow. Proceeds from the sale of the book went to benefit the Arizona Foundation for Children and the project was a raging success.

Dozens upon dozens of favorite (and I can attest, very tasty) recipes from family and friends were collected from players, staff, wives and even the Suns Gorilla. But the one that got the biggest reaction from Suns fans came from seven-foot, Suns center Rich Kelley, the cerebral, Stanford-educated iconoclast, who once described his own coiffure as "Hair by Weed-Eater." Kelley offered this for the cookbook:

"For some strange reason, most people have an image of me as the classic disheveled bachelor, running around at a frantic pace and leaving the home and the kitchen in a sloppy mess. Actually, I'm a very neat and fastidious person who stays at home all the time and loves to cook. My kitchen is spotless and well-appointed so these favorite recipes that I'm sharing with you might be too difficult for some beginner cooks.

Breakfast: The first meal of the day is the most important so I take extra care with breakfast. Enjoy this meal one morning!

Gulp down a large glass of orange juice and mix in the 27 vitamins suggested by our trainer.

Wolf down a bowl of TRIX.

Swallow a banana in two bites and rush out the door so as to avoid a tardy slip at practice.

Lunch: After straggling home from a hard day on the hardwood, I like to dig into something of substance – like a classic Dagwood special!

Toast two pieces of whole wheat bread.

Slice up tomatoes, Monterey jack cheese, and dill pickles.

Stack on bologna, liverwurst (that's right, liverwurst!) pastrami, etc.

Pile on condiments. Don't forget plenty of mayonnaise.

Toss the whole thing into the microwave for a minute or two.

Wash the meal down with a tall glass of milk.

Dinner: There is nothing like a romantic dinner with candles flickering and jazz whispering to win a lady's heart. Try this recipe sometime.

Slip into the back door of *Avanti Restaurante* and pick up a to-go order of fettuccini.

Once you get home, make sure you serve the meal on your own fine china and not in the Styrofoam container.

Don't worry about the wine. Beer is just as good and it's cheaper.

Good luck!"

NEW TECHNOLOGY

As a Stanford graduate, Rich Kelley always embraced new technology. In the early 1980s, "hi-tech" included telephone answering machines. When you called Kelley, you almost hoped he wouldn't answer the phone so you could hear his latest telephone message creation.

One of my favorites featured a woman's voice (or was it a high-pitched Kelley?) who spoke over a lovely piano melody..."Hi there, neighbor, this is Richie's mother talkin.' I'm sorry, Richie can't come to the phone right now. He's practicing the piano and then he's going to Little League practice, and then he has to come home and do his homework. Me and the mister, we're raising him pretty strict, ya know. My, he's grown up like a bean-pole, hasn't he? Well, I'll be seeing ya!"

NOT EXACTLY THE BATMOBILE

Mention "Old Hulk" to Rich Kelley and a smile will spread across his face. "Old Hulk" was a mildewed 1967 Plymouth Sport Fury convertible with 180,000 miles on it. The only thing that worked on the car was the heater, and sometimes, one of the windows. It was a curse of a car that seemed to follow him everywhere. Kelley often referred to it as the "Eighth Wonder of the World."

Suffice it to say, it was a unique set of wheels, as Kelley once described:

"It's the same convertible that I drove all through high school and college. My two brothers and their friends borrowed it and converted it into a low-riding van with a new paint job. Then they took out all the seats except for the driver's seat. All they left were mattresses. It was pretty obnoxious. They drove it around the country for three months a few summers ago and ruined the interior some more.

"My brother Bruce took it out to Princeton his senior year and it floated around for three semesters. Then, lo and behold, he left it there in New Jersey over the summer. Next thing I know I am traded to the Nets and Old Hulk is sitting there waiting patiently for me. I drove it around for a few months before I got a regular car."

One of his old Nets teammates, Eddie Jordan, remembered "Old Hulk" well.

"His car, man, Rich Kelley's car, oh man!" Jordan said. "I once rode in it. I got in it and at first I thought it was pretty funny, but I'm lying there next to Rich. Rich is driving the thing, we're talking and I'm too low to even look out the window. Suddenly I realized that I had no idea where I was. I mean, I knew I was in the car, but I had no idea where Rich was taking it. When we got to where we were going, I had to reach up to open the door and then I had to roll out.

"Kelley's crazy, but it is the best kind of crazy."

PAY ATTENTION

Lyn Steingard, didn't really like basketball all that much but she was the wife of the Suns team physician, Dr. Paul Steingard, who absolutely loved the game, loved the Suns, attended every game and sat in the front row. During one Suns home game, Lyn was idly gazing around the Coliseum, not at all into the game. With the game action to her left, she was actually gazing up into the stands to her right when Dr. Paul noticed and chastised her, "Lyn, they're playing down at THAT end!"

"Don't worry," she said, "they'll be back!"

OK TO LOOK

The Suns were about to take on the New Jersey Nets in a game at the Coliseum. It was early and I was standing in the tunnel where players would move back and forth from the locker rooms to the basketball floor. On the court were just a few players from each team, getting in some early shooting practice. One of our young, attractive, female employees was standing near the Suns bench marshalling a group of youngsters for some pre-game activity.

Two of the Nets players had finished their shooting and were walking off the court. One of them elbowed the other in the ribs and nodded in the direction of the Suns bench and the young lady. As they walked past me, the pokee said, "Whatchu lookin' at that for, man? I thought you told me you were married?!"

The other player just shook his head and responded, "I said I was married...I didn't say I was dead!"

WHISKEY ROW

For many years the Suns held their pre-season training camp at Yavapai College in Prescott, AZ. The camps were generally held during the first week in October. After a summer of brutal Phoenix heat, we'd always look forward to the cool, fall weather that was waiting for us in the high country. There were a couple of other camp traditions we also enjoyed. One was the occasional evening on Prescott's famous "Whiskey Row," and the other was the celebration of John MacLeod's birthday, which for some inexplicable reason, always seemed to fall on October 3rd.

One night, we combined the traditions. To celebrate Johnny Mac's birthday, we secured a private, upstairs room at the famous Palace Saloon. The fact that our space had once been used as the waiting room for a frontier-days bordello made it even more interesting...historically speaking, of course.

After a few libations, we heard a twinkling "fanfare" being played on a piano, but it seemed to be coming from across the hall. Suddenly the big double doors to our room flew open and here comes Al McCoy, playing "Happy Birthday" on an upright piano, with two guys wheeling in the piano and a third guy pushing McCoy on a rolling piano stool. Even as the piano moved across the floor, McCoy didn't miss a note as the coaches, trainers and staff all sang "Happy Birthday" to the coach.

BREAK OUT

It was the last night of the Suns 1986 training camp in Prescott. The following morning, after a light workout, the Suns would bus back to the Valley of the Sun. The grind of the regular season was just a few weeks away, but this was a night for the team to enjoy dinner out and maybe have some fun along Prescott's aforementioned Whiskey Row.

Nick Vanos was a 7'2" center from Santa Clara who played only 11 games in his rookie year. In his second Suns training camp however, he was beginning to show some maturity and real signs of progress in his development as an NBA player. Nick was a very nice kid, perhaps a bit shy, but a guy who was serious about his opportunity.

So forgive me if I was a little surprised when a bunch of us walked into a rollicking Palace Saloon that night to see Nick Vanos and several teammates up on stage rockin' with the house band! Nick was singing and playing the tallest air-guitar I have ever seen. It was a break-out night for Nick, who had enjoyed a good camp and would go on to be a regular contributor as a back-up center for the Suns during the 1986-87 season.

Tragically, less than a year later, Vanos was killed when a Northwest Airlines plane crashed upon takeoff in Detroit.

THE ORIGINAL CENTER

I started my career with the Suns in 1973, when the franchise was just five years old. Even though I had only limited exposure to the Suns during those first five seasons, it was pretty easy to play "catch-up" and become a resource regarding the team's early history. In doing so, I quickly developed relationships with a number of the players and coaches from those formative years. Dick Van Arsdale, for example, was still a key player in the Suns attack. Jimmy Fox and Dick Snyder would retire as players and settle in Phoenix.

Jerry Colangelo valued, and always respected, the players who wore the purple and orange, especially those who helped him put the franchise on the map in the formative years. By 1985, Colangelo decided the time had come for a major Suns reunion. We scoured the country and invited every former Suns player we could find to join us in Phoenix for a special weekend.

During that weekend, I had the honor, and the distinct pleasure of playing golf with George Wilson, the original Suns center. Although we had not met previously, my introduction to George Wilson was an educational, cultural and social experience. I remembered him from his college days on those great Cincinnati teams that won NCAA Basketball Championships in 1961 and 1962. He was also a member of the gold-medal- winning U.S.A. team at the 1964 Tokyo Olympics.

As we got ready to tee off at the Orange Tree Golf Club in Scottsdale, I watched George slather himself with a very high SPF sunscreen. I couldn't help myself and said to him, "George, do you really need to be doing that? Hasn't anybody ever told you that you're black?"

George laughed and, realizing that I obviously knew little about things "African-American," took pity on me. He patiently explained that, in spite of being a man of color, he was still extremely sensitive to the sun. If he did not "SPF-up" he would suffer from sun poisoning and break out in a rash. I apologized for being so culturally flippant.

> **"You're the PR man. Do you know the PR song?"**
> **- George Wilson**

Later on, he also explained to me why many black men cannot shave their beards with a razor in the manner TV ads depict. Instead, once a week or so, they would use the depilatory powder that you usually see on the bottom shelf at the drugstore under "shaving aids." Once properly foamed up, they would "shave" or scrape off their beard growth with a dull knife, or even a credit card, but never with a razor blade. I didn't know. Thank you, George! You are, and always have been a gentleman and a class act.

Later on that day George asked me, "You're the PR man. Do you know the PR song?"

"The PR song?" I responded. "I've never heard it. How does it go?"

He launched into a little ditty that went like this: (hint – to catch the rhythm, read lines three and four quickly)

The P.R. man,

The P.R. man,

He can make ya',

He can break ya',

He's the P.R. man!

IN THE PRESS ROOM

Due to deadline problems and the physical impossibility of being everywhere at once, writers covering NBA games often will bang out their stories in the arena press room and depend on the home team's PR staff to provide game statistics, a play-by-play chronology and quotes from the locker rooms. Frequently the PR staff utilizes journalism students from local colleges and universities as interns to collect the locker room quotes. We didn't need in-depth interviews. We just wanted the intern to pick up a quote or two from each coach and a player from each team as they were questioned by the assembled media. The intern would take notes and then bring them back to the media work area for transcription and distribution.

We were at the Coliseum and the Suns had just defeated the Lakers in a hard-fought playoff game. Our team of interns fanned out to collect quotes from the locker rooms as I waited at a typewriter to do the transcribing. As they returned, they would read their notes out loud and I would type what they had collected. This night, the process was taking longer than usual and I was getting a little impatient. Finally, the intern who had been dispatched to the Lakers' locker room returned.

"What do you have from (Lakers coach Paul) Westhead?" I asked.

The intern checked his notes. "He said, 'Winners smile, losers say dill!'"

"What?!"

"Winners smile, losers say dill!" the intern repeated.

"What? Are you saying 'dill' like in pickle?" I asked.

"That's what he said," came the response.

"I don't get it," I said "but if you're sure that's what he said... okay!"

"I'm sure."

And that's what went out on the quote sheet.

The next morning, I'm in the Suns office discussing the game with Suns statistician Barry Ringel and our chat gets around to the quote sheet.

"I still don't understand what this 'dill' thing is all about," I said. "I'm guessing that it's some sort of cliché, but I've never heard it before."

Just then, remembering our occasional Friday night poker outings, it hit us both simultaneously. What Westhead said was: "Winners smile, losers say DEAL!"

Of course!

It was DEAL, like in cards...not DILL, like in pickle!

We started laughing so uncontrollably about the misinterpretation that I barely heard the phone ring. When I finally answered it, I was almost gasping for breath. On the other end of the phone was Terry Day, a writer from the *Lompoc Journal* in California. Terry followed the career of Mike Bratz and would call occasionally for updates. I tried to get serious about his call, but I couldn't. Terry asked me what was so funny and I made the mistake of trying to explain it all to him.

The more I got into the story, the funnier it seemed to me. Finally, alternately sobbing and snorting with laughter, I had to put the phone down and try to regain my composure. The upshot of this laugh-fest was that Terry Day became a truly great friend, who, every year for the next 20 years, would send me a case of homemade pickles from his hometown of Chico, California. He called the pickles "Chico Gold" and they were awesome! Terry once told me that we held the Guinness Record for the world's "longest running pickle joke!" I never had a reason to doubt him.

WELCOME GUESTS

On his way to the main court for pre-game warm-ups, Suns star Paul Westphal once stopped by the Suns press room to say hello to one of his old writer buddies from his Boston Celtic days. As he walked in he saw all of the out-of-town scribes hunkered down over their free press room meals. It would not be a stretch to describe them as "at the trough." Westphal just shook his head and said in a voice loud enough for everyone to hear, "There they are...America's guests!"

No one even looked up.

ROOF LEAKS

The Arizona Veterans Memorial Coliseum was built in 1964 at a cost of $7.1 million. It had a distinctive "saddle" design and a suspended concrete ceiling that, in spite of being an engineering marvel of the time, would become a recurring nightmare for the Suns and for every Coliseum director for the next 40 years.

When the building was a year old, long before the Suns came to be, a giant 25-foot tall birthday candle was placed on the Coliseum roof. Why, you ask? Hey! Phoenix was a very small town back then. They were really proud of this gul-durn, bran' spankin' new Coliseum, and by golly, they were gonna' have a big ol' birthday party! So they put the candle on the roof, which negated any warranty, resulted in some roof damage and began a steady drip, drip, drip from the ceiling any time it rained.

❝There were over 600 patches on the Coliseum roof! ❞

The situation was exacerbated when they painted a big "smiley face" on the roof and then a few years later, painted that over with the USA bi-centennial logo. The different colors in the logos would expand, contract and ultimately crack at different rates. At one point it was estimated that there were over 600 patches on the Coliseum roof!

Contrary to popular opinion, it really does rain in Arizona. And when it does, it usually comes in hard, fast and relentlessly. On October 6, 1974, the Suns had to cancel a pre-season game with the Portland Trail Blazers due to extensive leaks. The game would have been the Arizona debut of the Blazers top draft pick, Bill Walton.

On March 1, 1978, the Coliseum roof leaked again during a game with the Pistons. It took a small army of men, working in the ceiling, to catch the drips and a larger detachment of ball boys, on the floor, to mop up what was missed. The Pistons "slipped" out of town with a win. Because of the recent collapse of an arena in Hartford, there was a lot of media coverage that week about the overall structural safety of the Coliseum and the potential dangers of this leaking roof.

Less than a week later, on March 5, during the second half of a nationally televised game vs. the Philadelphia 76ers, one of the soggy ceiling panels worked itself loose and began to fall. With the game going on at full-tilt, Suns marketing guy, Harvey Shank, happened to be looking up just as the ceiling panel broke loose. Sitting right behind the press table, Harvey leaped to his feet, pointed skyward and screamed, "LOOK OUT!!!"

The rest of us didn't know if it was just one panel coming down, the scoreboard cables had snapped, or the whole building was about to collapse! Fortunately, the 4'x6' panel that broke free was so light that it fluttered to the floor like a piece of paper gently drifting in the wind. It probably took five seconds for that panel to make the 60-foot trip from ceiling to floor. No one was hurt, but that day Harvey sure scared the living daylights out of a lot of people, including me! The game resumed without further incident, although it didn't do much for the image of the Suns or the Coliseum.

Arizona Republic writer Dave Hicks once described the Coliseum as "a West McDowell structure with a $400,000 scoreboard and a $40 roof."

GOING BALKAN

Jerry Colangelo was always willing to look at new ideas to make the Suns a better team. He first looked to Europe for talent before many NBA executives knew where Europe was located. In the fall of 1979, Colangelo brought in a prospect named Duje Kristilovich (Doo-jay Chris-til-o-vitch), whom Suns coach John MacLeod quickly dubbed "Dewey." He was from Split, Yugoslavia, stood about 6'8," weighed 210 pounds, and was a mainstay on the Yugoslavian national team.

He was rated among the top 15 players in Europe in 1979, averaging 20 points and 12 rebounds per game. The Suns gave him a long look during a week of informal workouts and even took him to training camp. But like many European players of that era, he was very mechanical and did not always appear comfortable in the up-tempo flow of the NBA game.

Ultimately, the Suns released him and he returned to Yugoslavia. If the Suns had kept him, he would have been the first European player to land a spot on an NBA roster. It was a worthwhile experiment but both Duje and Jerry were just a little ahead of their time. A few years later, Colangelo would go back to the Balkans for another prospect, Georgi Glouchkov.

THE BALKAN BANGER

In the seventh round of the 1985 draft Colangelo rolled the dice and picked a 6'8" power player from the Bulgarian National Team, Georgi Glouchkov (pronounced: your-ghee gloosh-koff). It was a bit of a gamble because the Suns were not sure they could even get Glouchkov out of Bulgaria, much less onto an NBA roster. Eventually, just as the NBA season was getting underway, Colangelo traveled to Sofia, Bulgaria to negotiate a deal with the Bulgarian Basketball Federation. After numerous negotiating sessions, with multiple toasts of "Nostrovia," punctuated with shots of vodka, Glouchkov became a member of the Suns.

> **"We were getting a lot of pressure from the local Bulgarian community!"**
> — Jerry Colangelo

From a PR perspective, Glouchkov was a legitimate story. He was the first player from behind the Iron Curtain to sign with an NBA team. He was an experienced international player and he played well in the Suns pre-season games. In one tilt against the Lakers and Kareem Abdul-Jabbar, Georgi had 18 points and seven rebounds in just 20 minutes of playing time. Colangelo needed to see if there was more where that came from and if Georgi could compete at the NBA level for an entire season.

But, from the beginning, we all knew this was a long-shot and we wanted to have fun with it. During the press conference to introduce Glouchkov, Colangelo was asked why he would go all the way to Bulgaria to find a prospect when there were plenty of good players here in the United States. Jerry smiled and quipped that "we were getting a lot of pressure from the local Bulgarian community!"

Imagine our surprise, the following day, when we started getting calls and we found out that there actually was a Bulgarian community in Phoenix... and it numbered in the thousands! They were ecstatic!

For the press conference we prepared a media kit which not only included Georgi's Bulgarian basketball statistics, background and credentials, but also a map of the Balkan Peninsula and a timeline of the history of Bulgaria, including its time under the flag of the Ottoman Empire. Also included was a primer of basketball terms, translated from English to Bulgarian. After going through the press information, Norm Frauenheim, Suns beat writer for *The Arizona Republic*, asked me if I included the map because I suspected that media people thought Bulgaria was located somewhere between Vermont and Connecticut.

Once Glouchkov had officially joined the team, we were off on an early season road trip with stops in cities that were important media hubs; specifically, Boston, New York and Atlanta. In Boston and Atlanta we didn't have days off so we held informal media opportunities for Glouchkov at courtside, a couple of hours before those games tipped-off.

In New York however, we had a day off before we played the Knicks, so we hosted a media gathering at our team hotel. At that press conference, it came out that Georgi's teammates, including prankster Rick Robey, were trying to help him with his English. When a New York reporter asked what Robey had taught him recently, Georgi proudly responded, "Today, I learn the difference between 'chick' and 'chicken!'"

Prior to the game against the Knicks, I had the opportunity to meet a New York sports icon, and a boyhood hero of mine, Madison Square Garden's public address announcer, John Condon. The title "public address announcer" is simply too industrial, too pedestrian to describe the consummate gentleman who was John Condon. With his clear, crisp and classy delivery, he was the voice of Madison Square Garden for decades and its most important ambassador.

As the Suns PR guy I had to confer with John to let him know just exactly how to pronounce, "Georgi Glouchkov." John was gracious and professional as he practiced the name a few times and asked me if he got it correctly. About mid-way through the first quarter, Georgi came into the game. Condon absolutely nailed the pronunciation, then he leaned back and looked down press row at me and gave me a nod and a "thumbs up" in thanks. For a kid like me, who grew up in New York and went to many games at the Garden, it was a very special moment.

One day, a CBS reporter came to a Suns practice to interview Georgi, but he quickly gave up after a long, one-sided conversation where he talked and Georgi just nodded. At the end, the reporter looked at Georgi and said, "You have absolutely no Idea what I'm talking about, do you?"

At that moment, Georgi perked up and responded, "Thanks to meet you!"

Georgi's contract was an agreement between the Suns and the Bulgarian Basketball Federation, which proved to be an unworkable arrangement. The deal was structured so that the Suns would first pay the Bulgarian Federation, which would then send Georgi an "allowance." Those wheels turned slowly, if at all, so the Suns adjusted things and took out a "living wage" for Georgi before transferring funds to the Bulgarians.

CALL ME BO

Another aspect of the relationship, was the presence of an official from the Bulgarian Basketball Federation who travelled everywhere with the team, sat on the bench during games and served as an interpreter between Glouchkov and Coach MacLeod. His name was Bozidhar Takev. "Bo," as he quickly became known, had a longtime involvement with the Bulgarian Federation as a coach and an official. He was in his 70's, spoke English proficiently and had wonderful stories going back to his days as a student in Europe during World War II. There was little doubt that he was enjoying this new assignment.

Once, on a Suns road trip, a group of us were walking through a hotel lobby on our way to dinner and there was Bo, sitting in a big leather chair, watching the world go by, contentedly puffing on a fine cigar and sipping a Wild Turkey on the rocks. No doubt, he was thinking, "I wonder what they're doing tonight in Sofia, Bulgaria?"

All we could say was, "Bo is goin' good!"

I have to give John MacLeod a lot of credit. He started learning basketball terms in Bulgarian so he could better communicate with Glouchkov on the court, since the more-often-used translation relay system from MacLeod to Bo to Georgi, then back to Bo and then to MacLeod, just wasn't working. How could it? By the time MacLeod got across what he wanted to say to Georgi, the play was over.

In a minor historical broadcasting footnote, Glouchkov became the first guest on Al McCoy's post-game show to require an interpreter.

Georgi wasn't overjoyed about the arrangement with Bo Takev because there was such a huge difference in their ages. It was kind of like palling around with a caretaker-grandfather. Enter 25 year-old Ruman Kosankoff of the local Bulgarian community. We arranged for him to help Georgi with his English, be a friend to whom Georgi could relate, and keep him out of trouble. Well, two out of three isn't bad! The two seemed to evolve into a real-life version of those "wild and crazy guys" from the old *Saturday Night Live* skit.

Georgi really took to America and especially Phoenix. Those who had the experience of driving around town with Georgi often described it as a cross between the Bob Bondurant School of High Performance Driving and a pedal-to-the-metal version of Mr. Toad's Wild Ride.

You could also say that Glouchkov's diet was like any normal American kid. He loved Whoppers™, Big Macs™ and Almond Joy™ candy candy bars. Though we never actually saw him slip an Almond Joy into a Big Mac, we wondered. When he ordered a soft drink, it was always simply, "Coke, no ice."

The following year, Georgi put aside the candy and junk food and, as Suns Trainer Joe Proski described, went on a "nuts and berries" diet. He lost over 25 pounds, going from a strapping 242-pound strongman to a skinny, 215-pound forward who could no longer hold his ground in the paint.

Proski also thought that the lack of availability of "Vitamin S" in the United States might have had something to do with Georgi's dramatic weight change. Since he was no longer playing or training behind the Iron Curtain, steroids were no longer easy to get.

According to Proski, one of Georgi's more peculiar habits was to put tons of baby powder in his shoes before each game. Proski remembered one game when Glouchkov went up for a rebound, came down hard and a big cloud of white powder shot out of his shoes. People in the stands went crazy.

When he realized that the Glouchkov experiment was going up in a puff of smoke (or perhaps it was a puff of baby powder), Colangelo used his contacts overseas and "traded" Glouchkov and the Bulgarian contract to a team in Italy. The move didn't garner much attention from the local media, but I believe that it should go down as a tribute to Colangelo's creative genius when it came to player personnel. To trade Georgi and his costly Bulgarian contract to a team that wasn't even in the NBA, was, in my opinion, a brilliant move.

"Nostrovia!"

BIRD

When we were on our East Coast Georgi Tour, one of the stops was Boston Garden. Because the team did not have a full day in Boston, we planned to have an informal, courtside media opportunity with Georgi, a couple of hours before the game. At about 3:30 in the afternoon, Georgi, Bo Takev and I took a cab from our hotel over to Boston Garden. Game time was 7 p.m. and our courtside media opportunity was scheduled for 5 p.m. We arrived at the Garden a little before 4 p.m. Georgi went into the locker room to get taped and dressed and I decided to just wait for him courtside.

One of the Celtics had come early and was shooting while one of the Celtic ball boys rebounded. The player was Larry Bird. He shot for close to an hour from every conceivable angle and he didn't miss many. During that time, no other player from either team showed up for any type of early shooting practice. I fully appreciated the fact that Bird was an NBA star who earned his super-stardom the old-fashioned way... he worked at it!

GOOD SPORT

As the Suns PR man I helped facilitate a story in *Sport* magazine featuring our own Truck Robinson and Elvin Hayes, Truck's former teammate with the Washington Bullets. "Hate" is such a strong word, so let's just say there was a really healthy rivalry between these two players. The writer followed each of them around for a few days before the Suns and Bullets met in a regular season game in Phoenix.

When the issue hit the newsstands a few weeks later, the story itself seemed reasonably well-balanced between the two rivals, but all the photos and the cover shot, featured the "Big E." Truck was furious.

A few weeks later, the local *Sport* magazine rep showed up at a game to present a special, commemorative, leather-bound copy of that issue to Truck, prior to tip-off at a Suns home game. Luckily for the rep I didn't let that happen.

When I brought the request to Truck, he suggested, in no uncertain terms, that I tell the guy to take his copy of *Sport* magazine, leather-bound and all, and use it as a suppository, right there at center court. Although Truck didn't use those words exactly, I got the message.

What I told the rep was something like, "You know, Truck doesn't want to do the presentation tonight because he wants to focus on the game, but he wants you to know how much he appreciates the gift." When the rep pressed me to perhaps have his photo taken with Truck after the game, I simply said, "That's probably not a good idea."

Sometimes the best presentations are the ones you don't make, although that one might have had some real entertainment value. I think I still have that leather bound edition of *Sport* magazine somewhere in my office.

SCHOOL NIGHT

The owner of the Cleveland Cavaliers was dating a very young lady. It had been circulating around the NBA that she was also very attractive. I happened to be on the trip when the Suns visited

Cleveland, so naturally I asked my PR counterpart with the Cavs if the owner's "babe" was going to be at the game that night. He hesitated for a moment... "H-m-m-m. What's tonight? Tuesday? N-a-a-a...she's got to stay home and do her homework!"

NO LUCK

On a night at the Coliseum, during the 1977-78 season when the Boston Celtics' John Havlicek was making his final appearance in Phoenix as an active player, Suns assistant coach Al Bianchi was a little leery.

"I don't like these farewell appearances," he said. "This reminds me of when I was with Syracuse and we played Boston at Bob Cousy's farewell. I knew we were in trouble during the pre-game ceremonies when I looked over at the refs and there were tears in their eyes."

Bianchi proved prophetic, the Celtics won 98-95.

And who said that the NBA doesn't have a sense of humor? Later that same season, the league gave the Suns another "Mission Impossible"... beat the Celtics in Boston on St. Patrick's Day. Oh, and just to make it a little more challenging, the league assigned a ref named Jake O'Donnell to lead the officiating crew. The Suns couldn't overcome the luck of the Irish and fell 115-108.

FEARLESS FOG

Then there was the day that the Sonics were fogged in at Seattle and could not get to Phoenix for a game because, according to Lenny Wilkens, coach of the Sonics, they "couldn't find a plane."

As the Suns PR director, I was asked by the media for a response to the situation and I just couldn't resist. I said that I thought "it was ironic that in Seattle, the city where they build airplanes...the Sonics couldn't find one." Wilkens was not amused. The game was rescheduled.

HANG TIME FOR WESTPHAL

Paul Westphal was an integral part of that magical "Sunderella" season of 1975-76. Five times he was an NBA All-Star, four of those appearances as a member of the Suns. Following five years with the Suns, Westphal signed with the Sonics for a few seasons before coming back to "re-up" with the Suns for the 1983-84 season. But following that year, he wound up suing the Suns over a performance clause in his contract.

The question was posed by the media if the Suns would be retiring Westphal's #44. With the lawsuit still pending, a Suns team official responded "Yes. Without a doubt, there will come a day when we will hoist Westphal's jersey to the Coliseum rafters...but right now, we'd like to do it with him still in it!"

OK. I confess. The team official, identified in news reports at the time only as "a press table wag," was me. I just couldn't help myself. Sorry, Westy.

About five years later, Paul Westphal was inducted into the Suns Ring of Honor in a halftime ceremony on April 15, 1989 and I had the honor of orchestrating the event. Paul signed a commemorative poster for me that night. It says, "Tom, thanks for making this necessary! Paul ."

FEELING GUILTY

Ultimately, Westphal would become a Suns assistant coach under Cotton Fitzsimmons and then succeed Cotton as the Suns head coach in 1992. During his days as an assistant, Westy was a guest on the show, *SportsLook*. When asked by host Roy Firestone why he stopped wearing contact lenses as an NBA player, Westphal responded, "I saw too many open men and had to pass them the ball."

PAUL WESTPHAL

THREADS

There are a few exceptions, but NBA PR guys and sportswriters are generally not known as snappy dressers. Don't get me wrong, writers and PR guys are hard working, dedicated professionals, but many of them don't fuss over clothes much. At league meetings, it was not surprising to see a hodge-podge of styles from the '70s, '80s and '90s... sometimes worn by the same person simultaneously.

One guy walked in late to an NBA PR directors' meeting wearing a particularly loud, plaid sport coat, totally uncoordinated with a patterned double knit shirt and vertically stripped trousers. Seeing this shocking vision of sartorial splendor, Wayne Witt of the Spurs leaned over and whispered to me, "Somewhere in this town... there's a cold quarter-horse!"

IT'S ALL RELATIVE

It was during December of 1973 and the struggling Suns were taking on the Boston Celtics. Traditionally, the holiday season was good for attendance at the 12,600 seat Coliseum. Harvey Shank and I were standing near the press table as the doors opened and fans started to file in, when I asked him what he thought the gate would be that night.

"Oh, we're going to have a great crowd tonight!" he said.

"How many?" I asked.

"It's gonna' be big," Harv said proudly, "seven or eight thousand!"

Harvey nailed it...7,362. That defined "big" in those days. Too bad more people didn't come that night. The game was sensational, with Charlie Scott leading a furious fourth quarter Suns comeback, hitting the winning basket at the buzzer for a 121-120 Suns win.

In future years at the America West Arena/US Airways Center, arena capacity was over 19,000 and the Suns would run off a consecutive sellout string of 153 games. That sellout streak started on March 3, 2006 and ended on November 1, 2009.

WILL THAT SUFFICE?

On another night, referee Manny Sokol was working a game at the Coliseum between the Suns and the Celtics. Sokol was a showman who clearly enjoyed his work and he often interacted with fans. That night, as was his style, the Celtics' Dave Cowens was literally man-handling Suns center Alvan Adams...holding, hugging and hacking. But few whistles were blown. The rotund Sokol was struggling to keep up with NBA athletes who were at least 15 years younger. As the teams raced upcourt, long-time Suns fan Bill Howard shouted from his seat directly behind the press table, "For cryin' out loud Manny, will you please watch Cowens holding?!"

Running at full tilt and without breaking stride, Sokol looked directly at Howard, nodded and with a somewhat crazed look on his face, said, "OK!"

On the very next Suns possession, Cowens bear-hugged Adams once more and Sokol finally blew his whistle. Sokol walked slowly toward the press table, focused on the official scorer and announced the call in his typical, demonstrative style.

"Numba one six...hold!" he said, loudly slapping his right hand against his left forearm.

Sokol then looked directly at Howard sitting in the seats and asked, "OK?"

Howard laughed and shouted back, "Thanks, Manny!"

JOHNNY MAC'S STREAK

John MacLeod was named Suns head coach in June of 1973. It was just a few months later, in October, that I joined the Suns as their director of public relations. We would both hold those same positions with the Suns franchise for the next 14 years. It was a professional and very friendly relationship. John was as straightforward as they came, so you always knew where you stood with him...something I really appreciated.

During those years, the Suns established a reputation for excellence and consistency both on and off the basketball court.

John MacLeod remains one of the most principled and disciplined people I have ever met. His 14 years at the helm make him the Suns coach of longest tenure by far. His 579 regular season wins are the most of any Suns coach in the 40-plus years of Suns history. It will be a long while before another Suns coach approaches that level of success.

One year, Coach MacLeod, an avid runner, set a formidable goal for himself. He decided that he would get in a run every day for an entire year. I'm sure there are lots of runners who can stick to a regimen like that, but I doubt that any of them are NBA coaches. The travel, the time changes, jet lag, games and practice schedules, not to mention the winter weather, all would conspire against such an ambitious goal.

But John MacLeod was nothing, if not determined and disciplined. Through blizzards in Denver, rain in Seattle, fog in Portland, wind in New York, sleet in Chicago and heat in Phoenix, he ran... day after day...week after week...month after month. The writers who covered the team began to take notice, although for MacLeod it was strictly a personal goal and he shunned any publicity about his quest. He hit his 365th straight day...then 366. Then, with his mission accomplished, he deliberately skipped a day.

When I asked him why he didn't just keep the streak going, John responded simply, "I don't need that kind of pressure!"

FROM THE WACKO! FILE – REALLY? ARE YOU NUTS?

KIDS COMMUNITY CLUB
Phoenix, AZ

Dear Mr. Ambrose,

...We as a country are faced with the same issues that have plagued us for years: crime, gang violence, teen pregnancy, drug abuse, dysfunctional homes and broken marriages to name a few. You now have an opportunity to equip our upcoming generation with the encouragement, discipline, training and help they will need to make our city a better place to live.

Tom, this is our advertising fundraising proposal to you. Early next year a billboard and media blitz campaign will sweep our city. We are taking 8 young people and strapping them to a 14 x 48 ft. billboard located at one of Phoenix's busiest intersections, right in the public's eye (actual location to be announced). These young people will remain strapped to the billboard for a period of two weeks or until our target amount is raised! We are out to get the public's attention and involve them in making a difference in the lives of children.

We are asking each of our partners to assist us with $3,000 to cover the initial cost of this event. This is your opportunity to participate in a city-wide event that will change the way America looks at crime. Don't let it pass you by!

The investment request in minimal, but will assist us in getting our mission accomplished, not to mention the exposure and recognition your organization stands to gain.

Sincerely,

KCC

DIVERSIONARY TACTIC

During the 1984-85 season the Suns were whacked hard by injuries. In fact, the Suns missed a total of 266 player/games due to injury or illness. Rick Robey missed 78, Walter Davis 59, Mike Sanders 58, Larry Nance 21 and Kyle Macy 17 to name just a few front-line players. Every player on the Suns active roster started at least one game during that tumultuous season, creating a total of 26 different starting lineups.

Even though they finished with a 36-46 regular season record, the Suns still qualified for the eighth and final spot in the Western Conference playoffs. Phoenix would face the top-seeded Los Angeles Lakers, whose 62 wins that season was the second best record in the NBA. This was when first round playoff series were a best-of-five, but the Suns had absolutely no shot at an upset. There was simply nothing we could do. Our best players were not able to play and the Lakers were healthy and in the prime of their "Showtime" heyday.

So, to make the case that the Suns had suffered through a miserable, injury-plagued season, I created a playoff press guide, whose cover resembled a Band-Aid ™ box, complete with a red cross. The media had a great time with the concept and I think they were generally sympathetic to our plight. Interestingly, during that series, I think I was interviewed about the press guide cover more than many of our players were interviewed about the series. As expected, the Suns were swept by the Lakers 3-0 in the series, by an average of 20 points per game!

JUST GET IT DONE

One night, the Suns were hosting the Boston Celtics, traditionally, one of the bigger home dates of the season at the Coliseum. As PR director, I have to make sure that the visiting media were well taken care of… notes, stats, food, workspace and most importantly, press table seating. The Celtics had a huge media entourage and had requested four seats for their television broadcast team, four seats for their radio broadcast team and four seats for their travelling writers. Of course, all of them wanted courtside seating. Problem was, I only had eight seats at the courtside press table. Obviously, somebody had to be "repositioned."

Fortunately, the Suns had an auxiliary press box at center court, about 16 rows from the floor. It was a great vantage point with plenty of seats for the overflow. I made the decision to put the Boston radio crew up there, much to the consternation of their legendary broadcaster Johnny Most, who ripped me up one side and down the other about being moved to this new, and in his mind, less desirable position. I seem to recall a reference to me as "a dollar-an-hour executive," but hey, that's why I got the big bucks! And by the way, who told him about my raise?

Nevertheless, here we were about two hours before the game. The set-up crew had already done their job of installing the phone lines and they'd gone home. The radio lines were set at the courtside table, so now I had to figure out how to move those lines 16 rows up. Surreptitiously working with an unnamed accomplice from the Coliseum staff, we gained access to a Coliseum storage room to secure the proper type of cable and a roll of… what else…duct tape. By this time, I had shed my sport coat and tie… this was turning into something that resembled real work.

We spliced the cable at the courtside location and I began running the line between the seats and up the stands to the upper press box, duct-taping everything down to keep fans from tripping over the cable and to keep the Boston radio broadcast on the air for the next few hours. After a frantic 30 minutes of work, it was done and I retreated to the press room to get myself cleaned up. As luck would have it, I ran into my team photographer and friend, Joey Beninato, who had been watching me pull off this minor miracle.

"Hey Tom, I just want to tell you that I was standing in the east staging area when you were working up in the seats and Jerry Colangelo walked up."

"Really?!" I beamed.

"Yeah!" he related, "Jerry said, 'Look at that Tom Ambrose. Something needs to be done and he just rolls up his sleeves and goes to work. The only thing that matters to him is getting the job done. That's the kind of guy I want working for me! That's a great effort!'"

"He really said that?"

"Na-a-a-h...Jerry never said anything. I just made that up!"

My pal, Joey.

JUS BAD

Kenny Glenn first started with the Suns as a 15 year-old ball-boy, assisting Harvey Shank with game night promotions. After a few years he moved into the Suns front office as an administrative assistant, taking care of just about everything that needed attention. His ride was a customized, 1972 Ford Maverick with two, 650 four-barrel Holley carburetors sticking out of the hood. It was a "street rod" featuring a Corvette yellow paint job with three stripes down the side and a personalized Arizona license plate that read "JUS BAD." It was every bit of that.

> **❝Jerry was going for a ride in JUS BAD. 〞**

One of Jerry Colangelo's cars had been in the shop, but was ready to be picked up. J.C. asked Kenny to give him a ride to the repair shop so he could reclaim his car. Instantly word flashed through the office that Jerry was going for a ride in "JUS BAD." As Colangelo and Glenn walked to the parking lot, every other Suns employee raced to my office window to catch a glimpse of the scene unfolding in the parking lot.

As Jerry stood by, Glenn backed "JUS BAD" out of its parking spot and into the middle of the lot. Colangelo opened the door and then, very carefully and deliberately folded his 6'3" frame into the tiny passenger's seat, which was laid back to about a 45 degree angle. To keep his hot rod running, Kenny was constantly revving the engine...B-R-R-U-U-U-M-M...B-R-R-U-U-U-M-M...B-R-R-U-U-U-M-M! Inside the office, we could not only hear it... we could feel it!

With the whole Suns office crew looking out my window, an almost reclined Colangelo, sat up, turned his head and glanced through the passenger's side window towards us. His expression reflected concern, perhaps even a hint of fear...a sort of "what have I gotten myself into?" look. It was at that precise moment that Kenny popped the spring-loaded clutch and "JUS BAD" screeched forward, the instant acceleration slamming Jerry's head back against the headrest. "JUS BAD" roared off in a cloud of dust, exhaust and squealing tires. In an instant, they were gone! But for those of us who witnessed Jerry's haunting look, it was an image that will last a lifetime!

JUS BAD

DOING PR

As the Suns front-line PR director for the first 17 years of my career, I thought that the essence of my job was to make it as easy as possible for the media to do theirs. But there was much more.

Within an NBA franchise, the PR person has a unique position, with many masters. An effective NBA PR director walks a virtual tightrope, balancing relationships with players, coaches, upper management and the media. Each group must know that they can depend on you...that they can trust you. But each of those groups can have vastly different agendas and mind-sets. Betray a confidence and your job just became much more difficult. On top of that, you have to work with the franchise's other departments, in addition to cooperating and coordinating with other NBA teams and the league office. Toss in interaction with the public, lots of writing and public speaking, as well as spot duty as the team's "official" spokesperson (usually just for bad news) and you have the basic NBA PR job profile.

In spite of the inherent stress of the job, it's always nice when somebody recognizes your efforts. That's why this note from the Lakers' legendary broadcaster Chick Hearn was extra special to me.

By the way, it was Chick Hearn who nicknamed the Arizona Veterans Memorial Coliseum the "Madhouse on McDowell." He was more than impressed by the volume and enthusiasm of Suns fans during the 1970 playoff series against the Lakers.

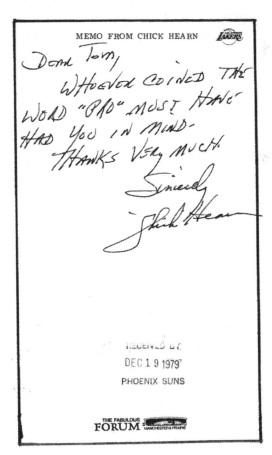

NO MUSCLES

In the late 1980s, Kheni White, a former team rep for Nike, joined the Suns public relations staff. Kheni was a fun-loving guy with a great personality and was a self-styled master of the malapropism. "K-dub" counted many Suns players as friends. Kheni was also an enthusiastic body-builder who fancied himself "the black Arnold Schwarzenegger." To promote the sport, he really pushed to have his body-building group put on a demonstration at half-time of a Suns game. I was not super-excited about it, but I said OK as long as it did not interfere with his game-night duties. I also knew that we'd make little progress on any PR projects until we put Kheni's exhibition behind us.

The big night finally arrived and, as the halftime intermission began, game ops rolled out some small risers to center court and the body-building show got underway. I was almost too embarrassed to watch. But once in a while, I did take a peek at the close-up, live coverage on the big screens in the Coliseum. Once, I looked up and there was Kheni, his skin completely greased down and glistening with some kind of oil. He had so much oil on him that I wanted to throw him into a big ol' frying pan... or maybe hit him over the head with it! He was flexing mightily and wearing only a skimpy, black Speedo ™. This was my assistant PR guy! On the Coliseum's big screen, Kheni's grimacing face was about 12 feet high!

Kheni's friends on the team were dying to see him in the exhibition, but they knew they'd be in the locker room until the show was over. So they designated Bernard Thompson, a Suns guard who was on the injured list, to watch the show and report back to them. I was standing near the locker room when the team emerged from their halftime meeting just as Thompson headed toward them with his eye-witness account.

One of the Suns players said, "B'nar, B'nar...wad he look like?"

Thompson shook his head in abject disappointment, "Shi-i-i... man. He ain't got no muscles, man! He ain't got no muscles!"

KHENI WHITE (L) AND TOM AMBROSE

SUDDEN IMPACT

As The Gorilla neared the end of a typically raucous appearance at a Phoenix elementary school, he wanted to give the kids an extra thrill. "Go" decided to make a dramatic exit by running towards the back of the auditorium stage and diving out of sight under the big velvet curtain. Unfortunately, his exit would be more dramatic than he thought because there was a solid brick wall just a few feet behind the curtain.

The sliding Gorilla flew under the curtain at full speed, hit the wall head first, and knocked himself loopy. He was bleeding profusely from a scalp wound, but inside the sweaty gorilla mask and costume, he couldn't feel a thing. Once he got outside, climbed into the Gorilla-mobile and took off his mask, he then realized that he was completely drenched in his own blood. "Go's" assistant, Kenny Glenn, took him to a nearby hospital emergency room for stitches and a noggin-check. They took X-rays of his head, but found nothing.

> **❝He was completely drenched in his own blood. ❞**

RESTRICTED AREA

When Steve Kerr was a rookie guard with the Suns, he was running late for a team flight. He parked his car in an airport lot at Sky Harbor but he was still far from the entrance gate where he needed to be. So he decided to save some time and take a shortcut by hopping a fence and cutting through a restricted area at the airport. He was immediately detained by airport security personnel.

It was a rookie move that The Gorilla spoofed in a skit at the Suns next home game. Wearing a blond wig, Kerr's warm-up jersey and carrying a suitcase, the Gorilla hopped a barricade set up at center court and was immediately apprehended by a platoon of Coliseum security guards and led off the court in handcuffs.

"I can't believe you guys did that to me," said a now doubly embarrassed Kerr.

Actually, Kerr was lucky that all this took place before 9/11/2001... otherwise he might have been shot!

THREE SECONDS

The Suns and Lakers were at the Coliseum, embroiled in one of the many battles in their long-standing, and often heated, rivalry. This was the Lakers' "Showtime" edition, featuring Magic and Kareem. Suns fans were frustrated that night, even more than usual, because it seemed that the officials were allowing the 7'2" Abdul-Jabbar to constantly spend more time in the three-second lane than the rules allow.

After a quarter and a half of watching Abdul-Jabbar operate freely and, for extended periods of time, directly in front of the Lakers' basket, the Gorilla had seen enough. At the next time-out, "G" came out wearing overalls and a construction hard-hat. He erected a fence around the Lakers' free-throw lane. Then he left the court momentarily and returned with a big stand-up sign from the Coliseum lot that said, "NO PARKING." He slammed it down in the middle of the lane and the crowd went nuts! Just then, the horn sounded, ending the time-out. The hard-hatted Gorilla picked up his lunch pail and walked off the court. It was another "G-rated" classic.

WATCHERS

If you think that NBA players don't pay attention to what's going on inside the arena during time-outs, consider this story.

It was another high stakes Lakers-Suns match-up at the Coliseum. The Suns were in the midst of a huge, come-from-way-behind rally late in the game, when the Lakers called a timeout to blunt the Suns momentum. It was a perfect time for the Gorilla to keep the roll going and keep Suns fans excited with his hot-footed, center-court dance to the up-tempo, hard-fiddlin' country classic, *Boilin' Cabbage*. Suns fans lapped it up and the Coliseum was absolutely rockin'.

But, L.A. mounted a late counter-surge and eked out a close win. As the jubilant Lakers headed toward their locker room, a disappointed Suns Gorilla was slowly shuffling towards his nearby dressing room. Lakers center, Kareem Abdul-Jabbar ran over to him, grabbed the Gorilla by the front of his warm-up jacket, slammed him up against a wall and screamed in his face, "DANCE NOW! M_____ F_____! DANCE NOW!"

Nice guy. Apparently, Abdul-Jabbar had somehow been offended by the Gorilla's dance performance... or maybe country music just makes him crazy.

Someday, I'd love to see Kareem on *Dancing with the Stars*, but only if he has to dance to *Boilin' Cabbage*.

INTERPRETATION

NBA legend has it that Wes Unseld was so wide that it was a five dollar cab ride just to get around him. There was no question he had a commanding presence on an NBA floor. When Unseld's Washington Bullets were visiting Phoenix one night, Suns Coach John MacLeod decided that the best way to combat this 6'6," 285-pound force of nature was to foul him every time he got the ball in the low post and let him earn his points from the free-throw line...certainly a time-tested NBA strategy.

> **❝Unseld was doing a slow burn. ❞**

For the Suns that night, things went even better than planned. The Bullets would dump the ball down to Unseld on the low block and an array of Suns centers led by Dennis Awtrey would then dutifully hack, grab and hold the Washington big man. Only problem was the refs seemed to be taking the night off. So, as the first quarter unfolded, with foul after uncalled foul, Unseld was doing a slow burn.

Finally a time-out was taken and Unseld angrily stormed toward the Bullets' bench. He was just three steps away from it when he whirled and headed directly for lead referee, Earl Strom, who was standing right in front of me at the press table at center court. Strom, sensing Unseld's displeasure, held up his hand and warned, "Don't come near me, Wes!"

Unseld stopped suddenly, his demeanor changed, and he said in a calm, measured voice, "I'm the team captain. I want an interpretation!"

Strom waved him forward.

It took Unseld just a couple of steps to reach Strom and then he wasted no time, putting his nose in Strom's face, poking his finger near Strom's chest and saying, "I just want to know…what is your interpretation of a FOUL?!"

In the NBA, a figure of lesser stature than Unseld would have been ejected immediately, and then fined heavily the following day, but instead, Strom just laughed and said, "Get outta here!" and waved him back to his bench.

But Unseld had made his point with a little humor and Strom heard him.

But wait! There's more!

Years later, I was attending one of the NBA annual meetings. Unseld had retired as an active player and was working for Washington in their Community Relations Department. I walked into an NBA Community Relations meeting and found the man, the legend, Wes Unseld, sitting by himself, waiting for the meeting to start. I sat down next to him, introduced myself and told Wes that he is the subject of probably my favorite NBA story.

"Really?" he said. "Tell me about it."

So I proudly repeated the tale. Over the years I've had lots of practice telling and re-telling this story, so I thought I did a pretty good job of expressing it to him. But after I was done, Wes looked at me sympathetically and deadpanned, "I'm sorry. I just don't remember that."

"A-w-w-w Wes, you're killin' me, man!"

It was a crushing blow, to this self-styled raconteur, that Wes wouldn't cop to the story. But I think he used that ploy so often with referees that he couldn't remember who, where or when. However, I stand by my recollection, which unfolded three feet in front of me at the press table that night.

LISTENING DEVICE

When *Republic* columnist Dave Hicks was previewing the 1978 NBA Draft, he revealed one of my heretofore best-kept secrets. Our team physician, Dr. Paul Steingard had given me a stethoscope, intended strictly for the stealthy purpose of eavesdropping on Jerry Colangelo's adjacent office. An inveterate fan, Dr. Steingard just HAD to have the "inside scoop" on all Suns trades and drafts.

Because of the stethoscope, in his preview, Hicks referred to me as "Thomas Ambrose, D.P. (Doctor of Publicity)" and observed that I was afflicted by the dreaded disease of "terminal curiosity."

But truthfully, the diaphragm on doc's old stethoscope was cracked and broken so it didn't really work as designed. I kept it hanging on my office door strictly for "show." It made for great stories… or in Hick's case, an excellent pre-draft column.

My greatest fear was that Hicks might one day expose my deception by announcing it through the quasi-government information agency which his fertile mind once created. He called it the "Department of Public Enlightenment," otherwise known as "D.O.P.E."

FROM THE WACKO! FILE – BEWARE OF HUMAN MUTANTS

DEAR SIR:

LAST YEAR HUMAN MUTANTS CAME INTO OUR NATION AND KILLED OVER FOUR THOUSAND PEOPLE.

AMERICA NEEDS TO BE A LEADER IN STOPPING ALL VIOLENCE AND ABUSE, ESPECIALLY TO HER OWN CITIZENS. ONCE UPON A TIME MEDIA PRAISED THE ACCOMPLISHMENTS AND TALENT OF WHITNEY HOUSTON AND NOW THEY ARE KILLING HER NAME TO THE PUBLIC. A TRUE AMERICAN NEEDS HELP AND MEDIA IS BOASTING ABOUT HER SHAME.

WHAT IS IT? DOES AMERICA ONLY GIVE PRAISE WHEN THEY CAN MAKE MONEY OFF A NAME AND WHEN THAT PERSON FALLS, THEY TRASH THEIR EXISTENCE IN LIFE?

PLEASE PRINT THE ATTACHED LETTER AND HELP OUR NATION TO LEARN HOW TO BE HEALERS OF EACH OTHER AND NOT MURDERERS WITH VERBAL ABUSE.

REGARDS,

WH

LONG SHOT

Today, the NBA Draft is just two rounds. With 30 teams in the league, that's 60 draftees and the entire draft takes about four hours. That's only because of the requisite TV commercials. Until 1984 however, the draft was a marathon of 10 rounds and a true test of patience. In the late rounds it was not unusual for somewhat punchy team GM's to draft college athletes who may have never played college basketball, take a shot at foreign players whose names no one could pronounce, or perhaps waste a pick honoring their own newborn children. Usually, it was a time for silliness.

That's one of the reasons why, in 1977, the New Orleans Jazz selected Lusia "Lucy" Harris of Delta State, in the 7th round. The Jazz weren't really planning to sign Lucy, they just were just showing a little respect for one of the country's best female players. Lucy could play, but the Jazz pick was more of a public relations maneuver than a basketball move.

Most folks would say that anyone selected at that point or later in the draft wouldn't have a snowball's chance in hell of making an NBA roster. But just two picks after Lucy Harris was "off the board," the Suns picked a 6'7"stringbean of a player named Alvin Scott from Oral Roberts University (7th round, 137th overall pick).

Scott, affectionately known as "Bone" to his friends and teammates, would not only make the Suns roster as a rookie, but would go on to enjoy an eight-year career in the NBA, all with Phoenix. Every year, it seemed like the pre-season prognosticators would label Scott "the man on the bubble," but he would consistently beat the odds. Alvin Scott was among the longest of long shots and a great NBA success story. He still resides in Phoenix and is a valued employee of Southwest Gas.

DAWN PATROL

Teams often hold their pre-season training camps in places outside of the team's normal routine. The idea is to eliminate "distractions" and have the team focus on basketball, while building team unity and camaraderie. At least that's what management has in mind... players sometimes focus elsewhere.

Prescott, Arizona is an easy, one and a half hour drive from Phoenix and the early autumn weather is about 20 degrees cooler. That made it an ideal site for training camp and the Suns trained there for a decade. During one of those years, after a few days at camp, I had to return to Phoenix for an early morning meeting. Not wanting to hit the heavy rush hour traffic in Phoenix, I decided to leave Prescott about 5:30 a.m.

As I started out, there weren't many cars on the road, so traffic going in the opposite direction was noticeable. After I saw a couple of big Mercedes sedans flash by, no doubt headed for Prescott, I began to think... "H-m-m-m, that car looked familiar... I wonder if that was..." Just then, a big, white Rolls Royce blasted up the hill toward Prescott and I realized that a bunch of our players were commuting back-and-forth from Phoenix to training camp on a daily basis! Let's just call it "dawn patrol." Most of our veteran players had fairly distinctive cars that were pretty easy to spot. And my guess was that workers in the Prescott area didn't usually drive to their early shift in a Mercedes or a Rolls Royce.

BELIEVE

❝You are guilty until proven innocent. ❞

There comes a time during lives and careers when circumstances force you to ask yourself, "What do you stand for?" I suppose that, after a while, even a job in pro sports loses a little bit of its luster. It is not quite as glittery as perhaps you thought it would be and there are always ups and downs, as in any other profession. But you build relationships with players, coaches and your co-workers. And you're proud of the good things that your franchise has accomplished both on and off the court. So when all that you know and respect comes under attack, it is only natural to react...to become protective... to defend what you believe. The so-called Suns drug scandal in 1987 was such a time for me.

I firmly believed that the Suns were a well-run and ethical organization. I believed that Jerry Colangelo and John MacLeod were highly-principled, moral men. I believed that if there was a problem, we would do everything in our collective power to correct it and take sincere measures to insure that the problem would never be repeated and I was willing to fight to defend that. Before the controversy erupted, I loved my PR job. And so, after the organization came under attack from police, local prosecutors and the media's investigative reporters, I was "all in"...fully committed, not only to my job, but to the Suns organization.

It was a stressful time. I remember walking out my front door to pick up the morning paper with a sick feeling in the pit of my stomach, because I was the PR guy and I had no idea what sort of attack on the Suns I would discover in that morning's edition. I quickly found that when a scandal breaks all the great relationships that you have spent years developing with national and local sports media people go out the window. In fact, those guys won't, or aren't allowed, to even talk to you. Instead, here come the "investigative reporters" who are very clear in their mission...you are guilty until proven innocent. And if you are eventually proven to be innocent, well, that won't matter much because they'll be long gone and on to investigate the next supposed scandal!

WALTER

It all started one morning in early December, 1985 when Walter Davis missed a team flight from San Francisico to Los Angeles. The night before, Walter was nothing short of sensational, scoring a career high 43 points, on 17-27 FG and 9-10 FT shooting. He drilled 29 points in the second half, to key a 123-113 Suns win at Golden State. When the team finally tracked him down, late the following morning, Walter was disconsolate and claimed that he thought he had a drug and alcohol problem.

Never a good thing in anyone's life, but an admission of drug dependency by an NBA player has a specific mode of treatment and there are very specific procedures to follow, as outlined in the league's Collective Bargaining Agreement (CBA). Consequently, Walter immediately went into a drug treatment facility for 30 days of counseling and detoxification.

In the real world, employee assistance programs involving drug abuse are confidential. Employees who come forward voluntarily get the help they need and hopefully return to their jobs as productive citizens. But in a business like professional basketball,

Walter Davis could not enjoy any anonymity about his situation. This was the biggest story to hit Phoenix in years. Following his month-long rehab session, Davis returned to the team to finish a prolific season on the basketball floor.

At that time however, the Maricopa County attorney's office was looking for high profile prosecutions to send a message to local drug dealers and users that they were "tough on drugs" and that they would go after anybody. Who, or what, could have a higher local profile than the Phoenix Suns? It seemed as if the county attorney's rationale was, "H-m-m-m, if Walter Davis admitted that he used drugs, he must've gotten drugs from somewhere... his friends? ...his teammates? ...the front office? We'd better look at everybody!" A grand jury was convened and multiple investigations were launched or expanded. Confidence in employee assistance programs and their foundation of confidentiality were clearly shaken.

WHOSE SCANDAL?

A year later, on Friday, April 17th, the day before the final game of the season, county attorney Tom Collins and Phoenix Police Chief Ruben Ortega called a news conference to announce that, as a result of their investigations and testimony before a grand jury, five current or former Suns players had been indicted for drug related offenses and that six other present or former Suns players were linked to the case. So voluminous was the paperwork for the indictments that the County Attorney's office wheeled them into the news conference in shopping carts, much to the delight of the assembled media photographers, whose camera whirred and flashed like the paparazzi. It was a feeding frenzy.

Condemnation of the Suns by the news media was immediate, overwhelming and devastating to the franchise. But, just a few days after the indictments were handed down, the entire transcript of the grand jury hearings and testimony was leaked to the press.

The transcripts were published in local papers and they revealed that the county attorney's entire case was built on a web of rumors, gossip, hearsay and innuendo. Public perception and sentiment quickly shifted from "drug scandal" to "witch hunt."

HOWARD COSELL

In the *New York Post*, lawyer-turned-sportscaster-commentator Howard Cosell, wrote a definitive column about the Suns "drug scandal." He was outraged at how the investigation and grand jury testimony was conducted by local prosecutors. He also chastised the Arizona media for its complicit role in their contempt for constitutional protections of grand jury deliberations. Cosell felt that these two groups had totally misplayed their roles and called for a deep introspection of their duties as law-enforcement officials and champions of the people's right to know.

❝Such testimony is always full of rumor, hearsay, and unsubstantiated charges. ❞

Cosell's objections focused on the fact the entire transcript of the grand jury testimony had been leaked to the media. Local newspapers wasted little time in publishing huge segments of the documents which, by law, are intended to be secret.

He pointed out that such testimony is always full of rumor, hearsay, and unsubstantiated charges. It is the jury's job, Cosell pointed out, to sift through everything, determine the truth and then indict, or not, depending on the evidence. In this case, Cosell felt that hard, factual, evidence was virtually non-existent.

We quickly reprinted Cosell's column and distributed it to all of our season-ticket-holders and key stake-holders. It was one of several independent opinions from outside Phoenix that we used to help turn the tide of public opinion in favor of the Suns.

SUPPORT OUR SUNS

I believe that because the Suns franchise had always tried to be exemplary citizens in the community and because the Suns gave back and consistently helped local non-profit organizations, when these troubling times hit the franchise, fans rallied to our support. As the Suns got ready for their final home game of that disastrous season, a meaningless contest against the L.A. Clippers, a Suns fan named Jeff Goldsmith formed an organization called S.O.S. – Support Our Suns. By whatever means he could, he reached out to Suns fans.

Goldsmith wrote:

Dear fellow Suns fans,

We are certain that most of you are angry, disappointed, and perhaps even disgusted about the latest revelations and the indictments of the accused Suns players, and to some extent we share those feelings with you. And while our initial reaction may have been to condemn and criticize, we have decided instead to offer them our support. There are too many fine people in the Suns organization who have already been hurt by the "guilt by association" syndrome. Enough damage has already been done, and we would like to help make tonight the first night on the road to recovery, rather than a continuation of their downfall.

The issue here is much more than the future of a few people and basketball players. The reputation of this city and our future economic growth is at stake right now. The entire nation is watching us tonight. If we abandon this team and ignore the 19 fine years they have given us, we will be sending the wrong signal to the rest of the country. Professional football and baseball may bypass and avoid the "Valley of the Sun" if we show ourselves to be "fair weather fans" who abandon their team when the chips are down.

Our friends are in trouble and they need our help. If and when the accused are found guilty (by a judge and jury rather than by the media), then they will deserve whatever punishment and criticism that comes to them. We do not and cannot condone or defend them for what they may have done. But in this country, the words "innocent until proven guilty" are supposed to mean something. We must support these players and this organization and stand behind them in their time of need. Tonight we are sending out an S.O.S. for the Suns organization. When you see the signs, Support Our Suns, stand up and let them know that you still care. Don't let your emotions cause you to abandon a friend in his/their time of need. Let the court system decide who is innocent or guilty and let basketball fans continue to support their team.

Sincerely,

Jeff Goldsmith and the
founding members of the
Support Our Suns Organization
April 18, 1987

That night, 10,578 very supportive fans were in attendance to watch an inspired Suns team defeat the Clippers 121-106. It was time to begin rebuilding a team and its image.

OVERBLOWN

Many felt that the Suns big "drug scandal" turned out to be more of a scandal of over-reaching local politicians and an over-stimulated media. At the beginning, there were dozens of indictments and thousands of pages of grand jury testimony.

In the end, however, there were no drugs confiscated; all drug tests administered to those involved, proved negative; there were no trials; not one player served a single day in jail, and, I might add, there were no apologies offered to the Suns by the media or by the county attorney's office.

THE REBUILDING BEGINS

Jerry Colangelo offered the media what would be prophetic words on that dark Friday in April, "We will not let this setback prevent this franchise from achieving, once again, the respect of its fans and followers, here and throughout the country. This is my commitment."

The organization went to work to rebuild the team and the trust of the community. Our existing season ticket holders were the first and most important group to reach. In a normal year, the Suns had a

90% renewal rate. In spite of the drug controversy, a less than stellar record and a future filled with question marks, the franchise was able to achieve a renewal rate of 87% after that tumultuous off-season.

Through newsletters and correspondence, we made sure that all of our key stakeholders had all the information they needed. Each season ticket holder received a video, narrated by Gary Bender, outlining the many positive accomplishments of the Suns franchise during its first 19 seasons and how we always remained committed to Phoenix. After a year of rumors, accusations and innuendo, I believe Suns fans appreciated an honest and direct approach from the organization, as well as Jerry Colangelo's commitment that the Suns would rise once again to be worthy of their respect and support.

FIT TO PRINT

As Walter went through his 30-day stint in rehab, the Suns organization, per NBA guidelines, was not allowed to have any contact with him. This frustrated Jerry Colangelo who wanted to reach out to help Walter in his time of need. The following year, Walter "relapsed" and *The New York Times* invited Jerry to write a column about his view of the Suns situation and the NBA's drug policy.

Jerry and I sat down to talk about it. He told me how he felt and I laid down the words. Although the NBA wasn't super happy with everything we had to say, *The Times* ran the piece verbatim. Many of the things that Jerry suggested for improvement of the NBA's drug policy were later adopted by the league through the collective bargaining process with the NBA Players' Association.

ROOM SERVICE

The press room is a great place to sit and absorb stories from visiting writers and broadcasters. It was there that I once heard a story about a first-round pick of the Clippers, in the mid-1980s, who was on his first road trip with his new team. A day or two after their first game, the Clippers' accounting department received a bill from the hotel for over $800 for "Room Service" ... the room that was registered to their prized rookie.

The team trainer was immediately dispatched to try to find out just exactly how the player had run up such a monumental bill in just one short night at that hotel. Management's thinking was, "That must have been one heck of a party!"

It turned out that when the rookie was checking out of his room, he opened up the mini-bar and with one big hand, swept everything into his gym bag. He thought it was a free service of the hotel! Or so he said.

CONFESSIONS OF A FORMER BALL BOY

A young man, who was once a Suns ball boy, was recently at the arena visiting with some of his old acquaintances. The subject of souvenirs and sports memorabilia came up and the young man sighed and said, "Yeah, I once had a pair of Kareem Abdul-Jabbar's basketball shoes when I was a ball boy, but I don't have them anymore."

We asked him what happened, since those shoes would have been valuable collectors' items.

"Well," he lamented. "I tried to autograph them but I spelled his name wrong, so I had to give them away."

Upon further interrogation, we discovered that he had spelled "Kareem" ... C-R-E-A-M.

Needless to say, before you purchase any type of sports memorabilia, make sure it is properly authenticated from a reliable source. And just in case, check the spelling.

ONLY ONE RULE

On February 26, 1987, with their record a dismal 22-34, the Suns fired John MacLeod, their coach for nearly 14 seasons.

The Original Sun, Dick Van Arsdale, was picked by Colangelo to move from the Suns broadcast booth and take over as interim head coach. It was a tough situation to walk into, but Van had played 12 years in the league and knew the game well. At the end of his first morning practice following the coaching change,

Van called all the players and coaches to center court. I was standing nearby, but out of earshot of what was, no doubt, an impassioned speech by Van Arsdale to his new team.

The building was hushed as Van made his points. Suddenly, there was a raucous explosion of laughter from the team, the meeting ended, and the players headed for the locker room, still laughing. As Van walked off the floor, I asked him what he had said to get that kind of reaction. His response was an NBA classic.

"I told them that I had only one rule on this team... and one rule only," Van told me, "NO FARTING ON THE BUS!!"

Van would lead the Suns to a 14-12 record over the season's final 26 games, but I can't confirm that the team always complied with the Van Arsdale Rule... or that they could consistently pass the "sniff test."

FROM THE WACKO! FILE – HUH? SAY WHAT!?

ELectronic Laboratory murdered people-sport
FLorence Griffith-Joyner-Thammara Shaikh-Yetunde
Price-Sierra Wright-Adam Petty-Conrad Mc Rae-Bison Dele
Becky Zerlentes-Craig Kelly-Robert Benson-Kenny Irwin
Kim Grallagher-John Lorton-Ben BLucknett-Cecil Dow
dy-Stephan Johnson-James Grogan USA-11-09-2001r USA
Fabrizio Meoni-Denis Zanette-Gianluca Signorini-Gaetano
Scirei-Marco Pantani-Simone BLanchetti-Antonio Maspes-
Vicenzo Polli-Giovanni Falcone Italy ALessio Galletti
Owen Hart-Greg Moore Canada-Zelijko Raznatovic Serbia
ALois Lipburger-Ulrike Maier-Ronald Ratzenberger Austria
Waldemaras Martinkenas Litwa-Yesso Uffo Samiou Benin
Sandra Schmitt-Dieter Lindemann-Stefan Hass-Rasa Schuls-
kyte-Germany-Andreas Escobar-Carlos Meza Kolumbia
Son Pele Edinho people-Ayrton Senna-Edvaldo ALves De Santa
Rosa-Edvaldo Izidio Neto Vava-Macir Barbosa-LibreLato
Bruno-Cleonicio das Santos Silva-Paulo Sergio de Oliveira
Silva Brazil-Whayne Wilson Kostaryka-Yvon Des Rochers
Marc-Vivien Foe Kamerun-Godiva Kuffoura Ghana
Sergiej ZoLtak Lotwa-Nili Natkho Israel-Paulo Pinto Portugal
Gonzalo Rodriguez Urugwaj-Einar Oern Birgisson IsLandia
Werner ELmer-Pascale Mathivet-Daniel Loetscher SwitzerLand
Mikael Ljungberg Sweden-Peter Cargill Jamajka-Otilino Tenorio-
Ekwador-Juha Tioinen-Timo Hayma Finland-ALem Techale Etiopia
Peter Dubovsky SLowacja-Arthur Lydiard-Possum Bourne NewZeLand
Hayel Belgium 1985r Liverpool FC-Juventus Turyn 39 murdered
Walery Lobanowski-Witalij Nesin Ukraine-Micham Zerouali Morocco
Jose Luis Martinez-Belby Marco Caneiry-Jesus Gil y Gil-Ramon
Moreno Grosso-Saul Morales-Jose Cano Lopez-Ladislao Kubala
Jose Jimenez-Salvador Farrando Spain-Brat Kachy KoLadze
Georgia-Omar Enrique Sivori-Jose Lois Cuciuffo Argentina
Tomas Vojtech-Emil Zatopek-Zuzana Krejcowa-Iwan HLinka Czech Rep
Anita Kulcsar-Miklos Feher-Laszlo Papp-Daniel Molnar Hungary
Rinus Michels-Michel Zanoli-Wim Jeremiase-Gerrie Knetean-Guus
Smit-King Fanów Feyenoord Rotterdam Holland-Jose Perez Spain
Regine Cavagnoud-Fabrice Salanson-Bruno Cauvy-Bill Fofana-
Richard Sainct-Gerard Bortage France-Jurij Morozow-Wiktor
KoLotow-Anatolij Firsow-Irmantas Stumbrys-Anatolij Ustiugow
Sergiej Bodrow-Walery Brumel-Aleksander Goliew-Lew Jaszyn Russia
Antonio ALexe-Cristi Neamtu-Catalin Haldan-Gelu Dascalu Romania
Representation of Zambia football team was murdered by them 2001r
Holly Wells-Jessika Chapman-Brian Clough-Norman Steng-Joey Dunlop
Emlyn Hughes-Jimmy Davis-Christopher Loftus-Kevin Speight England
Martin Sanchez Meksyk-7-07-2005r London England-Sharron Tate USA
President Sudan-Jair da Rosa Pinto Brazil-Ibrahim Ferrer Cuba
King Fagda Arabia Saudyjska-Minister Robin Cook England

TURN ON THE LIGHTS

There are 21 Native American tribes in the state of Arizona, covering 25% of the state's land and representing over 250,000 people. On the reservations basketball is nearly a religion. During the annual Arizona state high school basketball playoffs, games that feature teams from the reservations are usually the most hotly contested and, technically, they are among the best-played. Although they generally lack size, teams from the reservations play a solid brand of team basketball, and they play it well.

In the late 1980's, the Suns had a contract with the Dallas Mavericks to host a pre-season game. Instead of playing the game in Phoenix, Jerry Colangelo wanted to take the game to northern Arizona where many Suns fans, including the huge Native American population, rarely had the opportunity to see their team in person.

With the Suns training camp already scheduled for Northern Arizona University in Flagstaff, bringing a pre-season game to the nearby Hopi reservation, and its great NBA fans, would be a positive move for the Suns and a great opportunity for some national publicity.

In late spring, Bob Machen and I hired a small plane and a regular-sized pilot and made the one-hour flight up to the tiny airport at Polacca, AZ, to check out the facilities and the arrangements for the game. In case you've forgotten, Polacca is located between the villages of Chakpahu and Shongopovi and is just a few miles down the road from Kykotsmovi, where the game would be played. Put that in your GPS and see what you get! Machen and I flew up during the day, met with the tribal officials who ran the community center and we were impressed with the facilities.

When we toured the gym it was mid-day and there was plenty of daylight. We asked questions about the lighting, but when we saw that they had the same type of mercury-vapor lamps that illuminated most high school gyms in Phoenix as well as the Veterans Memorial Coliseum, we were more than satisfied. When we got back to Phoenix we even discussed the merits of possibly televising the game. But because of multiple technical challenges, we decided "no" on televising, but the game was most definitely "yes."

To his credit, Mavericks' coach Dick Motta did not want this to be just another pre-season game in a hard to reach venue for his club. He wanted his team to open their minds and embrace the Native American culture. So, the very first thing the Mavericks did, when they arrived at Kykotsmovi, was to go to the Native American Cultural Center, for a tour and an orientation. Naturally, this was big news on the reservation and there were a number of kids on hand to greet the Mavericks when they arrived. That's when I realized just how committed and knowledgeable these young Native American fans were when it came to NBA basketball. I stood nearby as the Mavericks got off their bus and the kids identified every one of them. "Look! There's Rolando Blackman!" one little boy said, "but, where's Uwe Blab?"

I thought, "Uwe Blab?!" I was an NBA PR guy and I wasn't sure who Uwe Blab was...but these kids sure seemed to know. When I asked them how they knew so much about the Mavericks, they said that they got all the NBA games on satellite. Later on, while driving through the reservation, it was not unusual to see a traditional Native American hogan, made largely of sticks, logs and mud, with a huge, modern satellite dish set up right outside.

When game night arrived, I took the Suns game stat crew from Flagstaff up to Kykotsmovi, early in the afternoon, to get everything set up. With tremendous cooperation from both the Hopi and Navajo tribes, things went flawlessly...until the sun went down. I don't want to say that the lighting in the gym proved to be a little dim, but I have been in nightclubs with brighter lights! It looked like the entire gym was illuminated by a single 60 watt bulb! When I asked if we could please turn up those mercury-vapor lamps, I was informed that they were already cranked to the max.

Fortunately, there was just enough light for the teams to see their respective baskets, but the whole scene was surreal to me. I was grateful that we had decided not to televise, but that didn't make it any better (or brighter) for the local TV crews who were on hand to cover the game.

The low lighting did not seem to bother the 3,000 Native American fans who packed the gym that night. They were literally beaming with excitement. The Phoenix Suns Gorilla was on hand and I think he got bigger and more frequent ovations for his antics, compared to anything that happened between the Suns and Mavericks. The game didn't count in the standings, but judging from the smiles in the gym, it scored a lot of points with the Hopi and Navajo tribes.

HARI-HARI

Today, NBA teams travel by charter jet, but it wasn't too long ago that everyone flew regular commercial airlines. Like other travelers, as the Suns moved through airport terminals, they were frequently the target of individuals handing out literature or soliciting donations.

Once, at Newark Airport, a clean-shaven Hari-Krishna, wearing a toga and sandals, held out his tambourine for a donation and approached Rich Kelley. Looking down at the Hari from his seven foot vantage point, Kelley said, "Sorry… I gave in another life!"

THE BIG PUSH

During the 1986-87 season the Suns were scheduled to play a game in Washington, D.C. but busing to the game was proving problematic because of near-blizzard conditions. The bus skidded off the road and became stuck in a snow bank. Everyone in the travelling party, players, coaches and trainers got off the bus and, working in concert with the driver, attempted to rock the bus out of the snow bank and back onto the road.

At one point, trainer Joe Proski looked up and there, sitting on the bus and looking out the window, was the Suns first-round pick, William Bedford. Somebody went back onto the bus and suggested to the rookie that he come outside and help. But because he was wearing a new suit and an expensive cashmere top coat, he refused.

His response? "I don't get paid to push buses!"

Apparently he didn't get paid to play much basketball either. Bedford was traded to Detroit after just one frustrating season with the Suns and did not enjoy an NBA career of any great distinction.

MISSING?

When promotional photo shoots required some young Suns fans, we never had to look beyond the children and families attached to the Suns front office. Such was the case when one of our sponsors, Carnation Milk, wanted to promote their Suns Benchwarmer Contest. My daughter Casey got the casting call and was one of two kids featured, along with Suns forward, Larry Nance. Their photo was featured on tens of thousands of Carnation milk cartons. Years later, when Casey told one of her teachers that she once had her picture on the side of a milk carton, the teacher asked, "Oh, you poor thing... were you missing?"

HIGH OCTANE

I guess you could refer to the 1980s as the "Muscle Car Era" in Suns history. Headed by Larry Nance, there were a number of Suns players who "muscled up" for some high octane automotive thrills between games and during the off-season. I'm not going to tell you that they would race illegally, but outside of a couple of drag racing tracks in the area, there really weren't any places where you can race without breaking the law.

Cruising Central Avenue on Friday and Saturday nights was a very big deal for hot rod enthusiasts from throughout the Valley of the Sun and Nance's cars were always on display. In fact, when the cruising crowd started getting a little out of hand, and the city clamped down on the activity, Nance served on a special committee, convened by the mayor, to clean up the abuses and turn cruising into a more wholesome activity for the community. That didn't stop some hot rod owners from challenging Nance to race. They would agree to meet at a certain time on a certain stretch of highway. Once the roadway was clear, Nance would proceed to blow their doors off.

Truck Robinson had a '69 hot rod Ford LTD convertible. Dennis Johnson had a 6.9 Mercedes sedan that looked somewhat sedate, but it was truly a "getaway car," in which Al Capone would have been proud to ride. D.J. didn't race often, but when he did, he usually kicked butt. James Edwards had an orange Roadrunner that he was constantly tweaking to add horsepower and increase performance. But Nance was by far the best driver and a full-blown motor-head. He owned a couple of very hot cars. One was a red Camero with black stripes and a 427 engine under the hood, while the other was an orange Nova II with a 454 power plant.

One day Nance beat Edwards in a race. Edwards protested on some technicality, so Nance suggested they just swap cars. They did, and Nance whupped Edwards again. Proving once and for all, that it's not the size of your engine...

PITINO

In 1987, in between the time John MacLeod was fired and before John Wetzel took over, Jerry Colangelo put the full-court press on Rick Pitino to become the new Suns coach. Rick had two big things going for him. First, he had been a highly successful college coach at Providence College and Colangelo loved to bring college coaches like Dick Motta and Cotton Fitzsimmons into the NBA. Secondly, and perhaps more importantly, Pitino was Italian.

I picked up Pitino at Phoenix' Sky Harbor Airport and, in between his meetings with Colangelo, I squired him around Phoenix during his visit. I showed him the Suns practice facilities, the Coliseum, and some high-end neighborhoods around the city where he might consider living. All the while, he was peppering me with questions about the team and the city but most importantly, Suns management and the recent drug issues. Also, if Pitino were to sign with the Suns, he had a list of contract requests that included private schools for his kids and limousine transportation to and from games.

Ultimately, Pitino perceived the fallout from the drug scandal to be too much and passed on the Suns opportunity. A few months later, he would sign with the New York Knicks as their head coach.

STRATEGERY

As the dark clouds hovering over the Suns franchise began to break up, in the months following the drug "scandal," the front office went to work strategizing how we could win back the goodwill of Phoenix in general and our fan base in particular. Of course, building a winning team would be a crucial first step but, being in position to tell our story in a positive way to that audience, was just as vital.

In PR, the first of those tactics included the creation of a new fan magazine called *Phoenix Suns Fastbreak*. Going back to the first year of the franchise, there had always been some type of newsletter, usually just a few pages, published quarterly. *Fastbreak* was much more ambitious. We would publish every month during the season and once during the off season...a total of nine issues per year. The format went from an 8 1/2" x 11" four page, fold-over, to an 11" x 14," 32-page, tabloid-style magazine.

After a year of researching, planning, staffing, bidding and writing, the first issue came out in late October, 1988. Local publishing entrepreneur Porter McKinnon was of immeasurable assistance in helping me pull everything together. I hired a staff of contributing writers and editors, headed by former *Phoenix Gazette* sportswriters, Larry Ward and Dick Dozer. Frequently, I would work with Jerry Colangelo, Cotton Fitzsimmons and our coaching staff to ghost-write their columns. The workload and deadlines were all-consuming, but I can't remember a time in my Suns career when I had more fun. Even better, under Cotton, the team began to turn things around on the basketball floor.

A second tactic was to retain the services of GO Media, a video production and news services company, to make sure that all of our team activities and personalities were covered for television. Headed by Gregg Ostro (the GO in GO Media), they were not only well connected in the local television market, but they were also making inroads into cable television and were producing good things for a new outfit called ESPN. If a local station was unable to cover a Suns news conference, or a community relations activity, GO Media made sure those outlets were covered with information and professionally produced video tape.

An interesting dynamic developed as a result of this relationship. The taint of the drug scandal made the Suns a bit of a local pariah, so the local stations seemed to shy away from Suns coverage, except for the occasional derisive "shot." But GO Media was having great luck in placing stories on the national networks and cable outlets. Stories on Colangelo, Fitzsimmons, Majerle, Chambers, Kevin Johnson and Hawkins, were all getting more attention from national outlets than from the local media. That seemed to be a wake-up call for the Phoenix stations and they eventually jumped on board.

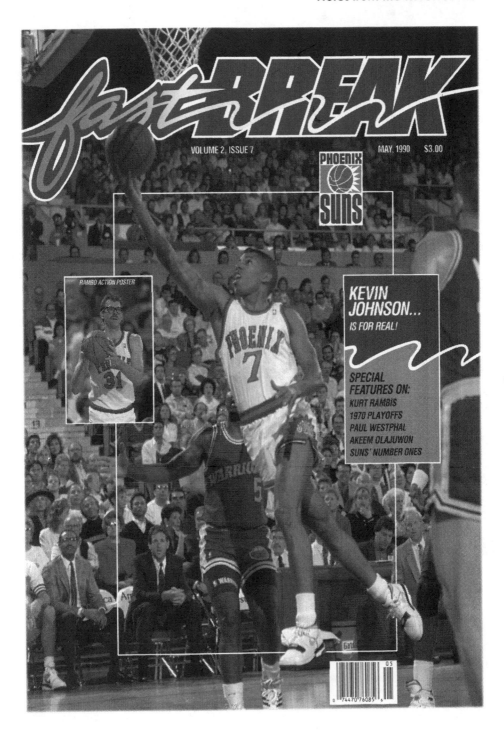

FAST BREAK

VOLUME 2, ISSUE 7   MAY, 1990 $3.00

PHOENIX SUNS

RAMBO ACTION POSTER

PHOENIX 7

WARRIORS 5

KEVIN JOHNSON...
IS FOR REAL!

SPECIAL FEATURES ON:
KURT RAMBIS
1970 PLAYOFFS
PAUL WESTPHAL
AKEEM OLAJUWON
SUNS' NUMBER ONES

0 74470 76085 6

I had cleverly (I thought) crafted the GO Media contract to be based on performance. Each local or national Suns story that they placed earned them a specific dollar amount. I had budgeted about $75,000 for the year for this purpose, but GO Media's success in placing stories went above and beyond my most optimistic projections. So much so, that I had to go see Colangelo to explain why that part of my budget had essentially doubled. I feared that it might be my last day with the Suns as I showed Jerry the reams of station broadcast affidavits, explaining when and for how long each Suns story ran on each station or cable outlet. I was just about to apologize for going over budget, when Jerry said, "Tom, this is fabulous! You guys did a great job!"

In Jerry's mind, it had been worth it to help change perceptions and rebuild the Suns reputation in the community. Not every NBA owner would see it the way Jerry did.

DIDN'T YOU USED TO BE

Of all the regular features in *Fastbreak* magazine, the one that I enjoyed the most was the column, "Didn't you used to be...?" It was an opportunity to sit down and visit with former Suns players about life after basketball. It also connected new Suns fans with Suns history and heritage.

Many Suns players have stayed in the Valley of the Sun after their playing days were over and established themselves in new businesses and careers: Jim Fox (Sport Court), Dick Snyder (insurance), Dick and Tom Van Arsdale (real estate), Dan Majerle and Nate Hawthorne (restaurants), Alvan Adams (facilities management), Jeff Cook (insurance), Alvin Scott (SW Gas), Joel Kramer (accounting), Eddie Johnson, Scott Williams and Tim Kempton (broadcasting), Truck Robinson (coaching), John Shumate (coaching and scouting), Neal Walk (archiving), Mark West (player personnel) and Connie Hawkins (being Connie Hawkins).

Every month it was great to catch up with old, but familiar, names like Kyle Macy, Curtis Perry, Ricky Sobers, Keith Erickson, Rich Kelley and Gar Heard. In the first 24 years of the franchise just 133 players wore the Suns purple and orange. Some came and went quickly, while others earned a permanent place in Suns history and in the memories of Suns fans.

Eventually, the tabloid-sized format for *Phoenix Suns Fastbreak Magazine* would morph into a standard magazine size. After a few more years, printed editions would disappear altogether and *Fastbreak* would become **suns.com**. It was a great ten-year run and *Fastbreak* accomplished what it set out to do...tell the Suns' story to our fans.

FU MANCHU

There was a time when a young boy about seven or eight years old was visiting the Suns offices with his father. They were looking at the yearly team photos which were displayed in the reception area. When the boy looked at the 1982-83 photo, he noticed that James Edwards, sporting a "Fu Manchu" mustache, was #53 that year. When he looked at the 1981-82 picture, he saw that there was a #53 on the team, also with a "Fu Manchu" mustache but that player was Rich Kelley. Confused, because both players were in the same location on the two photos, the boy looked up at his father and said, "Gee, dad, I didn't know that James Edwards wasn't always black!"

THE GREAT GORILLA HUNT

Just as the Suns Gorilla was beginning to earn widespread acceptance as one of the best mascots in the NBA, our original Gorilla, Henry Rojas, decided that he wanted to retire from the game. We gave him a well-deserved send-off late in the 1987-88 season. The Gorilla received a lifetime supply of bananas and some "Funky Monkey" ice cream, but his retirement left the Suns with a huge gap at the mascot position. That's when we started "The Great Gorilla Hunt," which I wrote about in this story, during the fall of 1988.

It is a fact almost too terrifying to contemplate, but they are out there. They lurk in the hot, humid jungle of the mind, just beneath the shadows of "normal" society. Their leathery faces are damp with perspiration; their liquid eyes dart back and forth, capturing images ...understanding. Their nostrils flare, pulling noisily at the air, cataloguing each scent. These dark, hulking beasts are not easily detected but, make no mistake, they are there watching, waiting for an opportunity.

Unknowing regular folks see them in their guises of architect, policeman, plumber or IRS agent. They could pose as an actress, a pilot, a professional person or a student, male or female. They might be a friend, a neighbor, or even (gasp!) a member of your own family. Each of them harbors a deeply-rooted psychological urge known as "furmania" or "transfurism"... the mysterious desire to wear a furry gorilla suit and mask.

They are the "secret simians."

But now, they have been exposed.

When the Phoenix Suns gorilla mascot of eight years waved a Mighty Joe Young-like goodbye to Suns fans at the final home game of the 1987-88 season, it left management not only with an entertainment gap but with a major decision. Should they continue with the gorilla character? Should they change to another style of mascot (perhaps a carrot or a weasel)? Should they scrap the mascot idea altogether?

"The gorilla character had become so closely identified with the Suns, we wanted to maintain that continuity," said the Suns vice president of marketing, Harvey Shank. "Although I don't really

know what relationship a dancing gorilla has to the Suns, to basketball or to anything else for that matter. All I know is that it worked for us."

And the Suns' Great Gorilla Hunt began.

Even before the Suns could establish any type of gorilla application process, unsolicited letters, video tapes and resumes began pouring in from around Arizona. When Suns President, Jerry Colangelo, appeared on CBS television during halftime of an NBA playoff game, and talked about the insanity of sitting down to negotiate a contract with someone wearing a gorilla suit, the applications began coming in from all over the continental United States, as well as Alaska and Hawaii, along with several inquiries from Canada.

In just a 30-day period, 525 of the "secret simians" emerged from the deepening shadows to apply for the job. Each was vying for the opportunity that would at last release them from the shackles of their silent frustration. Oh, to moon-walk at center-court in a fur suit and get paid for it!

"Although we didn't establish any prerequisites for the gorilla job, we indicated that prior experience in acting, dance, sports and gymnastics would be helpful," Shank continued, "but that didn't seem to stop anybody from applying."

In fact, the gorilla applicants cut a swath through all known socio-economic demographics. Men and women...black, white and Hispanic...actors and athletes...sales reps, sports producers and probation officers...loan collectors, bus drivers and boat-builders...electricians, music directors and advertising account executives...disc jockeys, bankers, coaches and teachers... cosmetologists, meat cutters and professional wrestlers.

An interesting assortment of active mascots also scratched out applications, including a rooster, a lobster, several devils, a hawk, a big-foot, a bear, a monkey and no fewer than six gorillas. Mercifully, on June 30th, the application period closed.

But once they're lured out into the open, how do you evaluate over 500 closet gorillas? An open audition, though initially tempting to Suns management, was rejected as impractical, if not a little ridiculous. Instead, a letter was sent to the simian hopefuls, outlining the mascot job, its full-time requirements and the *base salary of $25,000. Prospective gorillas, if still interested, were asked to produce a five-minute video tape audition displaying their skills in dance, non-verbal communication and any other talents they could bring to the act.*

One hundred and ten video tapes were submitted. Figure it out. That's 110 tapes at five minutes each, 550 minutes, or a total of nine hours and 10 minutes of nothing but cavorting gorillas. But there was no turning back. Each tape was carefully screened and logged by a bleary-eyed Suns staffer named Kenny Glenn. The tapes were then graded by the Suns Gorilla Selection Committee, comprised of Suns marketing and public relations executives... through careful scrutiny, evaluations and reevaluations, the group of 110 gorillas was pared down to 20 finalists, who were invited in for personal interviews...without their gorilla suits.

Who were these people, willing to give up jobs and careers for a life of monkey-see, monkey-do and bad jokes about bananas? One by one they came, drawn by their irresistible craving. Some were cocky and brimming with confidence; others were quiet and withdrawn. One was just plain crazy.

The finalists divided sharply into two groups, one creative and the other athletic. Personality and "coach-ability" were considered. Gorilla philosophy and the high ethical and moral standards that must be maintained by the character were discussed at length. But the final decision would not be made in the interviews. That would be reserved for the ultimate test, the live audition...the "fur finals."

It could have been a scene from a Fellini movie.

In a closed gymnasium locker-room in North Phoenix, on a hot Saturday morning in early July, a band of sweaty apes shuffled around in ill-fitting suits, their breathing labored through their rubber masks, as they nervously prepared for their final challenge. On the gymnasium floor, the panel of judges, an equally anxious group, composed of Suns staff and local media personalities, exuded the expected tension for such a critical event.

Each gorilla candidate would have seven minutes to go through a routine of his own creation, covering skills in dance, agility and communication. It was the essence of stand-up comedy and entertainment, though much of it would be neither funny nor entertaining.

Music blared, the cameras whirred and the onslaught began. They danced; they flopped; they fell. They walked on their hands. They dribbled; they shot; they missed. They tried to impress. They were innovative. They mimed. They slam-dunked off a mini-trampoline. One gorilla rolled out a piano and played Mozart; another calmly roller-skated around the gym floor. For the judges, it promised to be an extraordinarily long morning. For the candidates, seven minutes often seemed like an eternity.

But there was one. He raced across the court, dove head-first and slid smoothly on the hardwood...right into the middle of the center-court circle. In his non-stop, high-energy routine, he quickly established what the other apes did not...presence. The judges roared with laughter as he went through a number from the movie "Flashdance." And then came the unexpected finale. Clutching a basketball, he raced from one end of the court to the top of the key, hit a mini-trampoline in full-stride and soared Jordan-like toward the hoop. The judges gasped as he missed the slam, but he grabbed the rim and, in a single motion, swung his body up and climbed onto the heel of the basket. In the finest tradition of the gorilla family, he stood on the basket and pounded his chest with his fists. Then, reaching down, he grabbed the rim once more and executed a reverse flip onto a waiting pad in the middle of the key. Hitting the mat face-down and horizontal, he did not move until his attendants grabbed him by the feet and pulled him off the court. Thinking he was hurt, several judges left their seats on their platform to go to his aid. But the gorilla stood, waved them off and took a deep bow. It had been seven minutes of pure animal magnetism. The Suns had their new gorilla.

It had taken 13 weeks and countless hours of discussion and evaluation, but the Suns had fulfilled the dreams of one of the "secret simians."

But what of the other 524?

They return to the murk and shadows of their clandestine subculture...watching, waiting for their next opportunity. Beware.

FROM THE WACKO! FILE – ALL PROBLEMS SOLVED

TO: Solve your players' problems
DO THIS: Raise the basket 3 feet.

This will eliminate the height advantage (no more slam dunks). Also this will open up the game so smaller men, who are usually quicker, faster and more agile, thus making the game more exciting. It will broaden the players' base tremendously. Because of greatly increased supply of players, the salaries will be much, much lower.

Also you could have 3 or 4 leagues like baseball (a major league and 3 minors). Implementing these changes will greatly lower owner expense. Some of this could be passed on to the fans. Having 4 or more leagues would increase income tremendously. Any player negotiations would be far simpler. There are a myriad of shorter players who are terrific but are eliminated because of height.

Yours truly,

APS
P.S. I have copywrited these ideas,
but would sell for <u>my</u> price.

SUNS CHARITIES

After Jerry Colangelo pulled together a group of investors to purchase the Suns from the team's original owners in December of 1987, he had several key items on his "To Do List." First and foremost was to restore the team's winning ways. Second was to begin planning for a new arena in downtown Phoenix. Also high on that list was his commitment to increase Suns community involvement through the creation of a team foundation.

A few teams in the league already had foundations....Boston, San Antonio, Houston and Denver come to mind, but overall, within the NBA, the concept was in its infancy. I invited Jim Taszarek, general manager of the Suns flagship radio station, KTAR, to be our first chairman. Together, Taz and I visited several of the NBA's team foundations to explore best practices and then we invited select leaders in the community to join us as members of the board of directors.

As we prepared the legal paperwork, we realized that we needed a name for our new foundation. I went to Jerry Colangelo with a couple of suggestions, but he just said, "What about 'Phoenix Suns Charities?'"

What a great idea! Sold!

The primary mission of Phoenix Suns Charities (PSC) would be to help the children of our community maximize their potential. The team foundation would also create new opportunities to raise the team's profile when it came to charitable giving.

THE COURTSIDE CLASSIC

Working in collaboration with the Easter Seals Society, the Suns Charities board, along with Evans/Artigue Marketing & Communications, began planning the first major fund-raising event for our new foundation. "The Courtside Classic" was the result. It was a crazy idea... a formal, black-tie dinner-dance where everyone would wear high-top basketball shoes.

The first step was to get Nike™ on board to donate the basketball shoes. Cotton Fitzsimmons' friendship, with Nike Chairman Phil Knight, would play a key role. Once Nike agreed to join us, we were off and running (no pun intended).

As part of the invitation's return card, we asked guests to list their "athletic shoe size." Working with us right up to the day of the event, Nike supplied all of the shoes. As guests arrived at The Phoenician Resort, they stepped into an area that looked like a giant shoe store. On the shelves were hundreds of boxes of Nike basketball shoes, each labeled with a guest's name. The dress shoes came off, the Nikes were laced up, and the formal dress shoes went into the box and back onto the shelf to be picked up at the end of the evening.

My recurring nightmare during all of the planning was that no one, especially the ladies, would want to take off their fancy dress shoes and put on the Nikes. But the shoe exchange turned out to be a great ice-breaker and set a tone for the evening...

we were there to have fun. As the night unfolded, many of the lady guests came over to thank me...this was the most comfortable they had EVER been at a black-tie event!

The "Courtside Classic" theme endured for 10 years. During that time, PSC fund-raising from the event grew from $35,000 to over $300,000 annually.

And in 10 years, we only lost one pair of shoes.

FROM THE WACKO! FILE – IT'S ALL IN THE TECHNIQUE

A couple of our young sales managers spoke to a marketing class at Arizona State University. It was really a recruiting trip to build a pool of potential candidates who might be interested in a sales position with the Suns after graduation. During their remarks to the class, they offered some tried and true examples of sales and marketing techniques employed by the Suns.

About a week after their visit, they received this hand-written thank you note from one of the guys in the class.

> **Hello Nick & Jeff**
>
> **I just wanted to let you guys know that your presentation was "Dope." I enjoyed it. Thank you for coming.**
>
> **I picked up two girls with your selling tricks. I'll be sure to remember you guys when I make it big!**

PIVOTAL

On February 25, 1988, the Suns hosted the Cleveland Cavaliers at the Coliseum. Just a few hours before, the Suns and Cavs had agreed to a block-buster deal that would change the fortunes of both teams... for the good. As we waited for the NBA office in New York to call with approval of the transaction, tip-off was just a couple of hours away and we had to head over to the Coliseum to begin game preparations.

When the final OK came from the NBA, we hastily called a press conference in a seldom used executive conference room on the Coliseum's lower concourse. As they arrived at the arena, players involved in the trade were informed by their coaches and instructed to remain in their street clothes.

By the time we assembled the media and began the press conference, we could hear the crowd and the pre-game introductions just a short distance away.

I opened the news conference by stating that the Suns and Cavaliers had just completed a major trade involving multiple players. I then introduced "the architect of the deal," our Director of Player Personnel, Cotton Fitzsimmons.

Cotton outlined the trade: The Suns traded Larry Nance, along with Mike Sanders to the Cavs in exchange for Kevin Johnson, Mark West, Tyrone Corbin, a first-round draft pick in 1988 that would turn into Dan Majerle, not to mention a couple of second round picks in 1988 and 1989. Nance was the Suns best player, a former Slam-Dunk Champion and the Suns only All-Star. The deal did not set well with Suns fans, who had never heard of this Cav's rookie point-guard, Kevin Johnson.

For the record, the Suns won the game that night 109-103, with immediate-past Cavs Johnson, Corbin and West watching from the Coliseum's upper press box. But once those three new acquisitions suited up, Phoenix went 11-9 over their final 20 games. That set the stage for what would be one of greatest turnaround seasons in NBA history. Phoenix would go from finishing out of the playoffs with a meager 28-win season, to winning 55 games and earning a trip to the Western Conference Finals. With Nance, the Cavaliers would also improve dramatically, going from 42 to 57 victories the next season.

Utilizing 20-20 hindsight, it would prove to be a lopsided deal in favor of the Suns. But on that February night at the Coliseum, despondent Suns fans were ready to take Fitzsimmons and run him out of town on a rail. One year later, they would name the railroad in his honor.

CHAPTER 5

THE COTTON EXPRESS

POSITIVE THINKING

When I reflect on all my years with the Suns organization, one of the best periods for me personally, was 1988-1992. That was a four year stretch when Cotton Fitzsimmons coached the Suns and I was the PR man. I think it was a combination of Cotton's unimpeachable optimism and the team's incredible turnaround that made it so special.

There were two keys to Cotton's success. First, he was an unapologetic advocate of the power of positive thinking and second, he had the ability to see the whole picture. Of course he was a master motivator and a solid X's and 0's guy when it came to players and strategy, but he also recognized the importance of getting his team to cooperate with public relations, sales, marketing, and community relations. In 1988, as Cotton took over as coach, we were fighting our way back from a drug scandal, a 28-win season and the firing of two head coaches, MacLeod and John Wetzel, within a span of about 14 months.

Cotton was a sound-bite machine. The media loved him and I think Cotton was always honest and forthright with them. He had that folksy, "Missour-a" wisdom he was always willing to share, much to the edification, amusement and delight of everyone who came in contact with him.

On the court, he was well-aware of the importance of having your roster populated with star players like Tom Chambers, Eddie Johnson and Kevin Johnson, but he also knew it was equally important to have guys who he liked to call "dirt workers." That group included players like Tyrone Corbin, Ed Nealy, Kurt Rambis, Mark West and of course, Dan Majerle. All of Cotton's players were high-caliber people and talented players who knew their roles on his team.

ON COURSE

Cotton Fitzsimmons loved to talk. He was always ready to offer advice, deliver a verbal jab, tell stories, admonish, joke, laugh, coach, and sometimes he'd do it all simultaneously! On the golf course it was no different. If you were in his foursome, it was best if you just forgot about the normal courtesies of golf, like...no talking during the backswing...no talking while you are putting...no ridicule after you hit a poor shot. Nope...Cotton would keep up the chatter throughout. Cotton really enjoyed it when play was slow and you might have two or three foursomes waiting on the same tee box...it just made for a bigger audience!

I'm not that good a golfer to get upset when I don't play well, but I really enjoyed playing with Cotton. I adjusted to his constant chatter by thinking of it as a kind of "white noise"... or perhaps more accurately, "Whitey noise," similar to the sound of a distant lawnmower on the golf course. Cotton never made me nervous. His non-stop chatter actually relaxed me.

Speaking of golf, I'll always remember what Cotton used to say to me, "Ambrose, you're nothing but a lost ball in the high weeds!" But it was only recently that someone pointed out to me, "Tom, when Cotton said that...he wasn't talking about your golf game!"

Oh.

THE SWAMI

We were looking to build some excitement for the 1988 NBA Draft. The Suns were coming off a dismal 28-54 season. Cotton had been named coach and the Suns were in the NBA Lottery.

Someone came up with the idea to make Cotton a "swami," a sort of fortune-teller, who could predict who the Suns would get in the upcoming draft. Danny Manning of Kansas was, hands down, the top player in the draft that year. There was no question that if the Suns won the lottery and got the top pick, their choice would be Manning, a complete, all-around team player and a class act who also happened to be 6'10!"

Always the showman, Cotton played along and by the time we finished dressing him, he looked like a refugee from a traveling carnival sideshow, complete with a silky purple turban. We had a special Phoenix Suns teacup made so Cotton could "read" the tea leaves in the bottom of the cup. Cotton hammed it up for the cameras, swirling the tea leaves around the bottom of the Suns cup. He then offered the cup and its "results" to the cameras, and there, boldly printed at the bottom of the cup, not subject to any "reading" or interpretation, was the name, "DANNY MANNING."

Alas, in spite of Cotton's bold prediction, it was not to be. Manning was indeed the first pick in the draft, but he went to the Clippers. The Suns picked seventh and fourteenth, first selecting Tim Perry of Temple and then Dan Majerle of the Central Michigan "Chippewas." The "swami" retired, but the tea leaves proved somewhat prophetic when Manning signed with the Suns as a free agent in 1994.

OF BOOS AND MEN

One of Cotton's most memorable moments with the Suns came on draft day, 1988 when the Suns drafted an unheralded 6'6," 220 pound center out of Central Michigan, a kid named Dan Majerle. Once again, the Suns were staging one of those open–to-the-public draft day events, this time at the Phoenix Civic Plaza. All of the Suns pre-draft chatter led Suns fans and the media to the conclusion that at pick number fourteen, the Suns were zeroing-in on a player named Jeff Grayer, a talented forward out of Iowa State. That was however, a carefully calculated deception orchestrated by Fitzsimmons and Colangelo. Majerle's name was hardly ever mentioned as even a remote possibility.

> **"You people will be sorry that you EVER booed this young man!"**
> - Cotton Fitzsimmons

So when NBA Draft headquarters announced over our big screen TVs that "with the 14th pick in the first round of the 1988 NBA Draft, the Phoenix Suns select ...Dan Majerle of Central Michigan!" a lusty chorus of boos immediately went up from the assembled crowd of nearly 2,000 Suns fans. They felt deceived and angry. They had no idea who this MAY-JER-LEE guy was, or how to pronounce his name. Cotton grabbed the microphone and with boos still raining down, said, "We are very happy to select Dan Majerle. I cannot help how you feel. All I can tell you is this...We couldn't be happier and I think you people will be sorry that you EVER booed this young man!"

Cotton was absolutely right, Majerle went on to enjoy a very successful NBA career earning a spot in the Suns Ring of Honor, a reputation as a hard-nosed defender, one of the NBA's best three-point shooters and perhaps Phoenix's favorite Sun. He is currently a Suns assistant coach and a very successful restaurateur in the Phoenix area. And you just say, "MAR-LEE."

THE CLINIC FOR BLIND CHILDREN

Every now and then a community relations activity that starts out simply as a team obligation on a very busy schedule will transcend the ordinary to become something very special. The Suns Clinic for Blind Children was one of those events. It was St. Patrick's Day 1990 and the Suns were scheduled for a light practice and then they would host, on the Coliseum floor, a basketball clinic for a special group of kids from the Foundation for Blind Children.

We didn't know exactly how this was going to play out since many of the children had been blind since birth, yet many had become Suns fans by listening to our games on the radio. There were about 20 of these children at the clinic, along with their parents and foundation staff sitting in the stands nearby.

When practice was over, Coach Cotton Fitzsimmons and his players took the kids by the hand and led them out to the center of the Coliseum court where everyone sat down. The Voice of the Suns,

Al McCoy then started the program by talking to the youngsters about how he always tried to paint a word picture of Suns games for his radio audience and he especially wanted to do a good job for them. Cotton Fitzsimmons then gave a little background on how the game is played and then introduced each of the Suns players. When he told the children about the players' heights and weights, the youngsters gasped in amazement.

Cotton then had the seated children reach down to feel the floor...the wood...the grooves. Then he had the players distribute basketballs to the children and asked them to feel and smell the leather, touch the seams and then bounce the balls on the wooden floor. The kids were clearly enjoying every moment of this. Each player then took a couple of the children and walked with them up and down the court, so they could get a sense of how far the basketball players had to run when they went up and down the floor. Then, one by one, the players would lift a child up toward the basket and gave them the opportunity to touch and feel the net, the rim and the backboard.

For many of the players, working with these students was a very moving experience. Kurt Rambis in particular, found it easy to relate to the needs of these kids. "My vision is far from perfect without my glasses. That's why I have to wear them when I play," he said. "Becoming the 'eyes' for someone less fortunate than I am was a special moment."

"Rambo," who had just joined the Suns in mid-season, patiently worked one-on-one with one little girl in particular, Jenna. He took her down to the basket at the far end of the court and told her that he was going to guide her shooting and she was going to make a basket. Initially she protested and said she couldn't do it. But Kurt insisted that she keep trying. As Jenna put up shot after shot from the middle of the lane, you could hear Kurt at the other end, "A little higher...now a little to the left...Oh! You almost had it! Come on now...you're 'gonna get it!"

Pretty soon Kurt and Jenna had captured the attention of the parents, staff, the coaches, the other players and just about everyone else in the building. When Jenna's last shot dropped through the net, a tearful, happy cheer went up. No one could have scripted a better ending than that.

THE CAMP

As Cotton Fitzsimmons prepared for the opening of the 1990-91 season as the head coach of the Suns, his better half, JoAnn Fitzsimmons, was busy collaborating with members of the Suns PR and marketing staff to create the inaugural Cotton Fitzsimmons & Kurt Rambis Fastbreak Fantasy Camp. The camp, designed for hoopsters 30 years of age or older, would take place the following July at Lake Tahoe's Incline Village. The Suns would promote the camp on their radio and television broadcasts during the upcoming season.

After working on the project for several weeks with JoAnn, I told her that I would really like to go to the camp too.

"Tom, of course, we'll get a room for you and Alice," JoAnn said.

"JoAnn, you don't understand," I responded, "I want to be one of the campers!"

She was baffled.

"Why would you want to do that?" she said.

Having been a basketball and football player in high school and an admirer of Cotton's for many years, my response was simple, "I've always wanted to be coached by Cotton Fitzsimmons."

She laughed and said, "OK...if that's what you want."

I spent the next six months running, shooting baskets and getting in shape. Just after the Fourth of July, I headed for the airport and the flight to Lake Tahoe.

At first it was tough to pick them out of the airport crowd. But as I waited at the America West Airlines gate in Phoenix, they slowly came into focus.

The men, all over 30, appeared one by one, most were carrying gym bags and travelling alone. They were an eclectic mix of ages, heights, weights and builds. They were all bound for Lake Tahoe and the camp.

Cautiously, introductions began among the 16 strangers. Although their natural inhibitions soon disappeared, you could still sense that there was some subtle "sizing-up" taking place. Underlying it all was the trepidation of not really knowing what to expect...from the camp or the campers.

"Did you play college ball?"

"How many others are coming?"

"Will they run us?"

"What's the altitude at Tahoe?"

When our flight touched down in Reno, a bus was waiting to take us on the 45-minute ride to Lake Tahoe. As we wound our way through the mountains, we were treated to views of Ponderosa pine forests and the stunning beauty of Lake Tahoe's north shore.

We were welcomed at the Hyatt Regency by the brain trust of the Fastbreak Fantasy Camp, JoAnn Fitzsimmons, Linda Rambis and camp administrator, Barry Ringel.

At the orientation dinner Coach Fitzsimmons set the tone. We were going to work. We were going to learn. But most importantly, we were going to focus on having fun. Cotton introduced Kurt Rambis, whose sense of humor and laid-back style set everyone at ease. Also joining Cotton and Kurt on the camp's coaching staff was Suns' assistant coach Lionel Hollins.

Cotton asked every camper to stand up and tell the group a little about their backgrounds. The group turned out to be as diversified in occupation as they were in size and shape. The list of occupations included cardiologist, fireman, teacher, coach, salesman, homebuilder, executive, engineer, administrator, movie producer and more. Two more campers arrived from California to push the total in camp to 18.

The camp staff then distributed "the stuff." Each camper received a new pair of NIKE basketball shoes, a NIKE "Just Do It" athletic bag, a NIKE warm-up suit, two sets of camp practice uniforms, socks and supporters as well as a Fastbreak Fantasy Camp T-shirt and shorts.

The next morning, after breakfast, the first van was scheduled to make the short hop over to the Incline Village High School gym at 8:45. But by 8:30, every camper was in the hotel lobby and ready to go. Obviously, anticipation was high.

However, in a classic example of collective anxiety, the first workout was, at times, comical, as the group tried to bring new, or long-forgotten skills into play. Fortunately, we were saved by the appearance of Suns guard, Kevin Johnson, who put on an hour-long clinic, coupled with a question and answer session.

Cotton and Kurt designed the camp schedule along the lines of a pro basketball training camp, with two workouts per day and the time divided between stretching, instruction, drills and scrimmages. Tuesday through Thursday were set up in similar fashion while Friday's single session focused on the final camp game.

If it sounds like the camp was physical...it was. There were plenty of minor injuries. A strained knee, a bruised hip, a blood blister under a toenail, a bruised rib, a sore back, a pulled groin muscle...shall I go on to one of the other players?

Camp trainer Doug Landuyt was constantly rushing around taping injuries, distributing ice bags and setting up heat packs. Without Doug's work, I doubt that very many of the campers, including this one, would have made it to the final day.

Cotton, Kurt and Lionel worked patiently with each of the campers, teaching the basics of basketball as well as covering some of the nuances of the NBA game. They drilled us on ball-handling, footwork, shooting, the pick and roll, and they even installed a couple of plays. Even though it didn't always look like it...progress was being made.

All the campers looked forward to the 45-minute scrimmages which ended each practice session. Kurt and Lionel would each coach a squad, while Cotton would handle the officiating with flair and style all his own. In the beginning, the scrimmages had all the grace of a rugby scrum, but by week's end the drills and instruction made a dramatic improvement in the quality of play.

In one of those early camp scrimmages, I was pressing one of the guards defensively as he dribbled toward the baseline. The biggest man in camp at 6'8" and about 240 pounds, Steve Ginsberg stepped out to set a pick on me that none of my teammates called out. I blindly smashed into him and the impact was so hard that I actually saw stars! As I sat stunned on the floor, I took a quick inventory...nothing seemed to be broken or sprained. It had probably been 25 years since I had experienced that kind of collision...and the last time was while playing high school football. But I was OK! I jumped to my feet and chased after the play, knowing that I was alive and thinking, "That... was... GREAT!"

It was especially during those scrimmages that I questioned my original desire to be "coached by Cotton Fitzsimmons." I had my doubts because I frequently had to suffer the role of Cotton's "whipping boy." I recognize now that it was actually an "honor" to be selected by Cotton for that part. As tough as he was on me, it made for a truly unforgettable camp experience.

The key to the success of the camp was the coaching staff spending time to get to know every one of the campers. Whether it was at lunch or dinner, on a Lake Tahoe beach or maybe at a blackjack table in the casino, Cotton, Kurt and Lionel were always willing to talk and share their knowledge and experience. The camp dinners were restricted to campers and coaches only... no wives, friends or camp administrators. After a few beers (for purposes of hydration, of course) Cotton and Kurt would open up and share a treasure trove of great NBA stories with the campers.

The camp's final game on Friday morning was a hard-fought battle that was videotaped with play-by-play and commentary by Steve Pascente of KPNX-TV and Dick Van Arsdale of the Suns. That tape, along with a camp plaque and team photos were distributed to each camper, mementos of a remarkable week of basketball.

I still chuckle about the strange looks we received day after day as we tramped back and forth through the hotel lobby in our practice gear. In spite of our purple and orange practice uniforms, nobody mistook us for the Suns. Although we all secretly harbored the fantasy, not one of us was asked for an autograph all week.

I salute all the guys who joined me as "original" Cotton campers: Trent Adams, Bob Ballard, Dan Bingham, Mace Cohen, Pete Colla, Frank Denogean, Bob Field, Steve Ginsberg, Ricardo Gonzalez, Michael Lloyd, Michael O'Meara, Scott Raubenheimer, Steve Stordahl, Kevin Westrum, Dave Woodard, Callie Yeary and trainer, Doug Landuyt. Thanks, guys...it was an absolute blast!

OLDEST MAN

The Cotton-Rambo camps continued at Lake Tahoe's Incline Village for the next seven summers and I was happy to be a camper in all but one. The video of the final scrimmage remained part of the camp tradition. Cotton recruited his old buddy and play-by-play broadcaster from the Kings and Bulls, Neil Funk, to sit in and call the action for the "Big Game." Since Neil spent most of his off-season in Tahoe, he was happy to do Cotton the favor.

For many years, my duties with the Suns involved working with the visiting media and team broadcasters, so Neil Funk and I had a great relationship. But because I was really the only camper that Neil knew well, he felt comfortable giving me more than my fair share of abuse on the video play-by-play.

For example: "Tommy Ambrose reports in. He has been a regular at these camps over the years. I have only one question for him. Why, Tommy? Why?"

Or, this one...

"And here comes Tommy Ambrose into the game. I think that Tommy is the oldest man in camp this year. In fact, he may be the oldest man in Incline Village!"

(L TO R) FITZSIMMONS, AMBROSE, RAMBIS, HOLLINS AT LAKE TAHOE

A CULTURAL EXCHANGE

At the invitation of the Japanese, the NBA opened their 1990-91 season with a pair of regular season games in Tokyo. The two featured teams were the Phoenix Suns and the Utah Jazz. But before the Suns entourage left on the trip to Japan, the NBA made sure that we had at least a rudimentary understanding of business protocols when working in Japan. The Suns arranged for business cards to be printed with an English version on one side and the Japanese version on the other. In the "States" when business cards are exchanged, it is almost an afterthought... "here ya' go, pal!" But in Japan it is all about respect and the exchange becomes a ceremony. When you accept a business card from a Japanese business counterpart, you take the card with both hands...you look at it carefully...you bow a bit in thanks...you turn the card over to admire it...you take the exchange very seriously...you do not show your teeth in a smile.

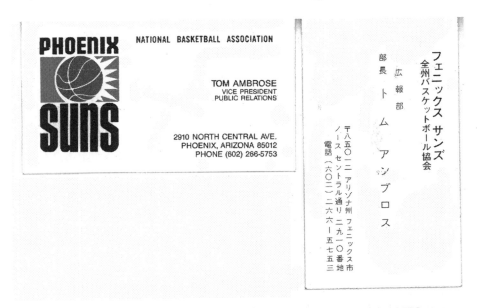

JAPANESE IS READ BY THE COLUMN, RIGHT TO LEFT, TOP TO BOTTOM

The possibility of actually doing this was all very exciting, but, honestly, the NBA's arrangements were so airtight and so protective, that on the team PR level, we really didn't have the opportunity to interact with any Japanese business people.

With the two games against the Jazz, team practices, government receptions, team meals and lots of other events scheduled during our stay in Tokyo, we were always on the move. One day, a team autograph session was scheduled for the rooftop garden of the C. Itoh Department Store in Tokyo. Understand that C. Itoh was the prime mover...the major sponsor who brought this two-game NBA series to Japan.

Cotton Fitzsimmons, Jerry Colangelo and I walked through a very busy downtown Tokyo district to the department store and then up to the rooftop garden. It was amazing. They had converted the expansive rooftop space into a giant, tented, NBA museum and store. All around were very well executed graphic displays on every NBA team, their location in North America and their star players.

> *What's the largest size shoe you have for sale?*

The place was packed with Japanese fans that were, of course, polite and reserved. But you could sense that underlying their polite exterior, they were about to burst with excitement. It was wonderful to see that kind of enthusiasm. There was also an NBA retail store stocked with jerseys, hats, pennants and other apparel from every NBA team. Even basketball shoes from the major manufacturers were for sale. I browsed the merchandise for a while as some of our players signed autographs. A thought occurred to me and I returned to the shoe counter to ask, "Excuse me, but what's the largest size shoe you have for sale?"

The clerk looked around the inventory for a few seconds before answering, "Seven and a half!"

Later on, I learned that the NBA did over one million dollars in merchandise sales in less than a week at that one location in Japan. I'm sure much of that came from the sale of tiny little basketball shoes.

Once the autograph session was concluded, we headed down the stairs of the department store and back toward our team hotel. When we got to the ground floor of the store, a young student with a backpack full of books, walked up to us.

"Excuse, please," he said in halting English, "Are you with...NBA?"

"Yes," I said proudly, "We're with the Phoenix Suns!"

He was very excited to meet us, bowing several times in respect. The conversation however, if you would like to call it that, came to a screeching halt at that point. But it suddenly occurred to me...give him one of my business cards! I had plenty of them!

So I held up my right index finger in the internationally known sign for, "wait a second!" and I swiftly went to my wallet.

I pulled out one of my two-sided Suns business cards and handed it to him. Being a student, he was immediately embarrassed that he had no card to give me in return. I assured him that I understood and it was not important. So he held my business card in his two hands like it was an ancestral wooden votive tablet from a sacred Shinto shrine. He focused his entire attention on it. He looked at the English side and nodded politely. He then turned the card over to the Japanese side and studied it carefully. Suddenly, while still staring at the card, his eyes opened wide and his jaw dropped, as he comprehended what the Japanese side of my business card said.

"O-o-o-o-o-o-o-o-o-o-o-o-o-o-o-o-o-o-o-o-o-o-o-o-o-o-o-o-o!!!!!" he exclaimed, "Vice plesident!!!!"

I immediately burst out laughing, no doubt showing teeth and thoroughly embarrassing the young man...a horrible cultural gaffe. I quickly bowed and apologized to him and said, "I'm so sorry, but you just showed my title of 'vice president' much more respect than I EVER receive in my own country. Domo arigato!"

JUST MAKIN' SURE

Ross Farnsworth, a great guy and one of the investors who helped Jerry Colangelo purchase the team in 1987, was on the Japan trip with us. When the flight attendant was making her routine pre-flight announcement about safety procedures, she mentioned that since we would be flying over the Pacific, life jackets were located under each seat. Reaching under his seat, Ross didn't feel his flotation device, so he unbuckled his seatbelt and got down on his hands and knees in the middle of the business-class aisle of our L-1011 aircraft to look under the seat and make sure his lifejacket was there. As a private pilot and an aviation buff, I tried to reassure him, "Ross," I said. "If we hit the ocean from 35,000 feet...I don't think you'll need a lifejacket!"

TITLES

Over his many years in the NBA, Cotton Fitzsimmons held a plethora of titles...coach, player personnel director, general manager, scout and consultant. But I think that the only title that ever really mattered to Cotton was that of "coach." In his mind, all the other titles were a little silly and pretentious. That's why, when he finally retired from coaching and took a job in the Suns front office, he declared himself "Senior Executive Vice President of Nothing." And that's exactly what the plaque on his door said. It should be what we all aspire to become.

COTTON-ISMS

❝You cannot make me have a bad day! ❞
- Cotton Fitzsimmons

At his core, Cotton Fitzsimmons was a force for positive thinking. One of his favorite sayings (after you gave him a piece of bad news) was, "You cannot make me have a bad day! If you want to mope around and feel bad about that, you go right ahead...but you are not going to make me have a bad day!"

If you passed him in an office hallway and asked, "Hey, Cotton, how you doin'?"

His response was usually, "If I'm on this side of the grass and I'm breathin' air...that's a good day!"

MORE COTTON

Once, when talking about his gift of gab, Cotton said of his own mouth, "Sometimes I open it and I don't know what's coming out."

"Coaches are hired to be fired. It's not a question of 'if,' it's only a question of 'when.'"

"Son, you ain't lived until you've been fired."

"You can't have too many good shooters."

"Whether you're winning or losing, it's important to always be yourself. You can't change because of circumstances around you."

"Rules can be bent, even broken, but principles are something you live by."

"No need for a contract...just a handshake."

"In my coaching career, the teams I've taken over are teams that need help. It's my job to fix 'em and do whatever it takes to turn things around."

"Read my lips...the Suns need better players!"

"Dirt workers...the guys who bring their lunch to work every day. Those are the guys that get the boards for you and play the game in the trenches."

"There has always been room for the little guy...even in the NBA. But the little guy has to be unique. He has to beat the odds...and there can't be any quit in him!"

"I love the game," Cotton once said, "We all started because we love the game, so why take that out of it? Go ahead and do your job, work hard, win...but have fun. Every day in practice I want to have fun."

"It's been a lot of years and I've traveled a lot of miles," Fitzsimmons said. "I've found out the grass isn't always greener on the other side. In fact, a lot of places I've been, there was no grass!"

ONE FLUSH

After a truly bad performance by his team or a lopsided loss, Cotton was known to come into the usually subdued locker room and without saying a word, walk into a toilet stall and give it a good, long flush. Then he'd come out and start his post-game talk by saying, "OK, men, let's just flush that one away!"

I understand it's a motivational technique adopted and now frequently employed by Suns assistant coach Dan Majerle.

ARSENIO

During the Lakers-Suns playoff series in 1990, JoAnn Fitzsimmons and Stacey Hornacek were sitting under one of the baskets in seats right next to TV personality, Arsenio Hall. Introductions were made, but Hall referred to Stacey and Jeff as "Horna-check."

She politely corrected him, "No, it's 'Horna-sec."

Hall said, "Well, never mind that. What I really want to ask you... what's the real reason they call Jeff, 'Horny?'"

Classy.

Later that night, in a jubilant Suns locker room at the Forum, Arsenio would give the Suns their "props."

"These guys shocked the world tonight!"

BETTER CHECK

After the Suns eliminated the Lakers in that playoff series, the team returned to Phoenix ... to an airport absolutely jammed with Suns fans. By some estimates, there were 9,000 people, pressed shoulder-to-shoulder, inside Terminal 3 at Sky Harbor International.

Airport officials became so concerned about the size of the crowd that they actually pulled out their blueprints, slide-rules and computers to check maximum load factors and the structural integrity of the concourses and the terminal building itself. That night, Phoenix fans truly offered some "heavy-duty" support!

PARAMETERS

Cotton was always jawing (OK, we'll call it "communicating") with the front office, the media, with JoAnn, but especially with his players. He always let them know where they stood with him and what kind of behavior was expected from them.

When the Suns travelled by commercial airlines, even before the team got off the bus at the airport, Cotton would be sure to say, "Remember, we don't own the plane. We just bought some tickets. The flight attendants aren't just here for you, they are here for all the passengers. Remember that. Be polite."

Upon arrival at the team hotel, he would once again offer some additional reminders, "We don't own this hotel. We are only renting some rooms. There are a lot of people staying here who have real jobs. They have to go to work in the morning and they don't want to listen to you all night...be respectful."

There were times when Cotton would delegate this "reminder" duty to one of the players, like Jeff Hornacek, who would do his very best Cotton imitation. Everyone loved it, especially Cotton. There were other times when the bus would pull up to the hotel and you might hear the entire team, like a bunch of unruly schoolboys, reciting out loud, Cotton's rules of behavior.

Kids and teams need parameters. Cotton made sure they were always in place.

MR. SLITHERS

Cotton always had good relationships with his players, but it might have been easier to just adopt Kevin Johnson for all the time Cotton and JoAnn spent taking care of him. K.J. had a beautiful home high on the south slope of Camelback Mountain in Phoenix. Desert environments frequently feature desert critters, as was the case one night when a panicky Kevin Johnson called JoAnn.

"Annie, I've got a snake in my yard!" Kevin told her. "Can you come over?"

JoAnn told Cotton about the call and was getting ready to head over to Kevin's when Cotton asked, "What are YOU going to do with a snake?"

"Well, I was kind of hoping that YOU would go with me," she responded.

So Cotton, amazed that they were actually going on a snake hunt, threw one of his golf clubs in the car and off they went.

When they arrived at K.J.'s mansion on the hill, they found Kevin huddled inside, peeking out the window into the yard where he had last seen the snake. And that's exactly where K.J. would stay during the entire adventure.

The distinctive patterns on the wet grass outside indicated that the critter was probably a "sidewinder," a poisonous snake common to Arizona ...sometimes called a "horned rattlesnake."

Cotton and JoAnn went forth into the yard to do battle, but the snake had relocated into some bushes. JoAnn fearlessly waded into the bushes trying to flush him out, an activity that Cotton quickly discouraged. Eventually, "Mister Slithers" showed himself once again and Cotton went to work. No one can confirm Cotton's club selection that night, but suffice to say that the threat to Cotton's prized point guard was eliminated, and Cotton's golf handicap only went up by a stroke or two.

K.J. watched everything from inside the house, safely ensconced behind a double-insulated picture window

When Cotton finally returned home that night, he collapsed into his favorite chair and with a big sigh said, "The things I do for that guy!"

I wonder how many NBA coaches today would do battle with a rattlesnake for one of their players.

By the time the sun came up the next morning, the hawks and scavengers had happily taken care of the "cleanup" of K.J.'s yard and life on Camelback Mountain returned to normal.

HEAVEN CAN WAIT

After stacking up a pile of technical fouls during his first year with the Suns, Cotton mended his ways and over his career, actually became better-known for his ability to keep up a steady stream of chatter with referees...without getting technicals.

One of his favorite sayings, especially after a call went against his team was, "In my next life, I'm coming back as an official and straighten this mess out!"

WHILE YOU WERE SLEEPING

Cotton had an unshakeable, game-day ritual of taking an afternoon nap before heading over to the arena. One afternoon, as Cotton slept, JoAnn picked up a call from the men's clothing store where Cotton had his advertising/trade agreement. The store clerk didn't know what to do because coach Chuck Daly of the Pistons had come in and asked if this was the store where Cotton Fitzsimmons shopped for his clothes. When he was told that it was, Daly proceeded to pick out some sweaters, ties and shirts. When he was ready to check out, the staff asked him how he would like to pay for the items, he said, "Just put it on Cotton's account!" Hence the phone call.

Not wanting to embarrass Daly or wake her slumbering husband, JoAnn told the store to go ahead and put it on Cotton's account.

That night at the game, Daly teased Cotton, "That was a nice store! I got some really nice things today! Thanks!"

CURSES!

One day, late in the 1990-91 season, a lady came to the Suns offices on north Central Ave, demanding to see Suns coach Cotton Fitzsimmons. She was dressed in the counter-culture fashion of the late 1960's. Sensing that perhaps this lady was "not all there," the Suns receptionist told her that Cotton wasn't available. The woman insisted that she be given the opportunity to see Cotton Fitzsimmons, or, using the special powers that she possessed, she would put a curse on the Suns and they will never, ever, win a championship!

The scene was getting a little uncomfortable and Suns video coordinator Todd Quinter was called to the front desk to see if he could help. No one remembers if she claimed to be a witch, a seer or a clairvoyant. They just remember that she was really angry that she couldn't see Cotton.

Todd escorted her out to the parking lot where she promptly backed her big pick-up truck into a chain-link fence... that locked onto her tow hitch. Had she pulled away at that moment, she probably would have take 100 feet of fencing with her, but Todd and some other Suns employees got her to stop. They then rocked her truck until it came loose from the fence and she roared off. Did she have enough time to invoke her curse? No one can say for sure, but a few days later Dan Majerle came down with a back problem, the first of a string of injuries to hit the Suns. The most serious one resulted in Kevin Johnson going on the injured list. Shortly thereafter, the Suns were bounced out in the first round of the playoffs by Utah. And Phoenix has yet to win an NBA Championship.

Hey, Morticia...or whoever you are...please...please...take off the curse!

STANDING PAYMENT

Sportswriter Dave Hicks covered the Suns for many years and not surprisingly, Cotton Fitzsimmons was one of his favorite subjects. In a feature story for *Fastbreak* Magazine, Hicks recounted a very unusual experience he once witnessed, while traveling with the diminutive Suns coach. Hicks wrote:

"Which brings us to a heretofore undisclosed milestone by the Suns coach... a feat worthy of research and scrutiny by the Guinness Book of World Records.

Fitzsimmons' press guide height is slightly over six feet (determined by standing on the press guides of every NBA franchise he has coached).

On a cold, snowy evening in Buffalo, Fitzsimmons, then general manager Jerry Colangelo and a Phoenix journalist who shall remain nameless, arrived at the Braves' arena by cab. The rookie coach announced that he would pay the fare.

As he dug into his pocket, Cotton determined that he needed more elbow room. So he stood up! Inside the cab! No retractable top involved. He stood in the cab! Never mind that he was weirdly contorted. He stood!

There was an immediate consensus: none of those present – driver included – had ever seen anyone stand inside a cab. Unquestionably, this was an NBA first that merited marquee recognition."

FATHERS, SONS AND THE SUNS

In 1976, my wife and I had just welcomed a baby girl into our lives. When our daughter was a little less than two years old, my mom and dad traveled to Phoenix from Connecticut to visit their granddaughter. My dad had been retired for a year or two and was having a few health problems, so we knew that this might be the last time he'd be able to make the trip. On one of those days, during their Arizona visit, I took my dad down to the Phoenix Suns offices, so he could see where I worked and get an idea of what his son was doing for a living.

As the treasurer for the National Association of Manufacturers, my dad had a high-pressure career in New York City and was not easily impressed. So, as he sat in a chair in my rather humble PR office, I banged out something really important on my typewriter...no doubt a vital press release about an upcoming promotion offering "free balloons for the kids" or some indispensible game notes about players long since forgotten.

At some point, my boss, "Top Sun," Jerry Colangelo, walked into my office. I immediately introduced him to my dad. Jerry was so gracious. He told my dad how fortunate the Suns were to have his son working in the organization and how valuable I was to the success of the franchise. I thought, "I am?" But Jerry's words clearly made a positive impression on my dad.

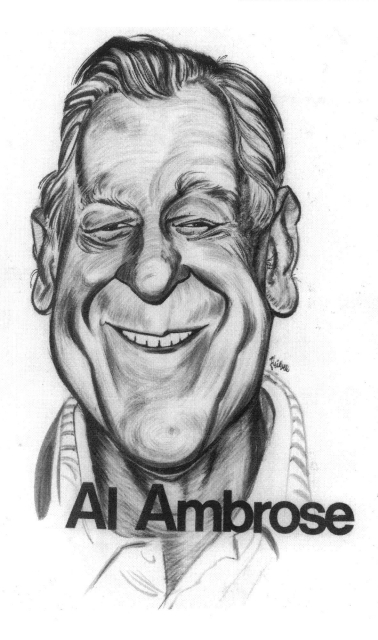

Al Ambrose

In retrospect, Jerry didn't have to say anything beyond, "Hi! Nice to meet you!" But he took that extra step... those few extra words. Knowing the difficult relationship Jerry had with his father, as he was growing up, made me appreciate his kind gesture even more. I will never, ever, forget that moment.

A couple of years later, my dad took a turn for the worse, was hospitalized and lapsed into a coma. At the time, I was with the Suns for a playoff game in Portland. Immediately after hearing my troubling news, Jerry and our team travel agent, Willis Neilson, coordinated all the arrangements for me, my wife and my brother Mike to fly back to Connecticut. Jerry told me to focus on my mom and family and not to worry about the job or the playoffs. My dad passed away the next day.

Weeks later, I tried to repay everyone for the travel expenses but they adamantly refused to accept any money from me. You don't forget kindnesses like that, but it was not unusual within the Suns family.

A few years after that, I was honored by the NBA PR Directors during the NBA All-Star Weekend in San Antonio. It was the typical PR directors' meeting...lots of cocktails to start, followed by a very informal and usually irreverent awards ceremony. But this time, Jerry Colangelo showed up to speak on my behalf.

Previously, no other NBA owner had *EVER* shown up at this awards ceremony to support his PR guy. I can't adequately describe what that meant to me...a guy who was only trying to do his job the best way he knew how.

NBA PR people are tough to impress, but I think Jerry's appearance that night had an impact on everyone in the room. In his remarks, Jerry, in his typical style, gently chided me for a few mistakes I had made, but then he took the time to say how professional I was in my job and how deserving I was of the PR award.

My ultimate wish would be for everyone, no matter what job or position in life they hold, to have an opportunity to work with somebody with the loyalty, the common sense, the leadership skills, the ethics, the integrity and the compassion of a Jerry Colangelo.

'DOWNTOWN JERRY'

JERRY COLANGELO

MAYBE YOU CAN FIGHT CITY HALL

One afternoon, after Jerry and I had attended a Suns community relations event, we were headed back to the office when
Jerry told me that we needed to stop by Phoenix City Hall for a
few minutes. He wanted to talk to one of the city councilmen
about the pending plans for the new downtown arena.

This particular councilman was not entirely sold on the idea,
especially the part about the city's financial involvement. The
three of us sat around a tiny, round table. The councilman was
more-or-less whining his reservations about the project, when
Colangelo suddenly jumped up, leaned across the table and
got right in his face. With his index finger jabbing the air in front of
him, J.C. said firmly, "All I'm going to say to you is this...if we want
this project to succeed...if we want to change downtown into
something special...it's going to take someone with some BALLS
to make it happen!"

I remember sitting there and thinking, "H-m-m-m, so *this* is lobby-
ing!"

DON'T DRIVE NO JIVE

One of the Suns young marketing guys, wearing a suit and tie,
had just finished a presentation at one of the local Boys and Girls
Clubs. He was headed for his car, in the parking lot, when he
overheard two youngsters, standing on the sidewalk outside,
talking about him.

"Hey, look man! That's the coach of the Phoenix Suns!"

"That ain't the coach of the Suns..."

"Yeah he is..."

"No he ain't...the coach of the Suns don't drive no *jive* Toyota!"

CHAPTER 6

SUNSET ON THE MADHOUSE

CHANGING TIMES

The Suns finished their 24th and final season at the Veterans Memorial Coliseum in fine style, setting a new regular season attendance record with sellouts for all 41 home games. They also tied a team record by forging an impressive 36-5 mark at home.

A few days later, on April 23, 1992, on the eve of the Suns' first-round playoff series against the Spurs, we called a news conference to announce that assistant coach Paul Westphal, would succeed Cotton Fitzsimmons as head coach, following the playoffs.

We set up the news conference in one of the Coliseum's exhibit halls. It not only marked the end of the line for the wildly successful "Cotton Express," but also signaled the end of the Suns era at the Coliseum.

It was a remarkably orderly transition for a major coaching change... a rarity in professional sports. It happened that way because, well in advance of that day, Colangelo, Fitzsimmons and Westphal had all agreed to the "coach in waiting" concept.

As the team's top assistant, Westphal had understudied Cotton for four seasons. "Westy" would prove to be a great choice to lead the Suns into a new era and... a new arena.

"Paul was an innovative player and he will be an innovative, successful NBA coach," Fitzsimmons said of his protégé. "I have no doubt in my mind about that."

Then, in a final tribute to the arena where he started his NBA coaching career, Fitzsimmons said, "I've closed a lot of joints in my day, but this place was special."

THE FINALE

The lights on the Coliseum scoreboard told one version of the story – Quarter **6**, Time **0:00**, Score – Portland **153**, Suns **151**. But those illuminated numbers didn't tell the whole story.

The scoreboard marked the last Suns game to be played at the venerable Coliseum, a place that had become known and loved by generations of Suns fans as "The Madhouse on McDowell."

As the game between the Suns and the Trailblazers ended, their hard-fought, double-overtime thriller had the potential to become one of those games that, years later, 100,000 fans would claim to have seen in person. But the 14,887 who actually were there, witnessed one hell of game.

A classic back-and-forth NBA tussle between two classy and very talented teams, the game was a fitting tribute to the mettle of a Suns franchise that had battled its way back to respectability after a debilitating drug scandal just a few years before.

For the fourth season in a row under coach Cotton Fitzsimmons, the Suns had won more than 50 regular season games and optimistically stormed into the playoffs. The Suns swept the San Antonio Spurs 3-0 in the opening round to earn a shot at the Trail Blazers.

Phoenix faced a solid Portland team led by Clyde Drexler, Terry Porter and Buck Williams. But the Suns countered with an equally talented lineup including Kevin Johnson, Jeff Hornacek, Tom Chambers and Dan Majerle.

The Suns would lose the first two games in Portland, but they bounced back by winning the third game of the series in Phoenix. During the final minutes of that Coliseum win, Suns fans drove noise levels to eardrum-splitting levels.

In Game Four, the Suns fell behind early but, as they battled back to tie the game late in the fourth quarter, players, coaches, and game officials were again forced to adjust their communication with one another, due to the relentlessly deafening crowd noise.

As Blazers' star Clyde Drexler reported to the official scorer at the beginning of the second overtime, a courtside reporter somehow got his attention.

"Hey, Clyde," the reporter shouted above the din, nodding toward the hyper-kinetic Coliseum crowd. "What do you think about all this?"

Drexler soaked in the noise and the atmosphere for a moment before responding, "I love it, man. I absolutely love it!"

He paused again before adding, "This is why we play!"

Game Four resembled two evenly matched heavyweights battling each other, blow for blow, for three and a half hours... before an exhausted Portland team finally eked out a decision.

K.J. led the Suns with 35 points before fouling out, while Tom Chambers added 29 points off the bench. In dramatic testimony to the physical play, five players fouled out of the game.

The effort by both teams, coupled with the raucous enthusiasm of Phoenix fans that night, was not only a tribute to the NBA, it was a respectful final salute to 24 years of Suns home games played at the Coliseum.

Even as the arena lights blinked off that night, fans could sense that an exciting new era for Suns basketball was just over the horizon.

A CHERISHED OLD FRIEND

Some will say that it was only a building. That it was just steel, concrete and glass. But for almost a quarter of a century the Arizona Veterans Memorial Coliseum was the very heart of the Phoenix Suns. Beginning with their expansion year in 1968, the Suns played over 1,000 regular season and playoff games at the "Madhouse on McDowell" and won an amazing two out of every three of them.

Although it has undergone numerous face lifts and changes since its opening in October of 1965, the Coliseum still evokes vivid memories of Suns days gone by.

Some of those memories once hung as banners from the Coliseum rafters: HAWKINS 42, VAN ARSDALE 5, ADAMS 33, WESTPHAL 44, the 1976 NBA Western Conference Championship, the 1981 Pacific Division title.

Player names and highlights still flash through the memories of longtime Suns fans. Last second victories, devastating losses, the routine, the bizarre, superstars and super plays... the Coliseum saw them all.

Remember? Dick Van Arsdale's drive to the basket to score the first points in Suns history...the 1968 Coliseum ticket prices were $5, $4, $3 and $2...the first Suns mascot was a sunflower...the Suns had cheerleaders during their inaugural season...the Dixieland sounds of The Desert City Six... Keith Erickson's miracle shot against the Warriors in the 1976 playoffs... Walt Frazier's MVP performance in the 1975 NBA All-Star game... the ceiling leaks... Tom Chambers' 60-point night... Connie Hawkins' gravity defying swoops... Jerry Colangelo's winning debut as coach... the playoff super-fan Superman... "Westy" and the "Oklahoma Kid" lead the Suns to two straight wins in the 1976 NBA Finals vs. Boston.

How about? Wilt Chamberlain's 30,000th point... the special tribute nights for Kareem, "Hondo" Havlicek and "Dr. J"... the annual egg tossing contest... Paul Westphal's mom singing the anthem on Mothers' Day... Hornacek vs. "Sleepy" Floyd... Goodrich vs. Kauffman... Neil Johnson vs. Everybody... John MacLeod's first pro win... the ladies' free throw contests... Diamond Vision... the Gorilla's impromptu debut... Butch van Breda Kolff's ejection from his first Coliseum game... visits by Captain Super... Van Arsdale's 15,000th NBA point...the theatrics, booming voice, big glasses and generous heart of Tom, the "Red Licorice Man."

Remember? The Suns score 173 points against Denver... 107 of 'em in the first half... Ronnie Lee's floor burns... Neal Walk's sideburns... back-to-back wins over Chamberlain, West and the Lakers in the 1970 playoffs... Walter Davis' buzzer-beaters... Gar Heard's block on Wilkes... "D.J.," "E.J.," and "K.J."

Don't forget… Cotton Fitzsimmons' first NBA win in 1970… his 800th win twenty-two years later and his NBA Coach of the Year award in 1989… the "Mean 13"… the annual Carnation-Boy Scouts Suns Booster Banner Contest…Suns in Six… Majerle's dunk over Bol… Truck Robinson's Coliseum debut and the toy truck… the rain-out… Stan Richards and the Voice of God… Pistol Pete's 51… "BEAT L.A.!"… the sellout season.

The Suns moved into their glittering new arena in downtown Phoenix in the spring of 1992. New Suns fans may not even be aware that the Suns played for 24 years at the Coliseum at 19th Avenue and McDowell, but old-time Suns fans will always remember the Coliseum as the place where the Suns were born, grew to maturity, worked hard, and achieved their first success.

The place was small by today's modern standards, but Suns fans made it one of the loudest buildings in the NBA.

All things considered…it was a great place to grow up.

EPILOGUE

As I verified facts for this book with longtime friends, fans and Suns employees past and present, invariably, I would come away from each meeting with material for two or three new stories. When the original manuscript grew to well over 400 pages, I made the decision to divide the material into two books.

The first book, **Notes from the WACKO! File... And Tales From the Madhouse on McDowell** covers Suns history from 1968 to 1992... the "Madhouse on McDowell" years, putting the focus on Jerry Colangelo, Dick Van Arsdale, Connie Hawkins and Cotton Fitzsimmons.

The soon to be released second book, **2WACKO! Echoes from the Purple Palace**, will cover the Suns since 1992, when they moved into America West Arena, originally nicknamed "The Purple Palace." **2WACKO!** will pick up where this book leaves off and will feature stories of Steve Nash, Tom Chambers and Charles Barkley among others.

I can guarantee that there will be some flashbacks, crossovers, double-dribbles and some chronological liberties taken between the two books, but if you are a Suns fan, old or new, I think you will enjoy the stories from both eras.

I trust you had a good time with this wacky look at the Suns first 24 years, and I hope you are looking forward to the sequel.

INDEX OF NAMES

10088535R00017